BRAVING THE TRUTH

ALSO BY RACHEL HELD EVANS

Wholehearted Faith

Inspired: Slaying Giants, Walking on Water, and Loving the Bible Again

Searching for Sunday: Loving, Leaving, and Finding the Church

A Year of Biblical Womanhood: How a Liberated Woman Found Herself Sitting on Her Roof, Covering Her Head, and Calling Her Husband "Master"

Faith Unraveled: How a Girl Who Knew All the Answers Learned to Ask Questions

What Is the Bible? (with Matthew Paul Turner, illustrated by Ying Hui Tan)

What Is God Like? (with Matthew Paul Turner, illustrated by Ying Hui Tan)

BRAVING *the* TRUTH

Essential Essays *for*
Reckoning with *and* Reimagining Faith

RACHEL HELD EVANS

Edited by Sarah Bessey

HarperOne
An Imprint of HarperCollins*Publishers*

Without limiting the exclusive rights of any author, contributor or the publisher of this publication, any unauthorized use of this publication to train generative artificial intelligence (AI) technologies is expressly prohibited. HarperCollins also exercise their rights under Article 4(3) of the Digital Single Market Directive 2019/790 and expressly reserve this publication from the text and data mining exception.

Excerpt from "Is God Male?" by Mimi Haddad. This excerpt first appeared in *Mutuality* in 2012. www.cbeinternational.org. Used with permission.

Excerpt from *Inspired: Slaying Giants, Walking on Water, and Loving the Bible Again* by Rachel Held Evans. Copyright (c) 2018 by Rachel Held Evans. Used by permission of HarperCollins Christian Publishing.

"The Risk of Birth, Christmas, 1973" from *THE ORDERING OF LOVE: THE NEW AND COLLECTED POEMS OF MADELEINE L'ENGLE* by Madeleine L'Engle, copyright © 2005 by Crosswicks, Ltd. Used by permission of WaterBrook Multnomah, an imprint of Random House, a division of Penguin Random House LLC. All rights reserved.

BRAVING THE TRUTH. Collection, Foreword, and Introductions Copyright © 2026 by Daniel Jonce Evans. Some material was previously published by Rachel Held Evans in another format. Text previously published on rachelheldevans.com Copyright © by Rachel Held Evans. All rights reserved. No part of this book may be used or reproduced in any manner whatsoever without written permission except in the case of brief quotations embodied in critical articles and reviews. For information, address HarperCollins Publishers, 195 Broadway, New York, NY 10007. In Europe, HarperCollins Publishers, Macken House, 39/40 Mayor Street Upper, Dublin 1, D01 C9W8, Ireland.

HarperCollins books may be purchased for educational, business, or sales promotional use. For information, please email the Special Markets Department at SPsales@harpercollins.com.

harpercollins.com

FIRST EDITION

Designed by Yvonne Chan

Library of Congress Cataloging-in-Publication Data has been applied for.

ISBN 978-0-06-289450-2

Printed in the United States of America

25 26 27 28 29 LBC 5 4 3 2 1

For all of us who felt a little less alone in the world because of the work and witness of Rachel Held Evans.

CONTENTS

Foreword by Dan Jonce Evans. xiii
Biography xvi
Introduction by Sarah Bessey xxi

PART ONE
An Evolving Faith: Essays on Doubt, Asking Questions, and the Cost of It All

Traveling Mercies for the "Consummate Ass". 3
The Scandal of the Evangelical Heart 5
They Were Right (and Wrong) About the Slippery Slope 11
This Was a Turning Point: A Reflection by Matthew Paul Turner 13
Why I Can't Stay Angry (Even Though I Want To) 15
The Power of Testimony 21
*A Christian Faith I'm Willing to Risk Being Wrong About:
A Reflection by Mason Mennenga* 24
Holy Week for Doubters. 26
The Thing I'd Love to Forget About the People I Disagree With . . .28
Jesus Started with the "Outliers" 31
"New" Masculinity: A Reflection by Mike McHargue. 35
I Don't Want an Easy Faith 37
On Borrowing Bravery: A Reflection by Shauna Niequist. 38

Changing Faith and Changing Relationships:
  Some Things I Learned the Hard Way. 40
She Was Just a Good Friend: A Reflection by Kathleen Gleason. . . . 44
Why Calvinism Makes Me Cry 47
"Ask a ___" Series: Editor's Note by Sarah Bessey 52
*The Familiar and the Stranger:
  A Reflection by Rev. Dr. Monica A. Coleman*. 54
The Cost 56
Let the World Change You:
  A Commencement Address Do-Over. 60
*About That Commencement Do-Over:
  A Reflection by Dr. Peter Held*. 64

PART TWO

That Unholy American Trinity: Essays on Patriarchy, White Supremacy, and Religious Nationalism

For the Sake of the Gospel, Let Women Speak 69
"... Your Daughters Will Prophesy" 81
The Troubler: A Reflection by Rev. Dr. Scot McKnight 85
Is God a Man? A Brief Response to CBMW's Accusation
  of Heresy 87
If Men Got the Titus 2 Treatment 91
Donald Trump and a Tale of Two Gospels. 96
A Perversion of the Gospel: A Reflection by Shane Claiborne 103
For the Sake of the Gospel, Drop the Persecution Complex. 106
Christians, MLK Day, and Historical Amnesia. 119
The Other Lie: A Reflection by Lisa Sharon Harper. 126
She Did That: A Reflection by Lisa Sharon Harper. 129

Calling Your Reps and Planting Onions:
  A Plan for Faithful Resistance 132
*Postelection Thoughts on Rachel and Feminist Solidarity:
  A Reflection by Candice Marie Benbow* *143*
Repenting of "Colorblindness" 145
*"Why Are You All Writing About Me?":
  A Reflection by Kathy Khang* *150*
On the World Vision Reaction:
  Some Bad News, Some Good News, and Some Ideas 153
World Vision Update 158
What Now? 160
Life After Evangelicalism 165
*Faith in God, Even in Disillusionment:
  A Reflection by Kelsey Hanson Woodruff* *170*

PART THREE

Casseroles, Evangelicalism, and the Kingdom of the Hungry: Essays on the Church

15 Reasons I Left Church 175
15 Reasons I Returned to the Church 178
So Our Church Plant Failed 181
Sunday Morning 184
*On Casseroles and Finding Community:
  A Reflection by Kristen Howerton* *187*
Blessed Are the Un-Cool 190
*Rachel Didn't Just Write About Including the Un-Cool,
  She Befriended Us: A Reflection by Shannon Dingle* *194*
On "Outgrowing" American Christianity 196
Why a Seminary Degree Doesn't Have to Make You a Jerk 200

x   CONTENTS

When Twitter Was Fun: Remembering RHE's Online Work:
    A Reflection by Rev. Emmy Kegler 205
Five Things You Don't Have to Leave Behind When You Leave
    Fundamentalism 207
Dear Pastors—Tell Us the Truth 211
Bringing Healing, Not a Cure: A Reflection by Tanya Marlow 213
Let's Build Bigger Banquet Tables 215

PART FOUR

All Right, Then, I'll Go to Hell: Essays on Gender and Sexuality

"All Right, Then, I'll Go to Hell" 221
Rachel Goes to Hell: A Reflection by Brian D. McLaren 225
Responding to Homophobia in the Christian Community 227
She Held Up a Lantern Ahead of Me:
    A Reflection by Jen Hatmaker. 235
The False Gospel of Gender Binaries 238
A Scandalously Inclusive Gospel: A Reflection by Austen Hartke . .244
The Absurd Legalism of Gender Roles, Exhibit D:
    "Biblical" Manipulation 246
If My Son or Daughter Were Gay 252
"Mom, I Want to Tell You Something.":
    A Reflection by Osheta Moore 255
Unstoppable Grace: Thoughts on the Gay Christian Network
    Conference 259
Her Questions, Her Invitations, and Her Critiques Flowed from
    Her Deep Love: A Reflection by Matthew Vines 264
How to Win a Culture War and Lose a Generation 267
I Was Listening: A Reflection by Micha Boyett 272

PART FIVE

Still a Bible Nerd: Essays on Scripture

I Would Fail Abraham's Test (and I Bet You Would Too)	277
The Bible Was "Clear"	284
How to Love Jesus Without Needing to Be Right About Everything: A Reflection by Zack Hunt	289
Everyone's a Biblical Literalist Until You Bring Up Gluttony	291
When Rachel Asked, She Gave Me Permission to Ask, Too: A Reflection by Matthias Roberts	297
Oh Beloved, Just You Wait: A Reflection by Rachel Kurtz	300
Sunday Superlatives: Rachel Was Both: A Reflection by Alise Chaffins	302
I Love the Bible	305
Her Nerdy Love of the Bible: A Reflection by Mihee Kim-Kort	309

PART SIX

Telling the Truth: Essays on Life in the Midst of It All

You Don't Hate Me. You Hate My Brand	315
Stay and Complicate: A Reflection by Glennon Doyle	320
Scattered Thoughts on My Life in the Christian "Industry"	322
Everything Will Pass: A Reflection by Cindy Wang Brandt	326
My Parents	328
She Never Had to Doubt Their Love: A Reflection by Rev. Carol Howard	332
What I Learned Turning My Hate Mail into Origami	334
The Afterglow Is Brilliant: A Reflection by Dr. Peter Enns	337
Ashamed	339

I Am Ashamed: A Reflection by Kathy Escobar 343
I Don't Always Tell You 345
Tending to the Spiritual Fire of Our Generation:
  A Reflection by Kaitlin B. Curtice 347
Hey Mommy Bloggers, Thanks 351
The Risk of Birth. 355
The Risks of Birth, and Life: A Reflection by Sarah McCammon. . . .360
Office of the Night Watch: A Meditation on Nursing 362
The Gravity of Real Life: A Reflection by Winnie Varghese. 365
Lent for the Lamenting 367
Her Last Act as a Blogger: A Reflection by Amanda Held Opelt . . .369

Afterword: Go Forth, Woman of Valor 371
Contributor Biographies. 375

FOREWORD

BY DAN JONCE EVANS

My fingers are cold as I sit here in my office. The sun is rising, revealing a pastoral view through the window. A distant barn. A field. The hint of snow flurries is present in the air.

It's January, and every new year brings with it a zeitgeist of priorities, commitments, and goals. I don't have an easily accessible mental library of favorites or firsts. In fact, it's something I want to get better at. To know myself a little more. If ever asked my favorite color, I tend to dodge and explain myself in contexts. "It depends on the object." I hide behind humor. "For cheese, it's anything not fuzzy and green." Or, occasionally, I will reference Rachel's favorite color of flower. Yellow. And agree with it.

It might surprise you to hear that Rachel was resistant to the idea of starting a blog in the first place. At the time, she'd been freelancing and had a few articles published in national publications. She had a column in our local paper, called "Shootin' the Breeze." She also had a book she wanted to write, and we were both in the process of learning the ins and outs of publishing. In this era of Xanga, many blogs were just that—a web log—focused on the author's personal life. And adding a public list of what Rachel had eaten for breakfast didn't seem, to her, like a needed addition to her work.

My strengths were those of a generalist who was technically minded enough to handle the tasks of creating social media accounts and websites. Her strengths were that of a gentlehearted, will-of-steel, intelligent, focused writer. I never knew what I wanted to be when I grew up. Rachel was a writer. I didn't know how to answer "what do you do?" when people asked. Rachel was a writer.

The new era we were entering happened to give us a way to combine our skillsets. In the age of these new social media services Facebook and Twitter, for a first-time writer to get a book published, it was easier if you approached a publisher with an existing audience. After a bit of good-natured debate over a few weeks, she agreed to start publishing a blog as long as she could do it in a way that she could be proud of. She wanted to treat it as a sacred place between her and a like-minded audience where she wrote full articles, things that could be found just as easily in a print magazine as on a dot-com.

So many Januarys ago, in 2008, we launched Rachel's personal website and blog. Yellow flowers had a few months before they would peak their heads above the soil. It was, as it is now, a time for beginnings. There were similar chills and smells in the air when she and I had discussions about putting her writing online.

Over the years, I saw her, at times, complete hours of research before writing and publishing a single essay. Reading and writing was part of how Rachel processed reality. It was connection to other souls, past and future, navigating their way through thoughts and doubts with words. It was something she was great at and something she would have done regardless of pay.

Her first blog article was dated December 2007. The fact that that's nearly twenty years ago now is difficult for me to imagine, and yet, after a look in the mirror, and the sight of a few extra wrinkles and some gray in my beard, it becomes perfectly reasonable.

Recently I've learned that I do have some favorites in life. My favorite part of a movie is the beginning. It's the instant the fanfare plays and the studio logos appear on the screen. It's the moment of immersion. A place where I've decided to let go of my reality temporarily and let someone else's story reveal things to me about myself.

My fingers are a bit warmer now. Above me, Rachel's vision board leans high against the wall on the top of a bookcase. It is full of sentences, bullet points, fragments of thought, all channeling the direction of her work and her focus.

Some of them were borrowed inspiration:

"One True Sentence."
"Moving forward lily pad by lily pad."

Some were original:

"The next sentence is not in the refrigerator."

Her decision to prioritize the reader, respecting us all as peers on similar but unique journeys, is what gave her the chance to reach so many. Because of her dedication, her blog wasn't just a blog. Rachel built a community. Of the inspiration found on her board, there's one that stands out to me. It's the one scrawled in Sharpie on a yellow sticky note.

"Write for the kindred spirits, not the critics."

In other words, she wrote these words for you. May you find Rachel's spirit in these pages. May you find yourself. May you find both hope and peace. May you find laughter. If you have been reading her work since the beginning, welcome back, old friend. If you have just found her now, welcome to the beginning.

Dan
January 2025

BIOGRAPHY

Rachel Grace Held Evans was born on June 8, 1981, in Birmingham, Alabama, to Peter and Robin (Greiner) Held. She was soon joined by a little sister, Amanda, and the two little girls grew up on Ruffner Mountain, spending hours outside in nature and at their local church, eventually attending private Christian schools.

When Rachel was fourteen years old, the family moved to Dayton, Tennessee, the home of the infamous and formative Scopes Monkey Trial of 1925. Rachel's father was a well-respected theology professor at Bryan College, and her mother was a beloved fourth-grade teacher.

Rachel attended Rhea County High School, graduating in 1999. She was a devoted fan of the Alabama Crimson Tide, a self-described "Bible nerd," and a youth group kid deeply committed to the Southern Baptist–influenced life of her community. After high school, she attended Bryan College, majoring in English literature. She had always aspired to be a writer, even dressing up as "an author" for career day, complete with her 1980s bangs.

Rachel met Dan Evans in a psychology class at Bryan College. When she sat beside him and asked his name, he asked why she wanted to know. Rachel retorted that he must be a Yankee because "around here, we like to introduce ourselves to one another" (confirmation: He was indeed "a Yankee," being originally from New Jersey). They became college sweethearts; Dan graduated from Bryan in 2002 and then Rachel in 2003. She was also the valedictorian of her class. They were married on October 25, 2003.

It was during her time at Bryan College that Rachel first began to question her evangelical faith. She wrestled with questions of theology; science, particularly evolution; community; and doctrine. After graduation, Rachel and Dan briefly moved to Chattanooga, Tennessee, where she interned for the *Chattanooga Times Free Press*, but they soon returned to Dayton, where she worked full time as a journalist for the local paper, *The Herald-News*. Eventually shifting from reporting to editorial and opinion writing, Rachel received the award for Best Personal Humor Column in 2007 from the Tennessee Press Association. She began blogging in December 2007 to develop a platform in support of her first book proposal about her own evolving faith and eventually transitioned to full-time self-employment.

The Evanses made their home in a bungalow and began to save money for a small piece of property with hopes of raising their someday-children near her family, on a green hillside near the trees. Despite many outsiders asking how a progressive daughter of a deeply conservative town could remain there, Rachel sincerely respected her neighbors and would make her home in Dayton for the rest of her life.

Described by *The New York Times* as "the voice of the wandering evangelical," Rachel became the bestselling and influential author of *Inspired: Slaying Giants, Walking on Water, and Loving the Bible Again* (2018); *Searching for Sunday: Loving, Leaving, and Finding the Church* (2015); *A Year of Biblical Womanhood: How a Liberated Woman Found Herself Sitting on Her Roof, Covering Her Head, and Calling Her Husband "Master"* (2012); and *Faith Unraveled: How a Girl Who Knew All the Answers Learned to Ask the Questions*, which was originally titled *Evolving in Monkey Town* and was released in 2010.

The reach and impact of Rachel's online writing continued to grow. Her blog was visited by millions, each post becoming appointment reading for her followers, with hundreds of comments and as many shares for each post. An unexpected voice of the millennial generation, this Southern woman with a deep love for the Bible and an allergy to bullshit wrote her way through her own evolving faith; American evangelicalism and politics; religious pluralism; feminism, particularly within the church; the Bible; planting a new church with friends and its eventual closure; and her personal life. An early adopter and avid user of Twitter (now called X), she developed a worldwide community of devoted fans and equally devoted critics on that platform, where she sparred and laughed, asked questions, and commented on the news of the day. In 2012, she was named one of the "50 Women to Watch" by *Christianity Today* and was considered a dangerous heretic by powerful conservative voices. Beloved for her curiosity, bravery, and unflinching honesty, she became one of the most popular faith bloggers on the internet.

Rachel and Dan welcomed their first child, a son, in February 2016. Just more than two years later, they added a daughter to the family. The Evanses purchased the property, just south of Dayton, for which they had been diligently saving and began to make plans for their modest dream home on the hill overlooking the trees. Dan was always Rachel's "behind-the-scenes" team, building her website, empowering her projects, supporting her efforts, and working alongside of her even as his own work in coding, computers, music, and video production grew. They referred to the family as "Team Evans," and their loving partnership extended to every aspect of their work and life together. Rachel often referred to Dan in her books and on her blog, holding up their marriage as an example of egalitarian partnership and mutuality.

Rachel's writing on church, faith, doubt, life in the Bible Belt, evangelicalism, and politics was featured in *The Washington Post*, CNN, *The Guardian*, and many other publications. She became a frequent podcast, radio, and television guest everywhere, from NPR to the BBC, the *Today* show, and *The View*, among others. She also served on President Barack Obama's Advisory Council on Faith-Based and Neighborhood Partnerships, even traveling to the White House in Washington, DC, to meet with President Obama and other politicians and religious leaders who were passionate about the intersection of faith and politics.

Rachel cofounded two conferences, Why Christian?, with Nadia Bolz-Weber, which ran from 2015 until 2019, and Evolving Faith in 2018 with Sarah Bessey, Jim Chaffee, and eventually Jeff Chu, which continues as a conference and online community to this day. In addition to her own conferences, she kept a robust schedule of speaking engagements at churches, conferences, universities, and communities across the United States. Even though she was a noted introvert, she loved meeting her readers, frequently staying past closing time at conferences to connect with them and listen to their stories, putting faces to the names from her blog comment section and Twitter feed.

Near the end of her life, Rachel left evangelicalism and became an Episcopalian, worshiping at St. Luke's in Cleveland, Tennessee, where she became passionate about the sacraments of the church, particularly communion. At her conferences, she often ensured that communion was offered to all, as an open table, even serving the bread and wine herself, embracing and blessing all who came forward.

To Rachel, one of the most important aspects of her work was a quiet one: her commitment to amplifying marginalized and ignored voices within Christian publishing. She became a generous advocate for women, especially women of color, and LGBTQ+ folks, steadily offering her expertise, introductions to influential leaders, endorsements, recommendations for speaking engagements, support, and friendship as well as her public support. She was deeply influenced by these friendships, associations, and good teachers; their impact on her life and work was profound.

Rachel suddenly became ill in April 2019; as her illness progressed, she developed complications and was placed in an induced coma. Despite the valiant efforts of medical teams across three hospitals, she died in Nashville, Tennessee, at Vanderbilt University Medical Center at the age of thirty-seven on May 4, 2019, just two weeks before her daughter's first birthday. At the end, she was surrounded by friends and family in prayer and song.

The outpouring of grief at her death was immense, causing the hashtag #BecauseOfRHE to trend worldwide for days as ordinary people shared story after story of how her life, work, and witness impacted their lives. Major media outlets such as *The New Yorker*, *The New York Times*, *The Atlantic*, NPR, *The Guardian*, and the Associated Press eulogized her. Thousands tuned in to the live stream of her funeral from Chattanooga, Tennessee.

After her death in 2019, her last unfinished manuscript was completed by fellow writer and friend Jeff Chu; *Wholehearted Faith* was posthumously published in 2021 and became an instant *New York Times* bestseller. She was also the coauthor, with fellow writer and friend Matthew Paul Turner, of several children's books, which were also completed after her death, including the *New York Times* bestselling *What Is God Like?* (2021) and *What Is the Bible?* (2025).

Rachel Held Evans is buried in Dayton, Tennessee, on a green hillside near a grove of trees. Dan finished building their home after her death and is currently raising their two children there.

INTRODUCTION

BY SARAH BESSEY

My dear friend Rachel Held Evans—RHE to many, but always just "Rach" to her friends—was an uncommonly gifted and prolific writer. From the dawn of her blog in 2007 until her sudden death in 2019, she wrote thousands of blog posts, posted countless tweets, published four books, and drafted even more. Simultaneously, she founded two conferences, spoke at hundreds of churches and universities, and contributed to America's most influential media outlets. Her output was as intimidating as her ability to process complex information and theological concepts while maintaining a sense of humor. She did all this from her unassuming faux-wood-paneled office in Dayton, Tennessee, while cultivating a diverse network of friendships and quietly advocating for dozens of marginalized and underrepresented writers.

Like many great origin stories these days, our friendship began on the internet. Back then, Rachel was in the early days of her blogging career, still an aspiring author herself. I was messily blogging my own way through my first experience with faith deconstruction and was in the early days of parenting tinies. I blogged for almost five years in relative obscurity before a post I wrote critiquing a then-popular Christian conference for its lack of women speakers sparked a minor firestorm. Amid the pushback, Rachel reached out to me to offer support. In what I would later learn was a common experience for many of Rachel's friends, she quickly and generously adopted me into a community of fellow misfit bloggers and writers—if she chose you, you were in for life.

We wrote alongside of each other for the rest of her life, blogging together, publishing books in shared lanes, and eventually starting a conference and online community together. For those sitting in the pews but barred from the pulpit, the new medium of blogging was appealing, and we flocked to it. We set up shop on Xanga, WordPress, or Blogspot. We learned the basics of HTML so we could add carefully chosen music to a MySpace profile. We were as likely to share a picture of what we ate for lunch as we were to opine on patriarchy's impact on the church or whatever nonsense a celebrity pastor tweeted out that weekend. We punched above our weight, criticizing leaders and institutions. We amplified each other's voices, joked around as early adopters of Twitter on each other's posts and tweets religiously, and read voraciously.

At the time, Christian publishing was dominated by megachurch pastors or seminary-trained theologians and influential conservative voices steadily steering the church toward religious white nationalism. Suddenly, because of the internet, those of us who were largely silenced, ignored, isolated, or purposely marginalized found a way past the gatekeepers. And boy, did we have things to say.

More and more of us began to write our way through our faith, our stories, our political shifts, our faith evolutions, the experience of being a person within our unique contexts and stories and identities. We began to realize that we were not as alone as we had once felt, and the church needed our perspectives—whether they were low-church mums like myself in western Canada, a gay man in Kansas who loved the Bible, a Black contemplative from the Northeast, or, like Rachel, a Southern white woman who had the gumption not only to wrestle with doubt but to do it in public.

Rachel launched her blog—rachelheldevans.com—in December 2007, hoping to build a platform for a book proposal she had started on her own evolving faith. By the time of her death in 2019, she had written thousands of blog posts. When people talk with me about Rachel, they are as likely to mention her blog or her Twitter presence as they are to reference her books or sermons.

Rachel was at her boldest and funniest on Twitter. She mostly eschewed the perfected curation of Instagram. Her books offered the most researched, most thoughtful, most creative versions of her.

But her blog? Her blog was basically a kitchen table where everyone could sit down to talk about whatever was top of mind, whatever was going on in the world or the blogosphere or the backyard. Her blog posts were never one-way missives. She never forgot about the very real people reading her words, whom she often responded to by name in future posts. She engaged vigorously in her comment sections—which often swelled to dizzying numbers—with her critics as well as her comrades. She initiated community conversations, hosted book clubs, invited pushback, wrestled with her own story, changed her mind, apologized when needed, flew off the handle now and then only to circle back and provide further nuance or perspective as she learned it, shared new learnings, and so created a community of fellow travelers who felt that they truly knew her as a friend and companion.

And as her actual, real-life friend, I'll be honest—they kind of did truly know her. Rach was the same person off the page as she was on the page. (Okay, fine, she swore a lot more in real life than most people knew. And there were few versions of Rachel her close friends enjoyed more than her occasional bouts of pettiness because good gracious, she was funny when she was mad.) If you knew Rachel through her blog, you sort of did know her. I have lost count of the number of people I've spoken to who tell me that they cried when she died, like they had lost a best friend. They felt seen, valued, even loved by her. I think that's a beautiful testimony to her work, her witness, and her life.

In the years since her death, many people—historians, scholars, and people who were *there* for this particular moment in time—have asked for a permanent record of Rachel's online writing in book form. Blogging as we knew it then has largely disappeared, and there's been concern that Rachel's blog posts would someday disappear into the ether of the internet.

At the request of her widower Dan Evans, I began to compile her blog posts for this book. I was honored to be asked—after all, I was there for almost every single post, in real time. But I'm not alone in that claim. There were hundreds of us writing alongside Rachel, beloved by Rachel, supported and cheered and bolstered by her, and intimately acquainted with her blog. I feel profoundly humbled by this project, not only because I deeply love and miss my friend, but because I want to do right by all of us who were there, too, all of us who can recall certain posts by memory to this day, knowing where we were when we read it, knowing all that her words ignited in our lives.

This project has been harder than I could have imagined, but it has also been more beautiful and healing than I could have hoped. My heart has been broken anew almost daily—but then stitched up again, bound by the thread of hope that Rachel herself weaves into each line.

Editing and compiling this book is the closest I've come to time travel so far. There are names of people I'd forgotten but whom I would credit as deeply influential in my own faith journey. There are allusions to controversies now forgotten, origin stories for writers you now know and love, and a lot of now-answered, but then-unknown, questions.

The book you hold in your hands is only a sample of Rachel's online work, so let me share some context for how I approached this impossible project. Beyond simply selecting the most viral posts, I decided to include representative posts from across the spectrum of her work, and to include the voices of those in her online community of writers and readers because her work was always part of a larger conversation. I reached out to dozens of her friends, fellow writers, teachers, and colleagues from that era, asking them to reflect on her work and contextualize these posts' influence. You'll find those reflections scattered throughout the book.

When people attributed her influence to her more controversial posts, Rachel retorted that it was much simpler than that: She was just a faithful writer who showed up to the empty Draft Post box on her blog every single day. Her readers knew they could count on her. From 2013 to 2016, she wrote daily, diligently, and consistently, and so you'll find that time period overly represented in this book. Her blogging began to slow down in 2016, after the birth of her son and as she prioritized her book writing and speaking commitments, but still, she blogged right up until the end.

I have had the impossible job of choosing what to include and what to exclude (this book was initially three times longer than what you currently hold in your hand—I'm sorry, and you're welcome). I made every effort to choose the posts that were not just the most popular, but also those essays that I knew she loved or that meant something to her. I've made only light edits to contextualize social media–oriented posts, update links and organize citations, refresh language where language has evolved, and provide background for new readers.

Finally, while the posts are organized thematically, rather than chronologically, I include the original posting dates at the end of each selection to allow readers to position each post in the context of Rachel's broader evolution. Opinions or perspectives she held at one time may have shifted altogether within a few short years, and, in many ways, her blog serves as a way for Rachel to demonstrate her evolution throughout those years.

IN THE FIRST EPISODE OF THE *EVOLVING FAITH PODCAST*, I mused that it was interesting to me how often Rachel was characterized as a rebel, as being *in opposition*. "But to tell the truth about Rachel is to recognize what she was really *for*," I said. "She was for sharing the love of God. She was someone who, inspired by Jesus's love for her, poured out an uncommon and wildly generous love. She was someone who called others to do the same and who worked relentlessly for the good of all people whether they agreed with her or not."

My friend and cohost Jeff Chu responded, "That was the thing about Rachel. All people were Rachel's people. Rachel was for an all-embracing vision of Christ's church, and the relentless inclusion of refugees and those suffering poverty, of LGBTQ+ people, of women and especially women of color. I think she recognized the real geometry of God. . . . She pointed us back to Jesus, to one another, and to the church."

You'll see that in the following pages. Rachel gave permission to an entire generation to quite simply tell the truth. She was a prophet in a cardigan, a friend to the misfits and wanderers, a hopeful voice, and an unrepentant questioner.

If I know one thing to be true about Rachel, it is that she would be the first person to reject even unofficial sainthood. I think she'd probably find the very existence of this book hilarious, maybe even a bit mortifying. She never bought her own hype. She was quick to elevate others when the attention was on her. So it is my earnest hope that you will not miss the story behind the story here: Rachel wasn't blogging alone. She was part of a community, one that she led well, not from a pedestal or a pulpit but right alongside of us and in real time.

This book is a testimony to Rachel and her work, yes, but I have come to realize that this book is also a memorial for all of us who were evolving alongside Rachel. It is an artifact of a moment in the life of the church and the internet. It is a love letter to her fellow bloggers, her commenters, her readers, even her critics. And it is the story of how one Southern millennial woman troubled the establishment, gathered up the misfits, told our stories, evolved in public, and helped us love God and each other just a bit better in real time.

If you want to understand the church today, you need to understand Rachel Held Evans. If you want to understand both the rise of what she used to call "the unholy American trinity of patriarchy, white supremacy, and religious nationalism," well, you can start here. If you want to understand why so many folks are deconstructing their faith, this is as good a place as any to begin. And if you want to understand why so many of us remember her, and will always remember her, with such love, this book is for you.

Sarah Bessey
Epiphany 2025

PART ONE

AN EVOLVING FAITH

Essays on Doubt, Asking Questions,
and the Cost of It All

Traveling Mercies for the "Consummate Ass"

Editor's note: This was Rachel's very first blog post, originally posted on December 28, 2007.

Whenever a friend returns from Florence or Venice or Rome, it inevitably happens. She publicly disavows herself from ever eating at the Olive Garden again. "Once you've had the real thing," she always says, "you just can't go back."

I always feel foolish when I unwittingly invite such a person for an evening of much-too-rich fettuccini Alfredo and way-overcooked-nothing-like-authentic linguini. If I gush over the gelato, will she think me uncultured?

Mark Twain said this about traveling abroad: "We wish to learn all the curious, outlandish ways of all the different countries, so that we can show off and astonish people when we get home. We wish to excite the envy of our untraveled friends with our strange foreign fashions which we can't shake off. The gentle reader will never, never know what a consummate ass he can become until he goes abroad."*

I think it is much the same with spiritual journeys. Having

---

* Mark Twain, *The Innocents Abroad* (American Publishing Company, 1869), 163.

recently "returned" from a long and difficult journey through doubt, I find myself reminiscing snobbishly about all the books I've read, all the edgy and intelligent questions I've asked, and all the exotic, complicated answers I've convinced myself I've found. Ask me anything about pluralism and I will wax eloquent. Suggest evangelism as a solution to Africa's problems and I will roll my eyes at your simplicity. Tell me you've done some traveling of your own and I will avert your gaze, worried you've been somewhere I haven't been.

As with the literal traveler, I think such arrogance is just a way of glossing over how out-of-place and scared I felt when abroad, when perched on those high peaks and lost in those shadowy valleys.

Spiritual pride is always a temptation for the believer, and I sincerely hope it is avoided on this blog. No one's journey is the same. There is much to learn from one another. So instead, I would like this little spot on the Web to serve as a sort of traveler's forum, a place for exchanging adventure stories, survival tips, and those priceless hole-in-the-wall recommendations that make a journey memorable. I look forward to sharing my own ideas, and I look forward to hearing from you.

So, in the spirit of humility, let us celebrate our wanderings, our little journeys without destinations—keeping in mind that even our most profound ideas are little more than dinners at the Olive Garden compared to the "real thing."

Twain continues, "I speak now, of course, in the supposition that the gentle reader has not been abroad and therefore is not already a consummate ass. If the case be otherwise, I beg his pardon and extend to him the cordial hand of fellowship and call him brother. I shall always delight to meet an ass after my own heart when I have finished my own travels."

The Scandal of the Evangelical Heart

It's right for God to slaughter women and children anytime he pleases. God gives life and he takes life. Everybody who dies, dies because God wills that they die.
—JOHN PIPER*

Belief in a cruel God makes a cruel man.
—THOMAS PAINE†

It's strange to think that doubt has been a part of my life for more than ten years now.

I remember when it first showed up—a dark grotesque with a terrifying smile that took up so much space, catching every prayer in its gravitational pull. That I could grow accustomed to its presence seemed impossible at the time, and yet I have. It hasn't changed in size, but somehow it occupies less space. I smile back at it now.

A lot of people, when they catch pieces of my story, assume my

---

* "What Made It Okay for God to Kill Women and Children in the Old Testament?: Interview with John Piper," Desiring God, February 27, 2010, https://www.desiringgod.org/interviews/what-made-it-okay-for-god-to-kill-women-and-children-in-the-old-testament.

† Thomas Paine, *The Age of Reason* (Barrois, 1794), Kindle Edition LOC 11487 of 14506.

doubts are of the intellectual variety. They assume I'm just a smart girl stuck in the Bible Belt asking pesky questions about science, history, and politics that my conservative evangelical culture, with a bent toward anti-intellectualism, simply cannot answer.

This is true to an extent. I've wrestled with a lot of questions related to science and faith, especially given my location a mere two miles from the famous Rhea County Courthouse where John Scopes was prosecuted for teaching evolution in a public school. While I no longer believe the earth is just six thousand years old, I still live in the tension of unanswered questions about the universe, and death, and brains, and Neanderthals, and whatever Neil deGrasse Tyson's got to say on public television about the earth getting burned up by the sun or our species going extinct after an asteroid hits. I have questions too about history and Christianity's emergence from it, questions about the Bible, questions about miracles.

But the questions that have weighed most heavily on me these past ten years have been questions not of the mind but of the heart, questions of conscience and empathy. It was not the so-called scandal of the evangelical mind that rocked my faith; it was the scandal of the evangelical heart.

If you've read *Evolving in Monkey Town*, you know that the public execution of a woman named Zarmina in Afghanistan marked a turning point in my faith journey. The injustice of the situation was troublesome enough, but when my friends insisted that Zarmina went to hell because she was a Muslim, I began wrestling with some serious questions about heaven, hell, predestination, free will, God's goodness, and religious pluralism.

Evangelical apologists were quick to respond. And while their answers made enough sense in my head, they never sat right with my soul.

Why would God fashion a person in her mother's womb, number the hairs on her head, and then leave her without any hope of salvation? Can salvation be boiled down to luck of the draw? How is that just? Shouldn't God be more loving and compassionate than I?

Oh, the Calvinists could make perfect sense of it all with a wave of a hand and a swift, confident explanation about how Zarmina had been born in sin and likely predestined to spend eternity in hell to the glory of an angry God (they called her a "vessel of destruction"*); about how I should just be thankful to be spared the same fate since it's what I deserve anyway; about how the Indian Ocean tsunami was just another one of God's temper tantrums sent to remind us all of his rage at our sin; about how I need not worry because "there is not one maverick molecule in the universe"† so every hurricane, every earthquake, every war, every execution, every transaction in the slave trade, every rape of a child is part of God's sovereign plan, even God's idea; about how my objections to this paradigm represented unrepentant pride and a capitulation to humanism that placed too much inherent value on my fellow human beings; about how my intuitive sense of love and morality and right and wrong is so corrupted by my sin nature I cannot trust it.

They said all of this without so much of a glimmer of a tear, and it scared me to death. It nearly scared me out of the church.

For what makes the church any different from a cult if it demands we sacrifice our conscience in exchange for unquestioned allegiance to authority? What sort of God would call himself love and then ask that I betray everything I know in my bones to be love in order to worship him? Did following Jesus mean becoming

---

* In Reformed theology, the phrase "vessels of destruction" refers to people or even nations who are destined for God's wrath and judgment. Rachel is referring to the practice of labeling people as such.

† This is a well-known and often referenced quote from R. C. Sproul. You can find references to it in most Reformed theologians' work. For instance: Tyler L. Fischer, *Omnibus I: Biblical and Classical Civilizations* (Veritas Press, 2005), 332.

some shadow of myself, drained of empathy and compassion and revulsion to injustice?

Perhaps in reaction to the "scandal of the evangelical mind," evangelicalism of late has developed a general distrust of emotion when it comes to theology. So long as an idea seems logical, so long as it fits consistently with the favored theological paradigm, it seems to matter not whether it is morally reprehensible at an intuitive level. I suspect this is why this new breed of rigid Calvinism that follows the "five points" to their most logical conclusion, without regard to the moral implications of them, has flourished in the past twenty years. (I heard a theology professor explain the other day that he had no problem whatsoever with God orchestrating evil acts to accomplish God's will, for that is what is required for God to be fully sovereign! When asked if this does not make God something of a monster, he responded that it didn't matter; God is God—end of story.) And I suspect this explains why, in the wake of the Sandy Hook tragedy, so many evangelical leaders responded like Job's friends, eager to offer theological explanations for what happened instead of simply sitting down in the ashes and weeping with their brothers and sisters.

Richard Beck has also observed this phenomenon and refers to it as "orthodox alexithymia":

. . . By "orthodox" I mean the intellectual pursuit of right belief . . .

Alexithymia—etymologically "without words for emotions"—is a symptom characteristic of individuals who have difficulty understanding their own and others' emotions. You can think of alexithymia as being the opposite of what is called emotional intelligence.

Orthodox alexithymia is produced when the intellectual facets of Christian theology, in the pursuit of correct and right belief, become decoupled from emotion, empathy, and fellow-feeling. . . .*

I encountered this recently after I spoke to a group of youth about doubt. In the presentation, I mentioned that upon reading the story of Joshua and the Battle of Jericho for myself, I realized it was a story about genocide, with God commanding Joshua to kill every man, woman, and child in the city for the sole purpose of acquiring land. I explained that this seemed contrary to what Jesus taught about loving our enemies.

Afterward, a youth leader informed me that when it came to Joshua and Jericho, I had nothing to worry about . . . and had no business getting his students worried either.

"I don't know why you had to bring up the Jericho thing," he said.

"Doesn't that story bother you?" I asked. "Don't you find the slaughter of men, women, and children horrific?"

"Not if it's in the Bible."

"Genocide doesn't bother you if it's in the Bible?"

"Nope."

He crossed his arms and a self-satisfied smile spread across his face. He was proud of his detachment, I realized. He seemed to think it represented some kind of spiritual strength.

"But genocide always bothers me," I finally said, "especially when it's in the Bible. And I get the idea that maybe it's supposed to. I get the idea that maybe God created me to be bothered by evil like that, even when it's said to have been orchestrated by God."

I'm not sure he and I will ever understand one another, but I've decided to quit apologizing for my questions. It's not enough

---

* Richard Beck, "Orthodox Alexithymia," Experimental Theology, May 16, 2012, https://experimentaltheology.blogspot.com/2012/05/orthodox-alexithymia.html.

for me to maintain my intellectual integrity as a Christian; I also want to maintain my emotional integrity as a Christian. And I don't need answers to all of my questions to do that. I need only the courage to be honest about my questions and doubts, and the patience to keep exploring and trusting in spite of them.

The bravest decision I'll ever make is the decision to follow Jesus with both my head and heart engaged—no checking out, no pretending.

It's a decision I make every day, and it's a decision that's made my faith journey a heck of a lot more hazardous and a heck of a lot more fun. It means that grinning monster, doubt, is likely to stick around for a while, for I know now that closing my eyes won't make him go away. It means each day is a risk, a gamble, an adventure in vulnerability and trust, as I figure out what it means to follow Jesus as me, Rachel Grace—the girl who cried for Zarmina, the girl who inherited her mama's bleeding heart and her daddy's stubborn grace, the girl who digs in her heels, the girl who makes mistakes, the girl who is intent on breaking up patriarchy, the girl who thought to raise her hand in Sunday school at age five and ask why God would drown innocent animals in Noah's flood, the girl who could be wrong.

It means I've got a long race ahead of me, but I'm going to run it with abandon. I'm going to run it as me. Because I think that's what God wants—all of me, surrendered and transformed, head and heart engaged.

I'm growing more confident in my stride, and I am running faster now, breathless, kicking up dust, tripping over roots and skinning my knees, cursing now and then, but always getting up and gaining ground on that bend in the path where I think I can see Jesus up ahead.

Originally posted on January 24, 2013.

They Were Right (and Wrong) About the Slippery Slope

They said that if I questioned a six-thousand-year-old earth, I would question whether other parts of Scripture should be read scientifically and historically.

They were right. I did.

They said that if I entertained the hope that those without access to the gospel might still be loved and saved by God, I would fall prey to the dangerous idea that God loves everyone, that there is nothing God won't do to reconcile all things to himself.

They were right. I have.

They said that if I looked for Jesus beyond the party line, I could end up voting for liberals.

They were right. I do (sometimes).

They said that if I listened to my gay and lesbian neighbors, if I made room for them in my church and in my life, I could let grace get out of hand.

They were right. It has.

They told me that this slippery slope would lead me away from God, that it would bring a swift end to my faith journey, that I'd be lost forever.

But with that one, they were wrong.

Yes, the slippery slope brought doubts. Yes, the slippery slope brought change. Yes, the slippery slope brought danger and risk and unknowns. I am indeed more exposed to the elements out here, and at times it is hard to find my footing.

But when I decided I wanted to follow Jesus as myself, with both my head and heart intact, the slippery slope was the only place I could find him, the only place I could engage my faith honestly.

So down I went.

It was easier before, when the path was wide and straight.

But, truth be told, I was faking it. I was pretending that things that didn't make sense made sense, that things that didn't feel right felt right. To others, I appeared confident and in control, but faith felt as far away as a friend who has grown distant and cold.

Now, every day is a risk.

Now, I have no choice but to cling to faith and hope and love for dear life.

Now, I have to keep a very close eye on Jesus, as he leads me through deep valleys and precarious peaks.

But the view is better, and, for the first time in a long time, I am fully engaged in my faith.

I am alive.

I am dependent.

I am following Jesus as *me*—heart and head intact.

And they were right. All it took was a question or two to bring me here.

Originally posted on January 31, 2012.

This Was a Turning Point
A REFLECTION BY MATTHEW PAUL TURNER

The first time I met Rachel was in 2010 when we co-headlined a presentation at the Southern Festival of Books, an event at which she discussed her debut, *Evolving in Monkey Town*,* and I read excerpts from my memoir, *Hear No Evil*. Prior to our book event, which was attended by exactly thirteen people, half of whom were related to one of us, Rachel and I had developed a growing connection over email.

Our shared experiences were too many to count for us to not become friends—both of us were writers who'd been raised in conservative churches, and we were now using our words to process our shifting beliefs about God and culture on our blogs and in our books. We were hardly the only ones doing this, but we most definitely were some of the most outspoken of the bunch. Moreover, both of us, at least according to members of our own families and some of the readers of our books and blogs, were on very slippery slopes.

Having grown up in a hyperconservative Christian environment, I was raised to believe that hell was hot, that the Bible was the inerrant word of God, and that the only thing worse than being on a "slippery slope" was becoming a slippery slope for other people.

---

* *Evolving in Monkey Town* was the original title of *Faith Unraveled: How a Girl Who Knew All the Answers Learned to Ask the Questions.*

And while I can't speak for Rachel, I remember feeling a lot of fear in those early days of riding down that slide, not necessarily because I was on it—but because I didn't want to be the reason why somebody else was on it. And certainly, on many occasions, my critics weaponized that fear. They told me that there was a special place in hell for people like me, people who used their influence to create "stumbling blocks" for other believers, a "false teacher" who led the faithful astray.

That's why Rachel's words about what those critics got right (and wrong) regarding the slippery slope connected with me in 2012 when she wrote them and why they have connected with me many times since. Because I believe this was a turning point for Rachel. These words represent a woman who was becoming comfortable in her discomfort. She was owning her place, not only as writer and as person of faith, but she was surrendering to them what was theirs and keeping for herself what she knew was hers. Rather than continuing to defend her story and her doubts by their rules and their beliefs, Rachel, in this post, was making an intentional effort to redefine the field of play, to stop being an outsider in their game, and to begin fully showing up in the story that God was creating in her and for her.

The first time I read these words, I was taken aback by Rachel's willingness to say the critics were right. Because they loved being right. And I hated giving them that satisfaction. But ultimately, Rachel's confession here helped to empower my faith journey, to let them have the parts that were always theirs, and to begin building and rebuilding on what was still mine—my faith in God. Releasing to them what was theirs was me letting go of their fears, their shames, and it was also me taking one more step toward letting go of my own.

Why I Can't Stay Angry (Even Though I Want To)

Sometimes I get angry.

I get angry when a young woman describes what it felt like to watch men stand up and leave the sanctuary when she approached the podium to give her first sermon. I get angry when evangelical leaders show more concern for protecting the powerful at Sovereign Grace Ministries than protecting vulnerable children.* I get angry when my most reasoned arguments are dismissed as "emotional" and "shrill" or when people question my commitment to my faith because I accept evolution or support women in ministry. I get angry when a young gay man cries into my shoulder as he recounts being turned away from his church.

I get angry when I overhear people at a restaurant talking about how they hope the verdict in the Trayvon Martin/George Zimmerman case will "teach those people to show some respect." (Yes, this happened.) I get angry when, like Paul, "what I want to do I do not do, but what I hate I do."

(And it's not just noble stuff either. You should see me when we lose our internet connection.)

I don't think anger is inherently wrong. Anger is part of what it

---

* Sovereign Grace Churches, previously Sovereign Grace Ministries, was embroiled in multiple scandals and lawsuits at the time due to a series of horrific abuse cover-ups.

means to be human, to be empathetic, to be engaged, to recognize sin for what it is, to be tenderhearted and vulnerable, to be awake in this world. Throughout Scripture we encounter a God who is angered by injustice and the neglect of the poor. Jesus expressed anger at those who exploited the poor and vulnerable, who harmed children, and who "shut the door to the Kingdom in people's faces" through religious legalism and exclusion. As N. T. Wright has said, "To deny God's wrath is, at bottom, to deny God's love. When God sees human beings enslaved . . . if God doesn't hate it, he is not a loving God."*

We are right to be angered by inequity and injustice, whether inflicted upon ourselves or on other people. And we have to be very careful of telling other people—particularly those in the process of healing—when they ought to be angry, when they ought to forgive, or when they ought to "move on."

But if Jesus is our example, if being fully human and fully God looks like this carpenter from Nazareth, we know that the evil within ourselves and in this world cannot be conquered by hate but must be overcome with love.

"You have heard that it was said, 'Love your neighbor and hate your enemy,'" Jesus says in a particularly annoying part of the Sermon on the Mount. *"But I tell you, love your enemies and pray for those who persecute you, that you may be children of your Father in heaven."*

I struggle with this. . . . like, big time.

A skeptic who is prone to cynicism, and a contemplative who is prone to indulgence, I find myself sinking into a state of bitterness from time to time. I lose hope—in myself, in others, in the church, in God. I forget that we know the ending to this story and that it

---

* N. T. Wright, "The Word of the Cross," ntwrightonline.org, sermon dated April 5, 2007, https://ntwrightpage.com/2016/03/30/the-word-of-the-cross/.

involves a lovely bride and a big banquet, and instead I assume the worst of other people, expecting the worst from this world.

But I know from experience that bitterness weakens a strong argument.

It breaks down dialog.

It gets in the way of change.

It weighs me down.

Anger, I think, is meant to wake us up, to provide clarity and direction. It's meant to be a starting point, the gun that sounds at the start of a race, a catalyst.

Bitterness lulls us back to sleep. It paralyzes us with "why bother?" and "it's no use." It grabs us like a riptide and pulls us away from shore. Eventually, it drowns us.

As a wise friend recently said, "Anger is supposed to be a flash fire that burns away the chaff and leaves clarity in its wake. To linger in anger or to make anger and wrath the first choice response is to burn out the humanity within you."

I recently bumped into a fascinating article by Hitendra Wadhwa about how Martin Luther King Jr. processed and harnessed his own anger, entitled "The Wrath of a Great Leader."

Recalling a particularly frustrating negotiation around the bus boycott in Montgomery, Dr. King wrote that *"on two or three occasions I had allowed myself to become angry and indignant. I had spoken hastily and resentfully. Yet I knew that this was no way to solve a problem. 'You must not harbor anger,' I admonished myself. 'You must be willing to suffer the anger of the opponent, and yet not return anger. You must not become bitter. No matter how emotional your opponents are, you must be calm.'"* [*]

---

[*] Hitendra Wadhwa, "The Wrath of a Great Leader: How Martin Luther King Jr. Wrestled with Anger and What You Can Learn from His Example," Inc., February 6, 2020, http://www.inc.com/hitendra-wadhwa/great-leadership-how-martin-luther-king-jr-wrestled-with-anger.html.

When his home in Birmingham, Alabama, was bombed by white extremists, he wrote: "*While I lay in that quiet front bedroom, I began to think of the viciousness of people who would bomb my home. I could feel the anger rising when I realized that my wife and baby could have been killed. I was once more on the verge of corroding hatred. And once more I caught myself and said: 'You must not allow yourself to become bitter.'*"

"You must not allow yourself to become bitter."

I'm writing that on a sticky note to put above my desk as we speak.

Dr. King didn't tell his followers not to be angry. He told them to turn their anger into constructive (nonviolent) action. In a 1968 article he said, "The supreme task [of a leader] is to organize and unite people so that their anger becomes a transforming force."

Or, as Gandhi famously said, "I have learnt through bitter experience the one supreme lesson to conserve my anger, and as heat conserved is transmuted into energy, even so our anger controlled can be transmuted into a power that can move the world."

As Christians work to find our prophetic voices in this culture, as we engage the world and one another in areas of disagreement, we must take these words to heart. Like it or not, we are called to a higher standard; we are called to forgive, to be peacemakers, to extend grace to those who don't deserve it.

And even as I type those words I don't want to do it—not for Mark Driscoll,* not for the folks defending Sovereign Grace, not for those jerks at the restaurant.

I've been thinking lately that the hardest part of fundamentalism for me to leave behind is the part that equates rightness with righteousness, the part that makes "winning" the goal.

---

* Mark Driscoll is a disgraced pastor who was highly influential at the time of Rachel's online writing. For more on his story, check out *Christianity Today*'s podcast series *The Rise and Fall of Mars Hill*.

Because I like winning arguments.

No, I LOVE winning arguments.

No, if I could marry winning arguments and cuddle with winning arguments every night while we watched *30 Rock* reruns together, I probably would.

And yet I feel God's presence most profoundly when I give up—not on making the argument, but on winning it. I know God's love with more certainty, not when I've proven it, but when I've experienced it and when I've extended it. I find the most peace when like Dallas Willard I "practice the discipline of not having to have the last word."*

It's possible, I suppose, to win an argument and lose your soul.

Jesus said we are to be wise as serpents and harmless as doves, and that bugs me because I like people to know I'm wise, that I'm not some naïve girl they can toy with, and I've convinced myself that the only way to prove my wisdom is to strike with venom in my teeth, to cause pain.

But Jesus doesn't say we are to be naïve. He doesn't say we are to be stupid as doves or naïve as doves or obnoxiously cheery as doves (no offense to doves here). He says we are to be harmless as doves. So if I'm going to become this awesome Jesusy-snake-dove creature, I guess I'm going to have to find something else to do with all this venom . . . like donate it to the antidote bank or something, as snakes do.

After all, the words Jesus promises at the end of this journey aren't "*Congratulations! You were right!*" The words Jesus promises at the end of this journey are, "*Well done my good and faithful servant.*"

Good. Faithful. Angry. Hopeful. Wise. Harmless. Cunning. Gentle.

---

* Dallas Willard, *Living in Christ's Presence: Final Words on Heaven and the Kingdom of God* (IVP, 2017), 42.

Now don't get me wrong: I'm not telling you not to be angry. You may be in an important season of healing in which anger is healthy and important and necessary for growth.

And I'm certainly not telling you to stop making the case for justice—for women, for LGBTQ+ people, for the poor, for the marginalized, for the abused, for yourself.

I'm telling you why *I* can't stay angry, even though sometimes I want to.

I can't stay angry because it debilitates me. It makes me unhappy and it makes the people around me unhappy.

I can't stay angry because I genuinely believe change is possible, and so I need to practice seeing that capacity for change in myself, in the church, in those with whom I disagree, even in my enemies. Only then can we draw it out together.

I can't stay angry because on good days I believe that love wins.

And I can't stay angry because even on bad days I can't get rid of the stubborn hope that maybe someday this little mustard seed of faith in me will grow into a tree after all.

Pope Francis recently told the enormous crowds who had gathered in Rio for World Youth Day, "You are often disappointed by facts that speak of corruption on the part of people who put their own interests before the common good. To you and all, I repeat: Never yield to discouragement, do not lose trust, do not allow your hope to be extinguished."

Reminds me of Jesus's words, "Do not let your hearts be troubled."

I'm not telling you not to be angry.

I'm telling you not to give up hope.

Originally posted on July 26, 2013.

The Power of Testimony
An Excerpt from Inspired

Editor's note: Rachel often posted excerpts from her books on the blog.

"There is deliverance in the music, there is healing in the music, there is love—there is love—in the music."

Tiffany Thomas had reached a crescendo. As the twenty-nine-year-old pastor concluded her riveting and rhythmic testimony about how the hymns of the Black church drew her to Jesus, the nine hundred people crammed into Saint Mark's Cathedral in Minneapolis rose to their feet and cheered.

That weekend, a dozen speakers, ranging from pastors to artists to teachers to scientists joined Tiffany in responding to the question, Why Christian? Why, with all the atrocities past and present committed in God's name, amid all the divisions ripping apart the church, in spite of all their doubts and frustrations and fears about faith, are they still followers of Jesus? What makes them continue to believe?

My friend Nadia Bolz-Weber and I posed the question at our inaugural Why Christian? conference in 2015 because it's a question that weighs on us every day and it's a question

Christians don't ask one another often enough. As each speaker approached the microphone to share their stories—some with the practiced cadence of working preachers, others with a quiet vulnerability, and all with the conviction of people whose faith has been hard-won—it became clear that there simply remains no greater apologetic for the Christian faith than a life caught up in the story of Jesus.

"I am a Christian," explained Episcopal priest Kerlin Richter, "because having a body wasn't always good news for me, but then I met Good News that had a body. In Jesus, I met a God who spits and kisses, who yells and cries. I am a messy and embodied person, and this is a messy and embodied faith."

"I am a Christian," declared Austin Channing Brown, an author and activist whose work focuses on racial justice in the church, "because God knows my pain, not in an abstract way, but in a real, bloody, enfleshed way."

"I am a Christian," said Rachel Murr, a researcher and counselor, "because the gospel is good news for gay people too."

"I am a Christian," explained Baptist preacher and human rights activist Allyson Robinson, "because I don't always know if this story is true, but I choose to live my life as if it were. I choose to live as if the things Jesus died for were worthy of God's sacrifice and therefore worthy of mine."

We were a diverse group: evangelical and Lutheran, Baptist and Episcopalian, Latina and Black and white and Indian and Korean, high church and low church, Catholic and Protestant, Reformed and Methodist, straight and gay and bisexual and transgender, pastors and scholars, writers and activists, crunchy dreadlocked mamas, tattooed and foul-mouthed priests, sweet-talkin' southerners, and stiletto-boasting fashionistas. Looking at us from the outside, you'd have no idea what we all had in common. While there were variations in the verses, our shared refrain remained unapologetically orthodox, undeniably Christian. We spoke of sin, repentance, baptism, confession, incarnation, resurrection, and Scripture. We proclaimed the great mystery of the faith—that Christ has died, Christ has risen, and Christ will come again. We served and received communion. We ran out of tissue.

When it came time for me to share, I spoke honestly about my doubts about the Bible and Christianity. I confessed my uncertainties about raising children in this broken and beloved community we call the church. I explained how gatherings like these help restore my faith because they pull me out of my head and into the lives of others, into the big, colorful, messy, and magical story of Jesus.

"I am a Christian," I concluded, "because the story of Jesus is still the story I'm willing to risk being wrong about."

I had forgotten the power of giving testimony, of publicly recounting our unique "gospels according to . . ." We can know a person for decades, share a pew with them in church every Sunday, without ever knowing their testimonies, without ever asking them, "Hey, why Christian?" We can spend a lifetime singing hymns and reading the Bible without honestly answering that question for ourselves.

Jesus invites us into a story that is bigger than ourselves, bigger than our culture, bigger even than our imaginations, and yet we get to tell that story with the scandalous particularity of our particular moment and place in time. We are storytelling creatures because we are fashioned in the image of a storytelling God.

May we never neglect the gift of that. May we never lose our love for telling the tale.

Originally posted on March 5, 2019.

A Christian Faith I'm Willing to Risk Being Wrong About

A REFLECTION BY MASON MENNENGA

I used to be a Christian because my interpretation of the Bible was something with certainty that I was right about, but then I experienced Jesus . . . through Rachel.

Like Rachel, I grew up evangelical. The first songs I learned were sung by the animated vegetables Bob the Tomato and Larry the Cucumber. I asked for Jesus to be my personal Lord and Savior when I was ten years old. When I learned about evolution in school, I wrote a paper defending Young Earth Creationism. I committed to saving sex for marriage. I went on a mission trip every year in middle school and high school. In many ways I was the ideal youth group kid.

Then I went off to a conservative, evangelical college, with the hopes of many that I would not be "corrupted" by the evils of liberal education. Growing up evangelical meant that I was certain about my faith, but it was during college that my faith began to unravel. I began doubting everything that I had been taught and grown up believing.

I truly thought no other Christian had experienced doubting their faith like this before. I felt alone.

And then I found Rachel.

Reading Rachel's books helped me feel a little less alone in my deconstruction. I wasn't sure if there were a lot of us who were deconstructing our faith, but at least I had Rachel.

There are many things over the years that Rachel said that made me see something I could never unsee. However, there is one that has remained with me more than others:

"I am a Christian because the story of Jesus is still the story I'm willing to risk being wrong about."

The story of Jesus is a radical one. It's a story of God becoming human in a poor, brown baby—in the lowliest of places. The Gospels share many stories of Jesus caring for the let down, left out, and left behind. He is executed by the world's largest empire, and because violence does not have the final answer, he rises from the dead three days later.

I grew up believing these stories about Jesus had to be historically true in order for me, or anyone else for that matter, to have faith in them. I read all of the Christian apologetics books about why the stories of Jesus historically happened. The case for Christ's power rested on the stories being factual.

However, Rachel taught me that the true mark of faith in the story of Jesus isn't in being certain about its literal historical factualness, but that it is worth willing to risk being wrong.

Even if none of the stories about Jesus ever historically happened, I would still be a Christian because that's how much the stories of Jesus have transformed my life and how much I think they can still transform the world.

Now, with a little help from Rachel, I have a Christian faith that I'm willing to risk being wrong about, and in doing so, hopefully I reflect the love and liberation of Jesus a bit more.

Holy Week for Doubters

It will bother you off and on, like a rock in your shoe,
    Or it will startle you, like the first crash of thunder in a summer storm,
    Or it will lodge itself beneath your skin like a splinter,
    Or it will show up again—the uninvited guest whose heavy footsteps you'd recognize anywhere, appearing at your front door with a suitcase in hand at the worst. possible. time.
    Or it will pull you farther out to sea like riptide,
    Or hold your head under as you drown—
    Triggered by an image, a question, something the pastor said, something that doesn't add up, the unlikelihood of it all, the too-good-to-be-trueness of it, the way the lady in the thick perfume behind you sings "Up from the grave he arose!" with more confidence in the single line of a song than you've managed to muster in the past two years.
    And you'll be sitting there in the dress you pulled out from the back of your closet, swallowing down the bread and wine, not believing a word of it.
    Not. A. Word.
    So you'll fumble through those back pocket prayers—"help me in my unbelief!"—while everyone around you moves on to verse two, verse three, verse four without you.
    You will feel their eyes on you, and you will recognize the concern

behind their cheery greetings: "We haven't seen you here in a while! So good to have you back."

And you will know they are thinking exactly what you used to think about Easter Sunday Christians:

Nominal.

Lukewarm.

Indifferent.

But you won't know how to explain that there is nothing nominal or lukewarm or indifferent about standing in this hurricane of questions every day and staring each one down until you've mustered all the bravery and fortitude and trust it takes to whisper just one of them out loud on the car ride home:

"What if we made this up because we're afraid of death?"

And you won't know how to explain why, in that moment when the whisper rose out of your mouth like Jesus from the grave, you felt more alive and awake and resurrected than you have in ages because at least it was out, at least it was said, at least it wasn't buried in your chest anymore, clawing for freedom.

And, if you're lucky, someone in the car will recognize the bravery of the act. If you're lucky, there will be a moment of holy silence before someone wonders out loud if such a question might put a damper on Easter brunch.

But if you're not—if the question gets answered too quickly or if the silence goes on too long—please know you are not alone.

There are other people singing words to hymns they're not sure they believe today, other people digging out dresses from the backs of their closets today, other people ruining Easter brunch today, other people just showing up today.

And sometimes, just showing up—burial spices in hand—is all it takes to witness a miracle.

Originally posted on March 27, 2013.

The Thing I'd Love to Forget About the People I Disagree With

I was talking the other day with a person with whom I disagree on just about everything—theology, politics, women in ministry, faith and science, biblical interpretation, doubt, hell, homosexuality, you name it. We were in the awkward process of making peace after some lines had been crossed and feelings hurt, and as we got to know one another a little better in that conversation, we had the chance to share more about our personal journeys and how we came to see the world in the ways that we do.

As we talked, I realized how much I had wanted to assume this guy was just taking the easy way out, simply toeing the conservative party line and falling in step with what everyone around him believed. But as his story emerged, I learned that he too had wrestled with his beliefs, that they had a profound personal impact on his life and his relationships, and that these beliefs indeed came with a cost. I had assumed he had taken the easiest path when he hadn't.

It bothers me when people make the same careless assumptions about me.

Just yesterday I was warned by someone that my support for women in ministry and my inclusion of LGBTQ+ voices on the blog represented an effort "to be liked by other people and win the approval of the world." I shook my head and released a sad laugh. This person had no idea how much hell I've taken from people in my evangelical community for writing about my doubts, my questions related to heaven and hell, my views on biblical interpretation and theology, and my support for women in ministry and other marginalized people in the church. For believing that the earth is more than six thousand years old, I've been called an idolatrous shrew who hates the Bible and has no business calling herself a Christian. I've been denied speaking and writing opportunities and banned from bookstores. I've wept as close friends slowly distanced themselves from me and well-meaning church people treated me like a project—someone to pray about, gossip about, and fix. Institutions that once welcomed me as a daughter have essentially disowned me. It's nothing compared to what many other people experience in the church, but it's painful. And there are indeed many professors who have lost their jobs, pastors who have lost their congregations, and others who have lost their families and friends as a result of their evolving perspectives on faith. *It's not a road you take because it's easy.*

I don't ask these questions and explore these issues because I want to be liked; I ask these questions and explore these issues because I want to believe what's true. I want to do what's right. I want my faith to make sense in both my heart and my head and I want to honor Jesus with my life, my words, my actions. You can dismiss my views as unfounded or wrongheaded or unbiblical, but dismissing my journey in arriving at them as simply "taking the easy way out" or "capitulating to culture" makes a lot of unfair assumptions about me and my story. It also underestimates the degree to which various religious communities can themselves function as subcultures, complete with expectations, economies, peer pressure, blacklists, marginalization, and spoken and unspoken rules.

And yet . . .

I do the same thing to those with whom I disagree. I assumed this hard-core complementarian Calvinist was just going along with the majority, just making the easiest decisions, just bumbling along without considering the views or experiences of other people so that his safe little religious world would remain intact.

And I was wrong.

It simplifies things when we can write off the thoughts and opinions of other people by assuming they've taken the easy way out, that they're just trying to be popular and liked. It's oddly affirming to tell ourselves that *we're* the ones living counterculturally, *we're* the ones taking all the risks for the truth, *we're* the ones getting persecuted for our right and true beliefs.

And it's a bit disconcerting to confront the reality that it's possible to wrestle with the same God and walk with the same limp and yet reach different conclusions.

Perhaps it is in the wrestling itself that we can find some common ground.

Originally posted on September 11, 2013.

Jesus Started with the "Outliers"

It was one of those Twitter conversations I probably shouldn't have gotten sucked into.

We were debating whether or not it's helpful to use language like "act like a man," or "true womanhood," or "real men" in our religious dialogs, and I was arguing that the goal of the Christian life is to be conformed to the image of Christ, not idealized, culture-based gender stereotypes. He was making the case that men are "hardwired" to protect women and women are "hardwired" to be protected by men, and so the lifeboats on *Titanic* prove that women should not teach or lead in the church. I suggested that perhaps the lifeboats on the *Titanic* point to a more general sense that the stronger in a dangerous situation are morally compelled to protect the weaker in a dangerous situation, and that mothers can be awfully protective of their children after all, and that a man who (for whatever reason) might be weaker than a woman in a given situation should not feel like less of a man if she protects him. "What about a husband who is confined to a wheelchair?" I asked. "Is he 'less of a man' because he may be dependent in some situations on his wife's assistance? And should we perpetuate the stereotype that 'real men' must be physically stronger than the women in their lives?"

"Yes, but that's an unusual circumstance," he responded. "We can't base our theology on the outliers."

When he said it, something clicked in my head in a way it hadn't before, something that seems pretty obvious when you think about it, yet is so easy to forget:

"Yes, but Jesus STARTED with the 'outliers,'" I said. "If it doesn't work for them, it doesn't work."

There is this tendency within certain sectors of Christianity to assume that if our theology "works" for the relatively privileged (often for white, upper-middle-class American men), then it should work well enough for everyone else, and everyone else should conform to it.

We see this a lot in the gender debates, especially among those who suggest that the only way a family can truly honor God is with a husband who functions as the family breadwinner and a wife who functions as a stay-at-home mom to their 2.5 children, regardless of finances or practicality.* This may work for some people, but it doesn't work for the family earning minimum wage, or the couple facing infertility, or this awesome church community of immigrants that shares the responsibility of child-rearing together.†

Same goes for theologies that suggest the poor are poor because of their sins, that if only the sick had more faith or gave more money they would be healed, that the tsunami or the earthquake or the flood that devastated a community was clearly the result of God's wrath on its gay inhabitants, that we can stop rape by teaching women to cover up better, that sex before marriage makes a person "broken" and "unwanted."

---

* Samantha Field, "Guest Post: Focus on the Family: Feminism Is 'The Way of Death,'" Patheos, last updated September 9, 2013, https://www.patheos.com/blogs/lovejoyfeminism/2013/03/focus-on-the-family-feminism-is-the-way-of-death.html.

† Liuan Huska, "It Takes a Church to Raise a Child," *Christianity Today*, March 15, 2013, https://www.christianitytoday.com/2013/03/it-takes-church-to-raise-child.

Sure, we don't always think about women who have been sexually abused when we preach that wives need to be super-sexy to keep the interest of their husbands, or about infertile couples when we talk about how "a woman's highest calling is motherhood," or about our African American brothers and sisters and our Indigenous brothers and sisters when we trumpet America's great "Christian heritage."

But maybe we should.

If the gospel isn't good news to the so-called outliers, then it's not good news at all. And, in fact, if our theology doesn't start with the "outliers," then maybe we're doing it wrong.

Jesus started with the outliers and made no bones about it:

> The Spirit of the Lord is on me,
> because he has anointed me
> to proclaim good news to the poor.
> He has sent me to proclaim freedom for the prisoners
> and recovery of sight for the blind,
> to set the oppressed free,
> to proclaim the year of the Lord's favor. (From Luke 4)

In the Sermon on the Mount:

> Blessed are you who are poor,
> for yours is the kingdom of God.
> Blessed are you who hunger now,
> for you will be satisfied.
> Blessed are you who weep now,
> for you will laugh.
> Blessed are you when people hate you,
> when they exclude you and insult you,
> and reject your name as evil, because of the Son of Man.

> But woe to you who are rich,
> for you have already received your comfort.
> Woe to you who are well fed now,
> for you will go hungry.
> Woe to you who laugh now,
> for you will mourn and weep . . . (From Luke 6)

Jesus talked theology with women. He hung out with sex workers and tax collectors. He drew crowds made up of the sick and poor. He criticized religious leaders who try to "slam the door to the Kingdom of Heaven in people's faces" (Matthew 23:13).

I think also of the Ethiopian eunuch (from Acts 8), a man who was ethnically and sexually "other," who was welcomed and baptized without question or hesitation into the early church, but who would no doubt fail all of Mark Driscoll's rigid categories for what makes a "real man" were he a part of the American evangelical church today.

Now, the point of this rambling reflection is not to further entrench the imaginary divide between the privileged "in" and the underprivileged "out." (It should be noted that with the center of Christianity shifting to the global South and East, and with the demographics of American Christianity changing so rapidly, white American Protestants will soon find themselves in a minority, which will make this whole conversation a lot more interesting!) The point is, we can't go around dismissing as irrelevant those for whom our pet theologies turn the good news into bad news. We have to start with them instead.

Because at the end of the day, we're all in this Kingdom thing together. We're all loved by God, all in desperate need of grace, all in need of one another.

In a sense, we're all outliers.

Originally posted on March 26, 2013.

"New" Masculinity

A REFLECTION BY MIKE McHARGUE

"Jesus Started with the 'Outliers'" contains such essential Rachelness. It is direct, thoughtful, unapologetic, and gracious. She dismantles the notions of what "real men" are like using the words of Jesus himself.

Her words rightly focus on the outliers—the marginalized—and you should go read them. But as I write these words, men have recently elected Donald Trump as president once again. In a prescient turn, this election has been framed by many pundits as a pursuit of "real masculinity."

The Civil Rights Movement, feminism, Stonewall, #BlackLivesMatter, #MeToo, and organizing work around the rights of Indigenous, immigrant, disabled, and other marginalized communities have made remarkable progress in righting systemic injustices.

But, many men have experienced this as a perceived loss of power and status. They feel as if their identity is wholly rejected by most of society. These men are lost, confused, and looking for role models. Figures like Joe Rogan, Elon Musk, Jordan Peterson, and yes, Donald Trump rush into this gap to show men what being a "real" man looks like.

I believe this is to our collective detriment, including men.

But what if Jesus, through his words recorded in Scripture, has already given us a new image of masculinity? Rachel selected two passages to illustrate the perspective of Christ on the marginalized, from Luke 4 and 6.

Rereading this piece after another heartbreaking election brought me to tears because we see a real man depicted in these passages. A real man sees injustice and corrects it. A real man is unafraid to be ridiculed for having a different set of priorities, for standing boldly and bodily with the poor, the outcast, and the oppressed. A real man sits in grief and sorrow and sees the folly in the pursuit of material wealth.

I miss Rachel every day. Though I have retreated from my platform (which Rachel helped me build), my commitment to being a real man has continued unabated. In that work, I admit I often feel lost and confused and am looking for a role model. I used to call her when I felt like that, but I am so grateful her body of work remains.

May a generation of real men emerge, and may we be as bold as Rachel in helping them to do so.

I Don't Want an Easy Faith

Some like to say that the bravest thing Christians can do is defend their faith, to stand their ground and refuse to change.

But it's easier to defend our faith than to subject it to scrutiny. It's easier to dig in our heels than to go exploring. It's easier to regurgitate answers than to ask good questions. It's easier to cling to our beliefs than to hold them with open hands. It's easier to assume we're always right than to acknowledge we may be wrong.

I don't want an easy faith, I want a brave faith.

I want a faith that takes risks, that asks questions, that experiments, that evolves, that thrives amidst change and obeys amidst doubt. I want a faith that engages both my heart and my head, a faith that operates out of love, not fear, a faith that leaps when it needs to and crawls when it has to.

I want the kind of faith that moves mountains precisely because it is small: small enough to need, small enough to grow, small enough to surrender to a God that is much bigger than it will ever be.

I don't want an easy faith.

Originally posted on October 5, 2011.

On Borrowing Bravery

A REFLECTION BY SHAUNA NIEQUIST

Rachel and I were friends for many years—friends who read early drafts of each other's work and cheered each other on when we had books come out, who hugged and caught up warmly at events where we were both speaking, who wrote back and forth over the years about both the joys and challenges of public-facing work.

But the most important role Rachel played in my life was not the role of a friend—she was a good friend to me, of course, but more than that, and more significantly, Rachel was a guide, a beacon. Rachel was *brave*, and when I needed bravery, I thought of her. I still do.

I still think of her when I'm afraid, which is so, so often. Courage isn't my strong suit, as much as I hate to admit it. I like stirring big pots of soup and gathering people up around my table, especially on hard days. I like being the safe place to land, the home team, the one you come to when you need putting back together a little bit. I'm a comfort girl—I like to say things like, *"I hear you. I get it. You're not alone."*

But what I learned from Rachel is that offering comfort matters only when it's offered alongside a robust practice of bravery. I think of Rachel's bravery so often these days, especially when I'm writing about the world we find ourselves in. And to be honest, I probably still haven't lived up to the bravery she modeled for me—even as I sit down to write about her, I feel a prick of conscience, a little kick in the pants . . . could you be a little braver? Wouldn't she?

It seems to me that one of the greatest gifts of friendship is that we get a chance to borrow those qualities that don't come naturally to us. We get to sort of draft off another person's faith or wisdom or playfulness. Whatever we have, whatever's been long-planted inside us, it's not just for us—it's for anyone who crosses our path, a little extra peace or creativity, or, in Rachel's case, a little extra bit of courage and boldness.

Rachel graciously allowed me—and so, so many others—to draft off her bravery, to be a little more courageous in the reflection of her courage. She gave me a living, breathing vision of something I wanted to be, something to aspire to.

Thank you, dear, dear Rachel, for being generous with your courage, so that all of us near to you could borrow it when we needed it. Thank you for giving this cozy girl a much-needed kick in the pants every time I needed it. Thank you for being an absolutely incandescently bright light—in your writing, in your friendship, and in your ongoing and very significant legacy. *Brava!*

Changing Faith and Changing Relationships: Some Things I Learned the Hard Way

We can't drag others along on our faith journeys. When we have dear friends with whom we've experienced notable life transitions—high school, driving, dating, college, marriage, kids—it's only natural to assume that they will be along for the ride when our faith changes. Perhaps the hardest lesson I've had to learn as I've raised questions about Bible-Belt Christianity is that no amount of passion or persuasion can convince others to ask the same questions. In fact, forcing such questions upon other people almost always makes the situation worse. Like many of you, I've grieved as some of the most meaningful relationships of my past have grown superficial and flat as we avoid talking about matters of faith. I desperately wanted these friends to join me on my journey because the road ahead was so lonely and frightening and new. But they couldn't, and it was unfair for me to try and drag them along.

A superficial relationship is better than no relationship. I'm terrible at small talk, so the prospect of spending the afternoon with a once-close friend talking about the weather is enough to make me physically ill. For several years, I resented the fact that those with whom I once trusted my deepest secrets did not want to hear about the things that were most important to me now.

(Some have refused to read my book!) But I've since resolved that if this is the kind of relationship they want, I must be willing to walk the extra mile and do my best at maintaining it . . . always leaving the door open for something deeper, if and when they are ready for it.

Online communities can really help. The nice thing about online forums like this one is that they let us know that we are not alone and they give us the chance to work through some of our new ideas without jeopardizing those "real life" relationships that are too fragile to handle brutal honesty. I'm not ashamed to say that some of the most important conversations of my life have happened right here on this blog.

New friends will come along. Online friends can't take the place of those face-to-face conversations over coffee or late-night talks about God. It took a few years, but as I grew more honest about my faith, a surprising group of new friends (and some old friends!) came out of the woodwork. Ironically, people who used to be turned off by my unrelenting confidence (and pension for proselytizing) suddenly felt comfortable engaging in conversations with me about faith. Now my circle of friends is more diverse than it has ever been, and I am a better person for it.

It's not always right to rock the boat. I get frustrated with Christians who seem to find it easy to believe everything their pastor tells them to believe.[*] It makes me especially angry when my friends refuse to even listen to new ideas because they are either too certain or too afraid to see things from another perspective. But I've learned that it is not my job to test other people's faith. My job is to be a friend to people who are already struggling through tough questions, to offer companionship on the difficult journey through

---

[*] Rachel Held Evans, "Why Do You Find It So Easy to Believe?," Rachel Held Evans Blog, April 7, 2011, https://rachelheldevans.com/blog/john-locke-easy-to-believe.

doubt. *I am to be a counselor, not a recruiter.* It's not always right to rock the boat.

. . . But sometimes it is. When friends engage in conversations that are anti-gay, anti-Islamic, or anti-immigrant, I speak up. When they speak with disdain about the poor or make general statements about people of another country or faith, I try to offer another perspective. Politics and theology are rarely worth arguing about, but when something cruel is said about another person or group, I think it's appropriate to offer a gentle correction. I figure that at the very least, it teaches people not to make those kinds of statements in my presence.

Don't feed the trolls. Online, trolls are people who show up to leave mean-spirited, off-topic comments that don't really contribute to the conversation. In real life, they may be acquaintances who suddenly take an interest in "fixing" your faith or in harassing you about issues related to politics and theology via annoying email forwards and Facebook statuses. Engaging such people is almost always a waste of time and energy. Don't do it.

"People who never get criticized aren't saying anything important." Dan offered those words to me once after I received a particularly hateful email in response to one of my posts. Questions, honesty, challenges to old ideas, and arguments for new ones—these things are almost always met with resistance. I can certainly be wrong at times, but I think I have some good things to say and that it's important that I keep saying them *in the right context and with the right spirit.* You should too.

Our lives are our testimonies. Living in a small Southern town has subjected me to a lot of hurtful gossip. Most of the rumors about my supposed theology are either untrue or exaggerated . . . and yet they are nearly impossible to dispel. I have learned by trial and error that it is a waste of energy to try and track down and correct the source of such rumors. Better to spend my time learning to follow Jesus as best as I can. If my life exhibits love, joy, peace, patience, kindness, goodness, faithfulness, gentleness, and self-control, people are more likely to doubt what they've been told about me. I can't control what other people say about me, but I can control my attitude. I figure that if my words can't convince people that I can be both Christian and a Democrat (or a Christian and an old-earther), then maybe my life can.

Avoid both blame and guilt. I have a bad habit of jumping to extremes, so I tend to see my failed relationships as either totally my fault or totally the other person's fault . . . when most of the time we both share some responsibility. I have to remind myself that it's okay to apologize and okay to be hurt when I don't receive one in return. It would be easier if there was a good guy and a bad guy, a black vs. a white, but relationships aren't supposed to be easy. In fact, they are valuable precisely because they are hard.

Originally posted on April 8, 2011.

She Was Just a Good Friend

A REFLECTION BY KATHLEEN GLEASON

Rachel was a protector of those she loved. I first met her in our dorm room our freshman year. The first thing I noticed, other than her warmth and her beautiful smile, was her faeries posted all over her side of the room. "The correct spelling is f-a-e-r-i-e," she told me. These were no sweet Cinderella faeries; these were wild, naughty faeries with haughty eyes. They were creepy. I loved them, and my parents hated them. My parents are Independent Fundamental Baptists, and they had learned to fear anything outside the norms of their church. They struggled to embrace difference, and that meant they often struggled to embrace me. I was often shamed for my bohemian clothing and big emotions; I think my appearance, taste, and behavior embarrassed them. With Rachel, I felt seen and embraced for my differences. She celebrated me. We spent the first night in our dorm room listening to Dave Matthews Band and Alanis Morissette and making up a stupid song for the receiving message on our voicemail. We stayed up almost the whole night laughing and reading music lyrics. It was pure joy and freedom.

I remember Rachel having a faith crisis our senior year of college. She was writing her thesis on *Tess of the d'Ubervilles*. The idea of injustice was really bothering her. I was a little afraid of her questions because I didn't want to have a faith crisis too. I made a mental note NOT to read that book. I wish I had been a better friend at that time, but I was consumed with myself. I think Rachel felt really alone, and I will always regret not being there for her.

After we both got married, we didn't see much of each other. Then, I learned she was part of an evangelical movement called the emerging church.* My pastor warned me about this movement and suggested that I could lose my salvation because "only those who stand firm to the end will be saved." That terrified me, so I distanced myself from Rachel for many years. I thought I was doing the right thing, all the while struggling with doubts about my faith. If only I hadn't listened to my pastor, I would've found great comfort in Rachel's writings. The church's spiritual bypassing, misogyny, racism, LGBTQ+ phobia, blind acceptance of predestination, and then allegiance to Trump eventually took their toll on me. I became completely fed up.

It was a scary time because I was leaving my community, and I was deconstructing my faith. A few women I thought were friends shamed me for causing division in the church, and had me convinced I was going to hell. I couldn't sleep.

I called Rachel, crying, and she told me to come over to her house. She fed my son goldfish crackers and put on *PAW Patrol* for him. She fed me cake. "Am I going to hell?" I asked her with tear-soaked cheeks. "Of course not," she confidently replied, and she embraced me in a huge hug. I sobbed and sobbed on her chest. We

---

* Editor's Note: The emerging church movement (sometimes emergent church), which was active within mid- to late-twentieth-century Christianity, developed within local communities and through books, conferences, and notably within the burgeoning online spaces of the early 2000s. Initially interested in the church's engagement with postmodernism, it heralded practice-based faith, generous orthodoxy, creative expressions, missional living, justice, and postevangelical thought. It was defined by leaders like Brian McLaren, Doug Pagitt, Phyllis Tickle, and others, but many of the early leaders—including Mark Driscoll—eventually distanced themselves from the movement, and many conservative Christians reacted against the emerging church conversations. Rachel never formally self-declared as part of "the emerging church," but she was influenced by its leaders and became a default leader for those shaped by emerging church or even emergent thought.

talked for several hours, and I left her house feeling a peace I never thought I would feel again. I knew I didn't have to be afraid and I wasn't alone. Rachel gave me many books to read, and she opened my world to so many writers, theologians, and free thinkers who are still guides and comforts to me today. I had the chance to apologize to Rachel for my distance, and I am forever grateful for that.

Unlike the pastors in my life, Rachel didn't think she knew everything; she was just a good friend, and she was more of a pastor to me that day than I have ever experienced. She knew what I was going through so well, and she loved me through it.

The last time I saw her was in my driveway. She was dropping me off after the Why Christian? conference in San Francisco. I knew she wasn't feeling well, and she was anxious to get home.

I wish Rachel was here with me. I wish we could sit in my living room and talk about everything going on in our world. We were forging a new path in our friendship, and I was so excited to dive deeper with her and be the friend I wasn't before.

Why Calvinism Makes Me Cry

This is not a post about Calvinism. Not really. It's not about TULIP or John Piper or predestination or the Reformation. It's not about why I think Calvinism is a theological system based on logical inferences rather than the clear, consistent teachings of Scripture. It's not about all of my nasty run-ins with hyper-Calvinists who have called me a "cotton-candy Christian" and an "enemy of the church" for not subscribing to their theology. It's not about John Calvin or the persecution of the Anabaptists or those "Jonathan Edwards Is My Homeboy" T-shirts.

This is not a post about Calvinism. It's a post about fear. It's a post about how our loudest protests and most passionate tirades tend to reflect our insecurities rather than our convictions.

I've been reflecting on this a lot recently, as I've been talking with loved ones about how to move past some of my "issues" (read—anger, obsession, deep-seated hatred) with some of the tenants of Reformed theology.

Here's the thing: I can talk about politics without raising my voice. I can debate young earth creationism vs. theistic evolution without shedding a tear. I can have differences of opinion with my friends about health care or global warming or eschatology or women in church leadership without taking it personally or holding a grudge. I generally accept differences in biblical interpretation with a shrug of my shoulders.

But I can't seem to talk about Calvinism without crying.

It happened again the other night when I was talking with my sister about Calvinism. She's not a five-pointer by any means, but she's much more sympathetic (read—patient, kind, understanding) toward Reformed Theology than I.

"If Calvinism is true, it means that God creates disposable people, people without any hope," I said, my voice steadily rising above the sound of the USC vs. Ohio State game on TV. (We Helds like nothing better than theological discussions, mixed with college football, topped with steaks on the grill.)

"It means that God not only allows, but sovereignly ordains, every war and every abortion and every rape of a child. It means that God does not love the world; he hates it. If Calvinism is true, it means that if that dying little girl that you held in your arms in India was not among the elect, then God did not love her. He never had any intention of loving her. She was nothing to him. In fact, he would delight and find glory in her eternal torture in hell."

Then I started to yell.

"And whenever I raise these points with Calvinists, all they can say is that I should be more grateful for my own salvation! It's like, 'as long as my eternal destiny is secure, as long as my life is all planned out and taken care of by God, who gives a damn about anyone else!' How can you be okay with that? How can anyone be okay with that? Why do I feel like I'm the only one who finds this morally offensive?"

I managed to get through the conversation without completely breaking down, but as soon as I got into my car to head home, I started to weep uncontrollably. I had to stop at the end of the street for about ten minutes because I was shaking and crying and my contact lenses were getting all fogged up.

For the past four or five years, I've believed that such a response reflected little more than righteous indignation. I figured I was so angry because these Calvinists were just so wrong. But as I've prayed and studied Jesus and talked with Dan and spent some time alone, I've realized that I cry, not out of conviction that the Calvinists are wrong, but out of the deep, paralyzing fear that they might be right.

You see, I grew up in a home in which the love of God was the foundation for everything. My father, in both word and deed, ensured that my concept of a heavenly Father was one that made me feel loved and cherished, and my mother instilled in me a sense of compassion for all people, especially the needy, the broken, and the lonely. Though my father had a degree in theology, he knew that having all the right answers wasn't really the point, so when I would pose a particularly personal or challenging question to him, he would often respond with, "You know what, Rachel—I don't know, but I know that God loves you." It's a phrase that I often repeat to folks who send me emails about how they are struggling with doubt. Though I can't always answer all of their questions, I know that I can say with complete confidence, "I don't know, but I know that God loves you."

That God loves everyone (and not just a select group of people) has always been the most important theological constant in my life . . . and I feel like Calvinism, were it true, would take that away from me. Replacing "for God so loved the world" with "for God so hated the world" (which I believe Calvinism requires) is so disorienting to me, so dark and frightening and hopeless, that I fear it would lead me to despair.

I realized how profoundly these fears had affected my life the week that Reformed pastor John Piper declared that the tornado that hit downtown Minneapolis (like the Indian Ocean tsunami of 2004, the Minneapolis bridge collapse of 2007, and even his own cancer) was an act of divine judgment toward the sinners involved.*

The night after I heard the news, I dreamed that I was in a beach house during a hurricane. (Yeah, so I know this is a little unrealistic . . . but so is flying airplanes shaped as turtles and living among the Sioux Nation as an algebra teacher, which are also recurring dreams of mine.) Anyway, in my dream, it was completely dark outside, and the wind had broken all of the windows of the house, so I was exposed to all of the elements. Water, funnel clouds, lightning, and debris swirled around me. I couldn't find Dan. Suddenly an eerie calm fell over the scene, and I looked out the broken windows to see a massive, roaring wall of water headed straight toward me. It was black, like the sky, and as I stared into it, the most terrible, lonely sense of despair rushed through my body. Somehow, I knew I was going to die, and somehow, I knew that the tsunami wave represented God.

I woke up in a panic. I had never dreamed about God like that before. As I wandered to the kitchen for a glass of milk, I realized why I was so upset about John Piper. I was upset because my single greatest fear is that God hates his creation, that he will never stop being angry with me, that he has chosen just a few for salvation, that the little girl in India is not among them, and that, perhaps, I am not among them either.

These fears are not so different from the fear I see in the eyes of protestors carrying signs that depict President Obama as Hitler, the fear I see in the red faces of angry preachers urging their parishioners to "take America back for God," the fear I detect in some of the books against the emerging church, the fear I detect in some of the books in support of the emerging church, the fear I hear in

---

* Rachel Held Evans, "Six Questions for John Piper," Rachel Held Evans Blog, August 20, 2009, https://rachelheldevans.com/blog/pipertornado.

the voices of both gays and the conservative evangelical activists who lobby against them when both sides consider for just a second the possibility that maybe they have it wrong.

No wonder James wrote that "the anger of man does not achieve the righteousness of God."[*] No wonder John wrote that "the one who fears is not made perfect in love."[†]

Originally posted on September 14, 2009.

---

[*] James 1:20, NIV
[†] 1 John 4:18, NIV

"Ask a ____" Series

Editor's Note by Sarah Bessey

Initially envisioned as a one-time series beginning in 2011, the "Ask a ____" series became a years-long intermittent project to break down barriers, heal divisions, inform, educate, and foster curiosity between different beliefs and communities.

Rachel intentionally included her readers in the experience. First, she would introduce a guest representing a community or belief, then open up the floor for her readers to ask whatever they've always wondered about in regards to their experience. The point, she wrote, was not to "proselytize or challenge, but to ask the sort of questions that will help us understand one another better." Then, the respondent would take a few days to thoughtfully respond in a follow-up post, creating further discussion.

By the time the series ended, Rachel's readers had "interviewed" a transgender Christian, an Indigenous theologian, a feminist, a Pentecostal, a nun, a pacifist, a pagan, a recovering alcoholic, a reformed pastor, conservatives and liberals in both Christianity and Judaism, a gay Christian, a Quaker, a Mennonite, a humanitarian, a Catholic, an interfaith couple, and even well-known teachers such as N. T. Wright or music artists such as Jennifer Knapp.

Through this series, Rachel was reminding her readers that everyone has a story and a reason for their beliefs. This was just one of the many ways that Rachel sought to model the very curiosity, empathy, understanding, and generosity that she hoped to foster among her readers and the wider church.

The Familiar and the Stranger

A REFLECTION BY REV. DR. MONICA A. COLEMAN

Teachers are often telling students, "There's no such thing as a stupid question."

That statement is meant for school classrooms—not for religion. Most of us are taught not to question our faith or what we are taught in church. Questioning is a sign of doubt, and doubt reveals a lack of faith. When the currency is faith, one cannot be found lacking.

So it takes a lot of courage for religious folk to raise their hand and ask questions. It's hard to say, "I want to know more." Even harder to say, "I don't know." When Rachel Held Evans opened her blog for people to ask questions, it was more commonly, "I've been taught that this is wrong or bad or unholy. Is it?"

Rachel was bold enough to ask folk who were not only learned in the questions, but who lived the questions. Thus many of the questions actually said, "I've been taught that YOU are wrong, bad, and sinful. Are you?"

This is how I first met Rachel. She asked me to respond to questions as a liberation theologian. Yes, I am a professor of theology, but I also deeply believe in and identify with liberation theology. Nevertheless, I did not feel attacked—nor, I imagine, did any of the others who answered in Rachel's column: a gay Christian, a transgender Christian, a Mormon, a Reformed pastor, a Unitarian Universalist. I felt like people were genuinely curious. When questioners pushed back, it was with more questions. They trusted me and others who were strangers because they trusted Rachel. Rachel was trustworthy because she was them. Rachel often admitted: I have some of the same questions too. Leaders lead well because they are their community.

Rachel modeled a faithful life that asks questions. She shows us how questioning helps us to grow, not shrink. She gave space for everyone else's questions. Rachel reached out to people she didn't even know . . . and helped us strangers to feel safe among people of our own faith who were unfamiliar with us and how we could even exist. They didn't know how we could be one of them, how we could be neighbors. But they wanted to know.

Rachel did not seem to think of herself as a pastor or a minister. There were no potlucks, vacation Bible schools, or choir. At its best, church creates a safe place for the familiar and the stranger. That was evident every time we asked some kind of Christian the questions we were taught to silence.

The Cost

They say I've taken the easy way out.

They say I've given in to the culture in an effort to be welcomed and liked by my peers. They tell me I've counted the cost of following Jesus and considered it too much, so I've jumped on the liberal bandwagon—embracing evolution, feminism, LGBTQ+ equality, and theological views that veer from the evangelical norm—because it's the easy, convenient thing to do.

And I want to shake their shoulders and ask, *What culture do you think I came from? Who do you think are my peers?* This church, this community, was once my whole world until it took the questions I offered with trembling hands and smashed them against the wall. *How dare you say I took the easy way out when these questions have cost me relationships, reputation, status, and security? How dare you say I took the easy way out when this path has been so lonely and treacherous?*

There has been a cost: Professors who once beamed with pride at my writing chastise me for not devoting myself to worthier female vocations. A community that once celebrated and encouraged my gifts has asked me to keep my distance. I am the subject of gossip in the grocery store aisle and a topic for critical discussion in Sunday school. Friends have compared me to an addict and told me they need to step away.

Oh, this has come with a cost.

Even so, mine has been a relatively easy journey. My parents are supportive and I have many faithful friends. I've found success and solidarity in my writing, and my husband has never left my side. But there are science teachers who have lost their jobs for teaching that the Earth is more than six thousand years old and biblical scholars who have been labeled heretics for suggesting Genesis 1 is not a scientific text. There are teenagers who have faced homelessness after coming out to their parents, and parents who have faced excommunication from their church for standing by their gay kids. I know women who can remember the way their hearts sank when a row of men stood up and left when they approached the podium to speak. I know writers who have lost book deals and pastors who have been run out of town.

We aren't "giving in" to the culture; our culture is evangelical Christianity. We're struggling with that culture, and doing so comes with a cost.

You're the ones taking the easy way out.

That's what I tell my detractors.

You're the ones who have given in to the culture in an effort to be welcomed and liked by your peers.

I convince myself that the people with whom I disagree hold their convictions because they haven't really thought them through or because they're afraid to challenge the status quo. They've chosen willful ignorance over thoughtful inquiry, I say, the safety of fundamentalism over the risk of inclusive love. They've counted the cost of *really* following Jesus and considered it too much. *They're* the ones taking the easy way out, not me.

And I get to feel all vindicated and righteous for about seven minutes before the weight of the log in my eye starts to pull my whole head down.

Because the truth is, their convictions come with a cost too.

It's painful to see your beliefs mocked in the media and satirized on TV. There's a cost to sticking with your values when they strike others as old-fashioned or strange. It hurts like hell to be the butt of jokes at your office or called a "bigot" or "extremist" on your college campus when nothing could be further from the truth. It takes guts to raise your hand and challenge the professor in a secular classroom or walk away from a compromising situation when it may mean damaging relationships that have been hard-won. And it's got to sting to be called a fundamentalist by other Christians (like me) when you're just trying to do the right thing and do it in love. It must hurt to be subjected to the rolled eyes and the know-it-all attitude we progressive-types can conjure as well as anybody.

I have made assumptions about my siblings in the faith, only to learn that they too have struggled through big questions; they've just arrived at different answers. I've spoken with twenty-somethings whose families ridiculed them when they came to Christianity and with women whose professors sneered at them when they challenged feminist teachings. Once, after I told someone he must certainly have never met a gay person in his life, he responded that his ex-wife was a lesbian and he struggles with how to raise his children with her in a gracious and loving way.

How little I know of other people's stories. How swift I am to judge based on where we met in the path without bothering to ask where they've come from.

I've been thinking . . .

We fight like family because we *are*. We've all been adopted into God's family.

Maybe we don't have to change each other's minds to lighten one another's load by not assuming motives, by giving each other the benefit of the doubt that we arrived at our beliefs through honest searching.

There's a cost to every conviction.

What mine have cost me may be different from what yours have cost you, but the sense of loss is the same. And so is the hope that comes with breaking bread together in spite of our theological and political differences and settling into the sweet certainty that following Jesus doesn't have to cost *this*. It doesn't have to cost our love for one another.

Not if we don't want it to.

Originally posted on February 17, 2014.

Let the World Change You: A Commencement Address Do-Over

Way back in 2003, when people still left voicemails and Mark Zuckerberg's "Facesmash" was just a mildly sexist college experiment, I was chosen by my classmates to deliver a commencement address at graduation ceremonies for our conservative Christian university.

I took the honor seriously, prepping for weeks amidst all the final exams and senior parties, working through multiple drafts and soliciting feedback from my parents and professors.

And I did okay (though, to this day I still have nightmares about approaching that podium only to look down and realize I left my notes . . . or my pants . . . in my dorm room). I admonished my classmates the way any other twenty-one-year-old evangelical would admonish her peers:

I told them to go out and change the world.

I told them that as Christians, fresh off four years of apologetics training, we were uniquely equipped to speak the truth in love—

that the world is dark, and we are the light,

that the world is sick, and we have the medicine,

that the world is lost, and we know the way.

Granted, it was a different time. The ash of 9/11 still clouded the air. American forces had just unleashed "shock and awe" upon Baghdad and we were sure to be out of there in a matter of months. Evangelicals elected presidents and Pluto was a planet.

It was easy to be overconfident.

So I try to give my younger self some grace, especially since "go out and change the world" is a perfectly suitable message for a commencement address—it's given all the time.

But if I had it to do over, if I could somehow transport thirty-four-year-old Rachel back to that sunny morning when things were simpler and I thought myself so much smarter, I would add:

Class of 2003, let the world change you too.

Because that's exactly what happened after I descended that platform and walked into a world inhabited not by the straw figures I'd been taught to defeat and convert, but by flesh-and-blood human beings who didn't stick to the atheist/Muslim/feminist/gay/liberal/poor/skeptic/foreigner script, a world less characterized by black and white certainties than by mile after mile and year after year of thick, impenetrable gray.

I thought I was called to challenge the atheists, but the atheists ended up challenging me.

I thought God wanted to use me to show gay people how to be straight. Instead God used gay people to show me how to be Christian.

I thought the world needed my answers, but as it turns out, I needed the world's questions. I needed to learn how to doubt well, listen better, and be humbled by how little I know. I needed to discover that evangelicalism is just one table in Christ's banquet hall, the Great Cloud of Witnesses far more sprawling and diverse than I'd ever imagined.

The world, it turns out, is not all weeds. There is evil growing, certainly, and fear and hate and prejudice. But I've found life sprouting out of all sorts of unlikely soil, wheat enough for a lifetime of harvests.

I am so thankful for the feminist coworker who mothered me through my first reporting job, for the library where I discovered Richard Rohr and Marilynne Robinson, for the physicist who helped me embrace evolution, for trips to India and Bolivia, for conversations lasting until 2 a.m., for the foul-mouthed and tattooed Lutheran pastor who gave me permission to love the church again.

These people and these things changed me for the better. They challenged everything I thought I knew, and I'm glad.

Oh, I resisted at first. Worried about compromising my beliefs, I clenched them more tightly and dug in my heels. So convinced it was my job to be Jesus to others, I nearly missed the chance to let others be Jesus to me—to teach me, heal me, love me, and call me to repentance.

And lest you think I count myself finished, know this: When I was a Bible-thumping, church-going, know-it-all Republican, God used bleeding-heart, politically correct, question-everything liberals to teach me to be human, to challenge my notions of who the enemy is. But now that I'm a bleeding-heart, politically correct, question-everything liberal, God insists on using Bible-thumping, church-going, know-it-all Republicans to teach me to be human, to challenge my notions of who the enemy is.

God, it seems, is rather stubbornly committed to extracting me from the notion that this is all about being right.

Now, the twenty-one-year-old me would point out that Scripture warns against "conforming to the patterns of this world." Indeed, the world of the early Christians and the world of today tend to favor the destructive patterns of power over humility, materialism over generosity, retribution over forgiveness.

But even the first apostles allowed themselves to be changed by goodness in the world. When the law-abiding, kosher-eating, Roman-hating Peter encountered a Roman centurion who feared God and gave to the poor, Peter—to his own astonishment—says, "I now realize how true it is that God does not show favoritism but accepts from every nation the one who fears him and does what is right." He even goes so far as to share a meal with his new friend. "You are well aware that it is against our law for a Jew to associate with or visit a Gentile," he tells Cornelius. "But God has shown me that I should not call anyone impure or unclean."

What a delight it is to be surprised!

So if I had it to do over again, I would tell my classmates:

Before you can make your mark on the world, let the world make its mark on you. Be curious. Stay open. Nurture the humility it takes to admit you can get it wrong.

And I would tell myself:

"Rachel, in a few years, you're going to doubt everything you said in your speech just now, and—guess what—you're going to be okay."

Originally posted on May 21, 2016.

About That Commencement Do-Over
A REFLECTION BY DR. PETER HELD

It was a cool, breezy, East Tennessee Saturday morning in May 2003. Dressed in my academic regalia I took my assigned place with the college administration on the makeshift outdoor stage. Having spent my entire professional career in education I have participated in countless commencement ceremonies. This one was different. This time my daughter was giving the commencement address and I had a front row seat. Like any father in that situation, I was bursting with pride. Rachel employed the communication skills she would later become known for, and with all the enthusiasm of a new graduate she challenged her classmates to go out and change the world.

Years later, if given a do-over, she wished she had included a simple but profound addition: "But first let the world change you." I resonate with her sentiment. My journey after college included seminary followed by further graduate education, a basic requirement in the world of academia. Seminary exposed me to so many authentic truths and genuine answers. But after seminary, graduate school and life as a father and husband taught me I still had much to learn about the questions.

Rachel was often criticized for having no formal theological education. How could someone with only a college degree be taken seriously? What qualified her to address the tough questions of life? Here's my observation (biased as it may be): I watched my daughter graduate from college, but then I watched her become a student of the world. She read widely, studied voraciously, and intentionally sought out and dialogued with all kinds of people and viewpoints. She worked hard and demanded more of herself than any graduate professor ever would.

Rachel's curiosity, her doubt and her passion, galvanized her to pursue the questions and drove her to continue learning and growing. Because of Rachel's example, I too was encouraged to continue asking questions. I believe I became a better teacher because of Rachel. It seems when we stop asking questions, we grow stagnant, as if we're merely existing on life support. Ephesians 4:13 (nlt) tells us that a life of growth "will continue until we all come to such unity in our faith and knowledge of God's Son that we will be mature in the Lord, measuring up to the full and complete standard of Christ."

Moving along on this journey of learning and growing, don't we all wish we could have do-overs? As for me, I wish I could hug my daughter one more time and tell her once again, "I love you, and I'm so proud of you."

And if I could go back to that day in 2003, I would add, "Rachel, you *will* change the world. I promise you will."

PART TWO

THAT UNHOLY AMERICAN TRINITY

Essays on Patriarchy, White Supremacy, and Religious Nationalism

For the Sake of the Gospel, Let Women Speak

Editor's note: This essay was part of a wider "synchroblog" that Rachel hosted online called One in Christ: A Week of Mutuality. For the uninitiated, a synchroblog was hosted by an originating blogger—here, Rachel—who would declare a theme or prompt that other bloggers would then rally around or respond to. She originally opened this post with that context: "This is the seventh post in our series One in Christ: A Week of Mutuality, dedicated to discussing an egalitarian view of gender—including relevant biblical texts and practical applications. The goal is to show how scripture, tradition, reason, and experience all support a posture of equality toward women, one that favors mutuality rather than hierarchy, in the home, Church, and society."

It's time! Today we discuss one of the most controversial passages of Scripture: First Timothy 2:11–12, where the apostle Paul writes that "a woman should learn in quietness and full submission. I do not permit a woman to teach or to assume authority over a man; she must be quiet."*

---

* Rachel included this note in her original post: "Now, I've heard from a bunch of folks who are eager to point out that most modern scholars are doubtful that the apostle Paul actually wrote the pastoral epistles. I've done a little research on this, and indeed the evidence is compelling. However, for our purposes this week, and

HOW DO WE READ THE EPISTLES?

I think Paul would roll over in his grave if he knew we were turning his letters into torah.

—F. F. BRUCE*

We forget sometimes that the epistles are just that: letters.

In our rush to find proof texts to support our various positions, we tend to skip past the initial greetings that designate the recipients of the message—*"to the church of God in Corinth," "to the churches in Galatia," "to God's holy people in Ephesus," "to Timothy," "to Titus"*—or those odd little details that remind us that we are essentially listening in on someone else's conversation—*"I have made a fool of myself," "I don't remember if I baptized anyone else," "When you come, bring the cloak that I left with Carpus in Troas, and my scrolls, especially the parchments."* (You don't see that last one on many desk calendars.)

I've never once heard a sermon preached on the passage in which Paul tells Titus "Cretans are always liars, evil brutes, lazy gluttons" (Titus 1:12), and yet, if these words are truly the inerrant and unchanging words of God intended as universal *commands* for all people in all places at all times, then the Christian community needs to do a better job of mobilizing against the Cretan people, perhaps constructing some "God Hates Cretans" signs!

Hyperbole aside, it's important to keep in mind that while the epistles are certainly written *for* us, they were not written *to* us. With the letters of Peter, Paul, James, John, and the other apostles, we are given the priceless gift of seeing how early followers of

---

with my particular audience in mind, I've decided to stick with the assumption that Paul is the author of these texts."

* Bruce quoted in Scot McKnight, *The Blue Parakeet: Rethinking How You Read the Bible* (Zondervan, 2008), 206–7.

Jesus applied his teachings to their unique circumstances. While these letters are packed with important theological observations—*"If anyone is in Christ, the new creation has come," "Conduct yourselves in a manner worthy of the gospel," "Have this attitude in you which was also in Christ Jesus"*—they also include lengthy discussion concerning how first-century house churches should operate, how unprecedented influxes of poor widows should be handled, how women should cover their heads when they pray and prophecy, how slaves should behave toward their masters, whether Christian converts should be circumcised, whether Christians should eat meat sacrificed to idols, how to endure persecution, how not to offend the surrounding culture, and how to follow Christ with conviction while avoiding unwanted attention from the suspicious Roman officials.

In other words, these letters have contexts. They are addressing very practical problems.

The epistles were never meant to be interpreted and applied as universal law. Rather, they provide us with an instructive and inspired glimpse into how Jesus's teachings were lived out by *real* people, in *real* communities, facing *real* challenges. It is not the details found in the letters that we should seek to imitate, but rather the attitudes. The details (head coverings, circumcision, meat offered to idols, widow management, hair length, etc.) are rarely timeless, but the attitudes (*"as much as it depends on you, live peaceably with all men"* [Romans 12:18], *"do not cause your brother to stumble"* [Romans 14:13], *"avoid the appearance of evil"* [1 Thessalonians 5:22]) provide guidelines that can instruct us as Christians today. So the questions we should be asking ourselves today are not: *Should we eat meat offered to idols?* or *Should women wear head coverings?*, but rather, *How can we find peace when Christians feel convicted in different ways?* and *How do we avoid unnecessarily offending others by our appearance?*

When read this way, I am constantly impressed by the degree to which these early Christians were willing to sacrifice beliefs and traditions they held dear for the sake of love and for the sake of advancing the gospel. Such a reading does not devalue Scripture, but rather honors it for what it is, not what we try to make it.

WHAT'S WITH THE WOMEN AT EPHESUS?

Just as I've never heard a sermon against Cretans, I've also never heard a sermon on 1 Timothy 2:8, in which Paul tells Timothy, "I want men everywhere to pray, lifting holy hands without anger or disputing," which included a universal dictum that all men everywhere must raise their hands whenever they pray. Nor have I heard a sermon on one of the most common instructions found in the epistles, to "greet one another with a holy kiss" (1 Corinthians 16:20). Nor have I ever heard of a pastor being removed from the position, in keeping with Titus 1:5–6, because one of his or her children had left the faith. (It's an uncomfortable reality, but if complementarians were as consistent in their application of biblically based pastoral qualifications as they claim to be, a few of their most prominent spokesmen would have had to resign from their pastoral positions when their children left the faith. They didn't.)

I haven't heard any sermons on all of *those* biblical instructions, but I've heard more than I can count on 1 Timothy 2:11–12, which says, "a woman should learn in quietness and full submission. I do not permit a woman to teach or to assume authority over a man; she must be quiet."

So what was the context of these words? Were they really meant to be applied universally to all women everywhere?

Some context: In keeping with the trend of early Christianity, the first-century churches at Ephesus and Corinth attracted a lot of women, particularly widows. As a result, large portions of the pastoral epistles tackle the mounting logistical challenges of caring for so many unmarried women. Of particular concern to Paul was a group of young widows who had infiltrated the church and developed a reputation for dressing promiscuously, sleeping around, gossiping, spreading unorthodox ideas, interrupting church services with questions, mooching off the church's widow fund, and generally making common floozies of themselves (1 Timothy 5).

Many scholars believe these women were likely influenced by the popular Roman fertility cults of Artemis that encouraged women to flaunt their sexuality and freedom to a degree that scandalized even the Roman establishment, hardly known for its prudish morals. Worship involved deviant sex, shirking off marriage and childbearing, possible abortions and infanticide, and immodest dress that made adherents indistinguishable from prostitutes. (This trend inspired Caesar Augustus to pass legislation regarding what respectable women ought to wear . . . and, oddly, what prostitutes and adulterers ought to wear!) It seems that enough of these women had joined the church to tarnish its reputation, repelling potential converts and giving the Roman authorities yet another reason to be suspicious of the church, which was the last thing the early Christians needed.*

"Give proper recognition to those widows who are really in need," Paul tells the elders at Ephesus. But "younger widows," he says, are "to marry, to have children, to manage their homes and to give the enemy no opportunity for slander" (1 Timothy 5:14). I suspect that Paul didn't want the church, so full of unmarried women, to be seen as just another Greco-Roman cult. He also didn't want pagans unfamiliar with the teachings of Christ and the Jewish culture interrupting services with questions or bossing

---

* Rachel included this note: "If you want to learn more about the cults, your best bet is *Roman Wives, Roman Widows: The Appearance of New Women and the Pauline Communities* by Bruce Winter. See also *The Letters to Timothy and Titus* by Philip Towner.

around other converts. Is it any wonder, then, that he expected some women in Corinth to prophesy but challenged others to "remain silent," or that he advised the women at Ephesus not to seize authority over men but to "learn in quietness and full submission"? (Remember, the guys would have been seriously outnumbered!)

"We are thus led to the conclusion that when Paul asks women to be silent . . . he is not talking about ordinary Christian women; rather, he has a specific group of women in mind," writes Scot McKnight in *The Blue Parakeet*. "His concern is with some untrained, morally loose, young widows, who, because they are theologically unformed, are teaching unorthodox ideas." It is reasonable, then, to assume that once these widows were trained, they could resume speaking.

WHAT ABOUT ADAM AND EVE?

Things get a little trickier as Paul goes on with his letter. "For Adam was formed first, then Eve," he writes. "And Adam was not the one deceived; it was the woman who was deceived and became a sinner. But women will be saved through childbearing—if they continue in faith, love and holiness with propriety" [1 Timothy 2:13–15, NIV].

Now, I'll readily admit that the fact that Paul appeals to the creation narrative to support his point about Ephesian women complicates things for egalitarians. (Actually, the part about being "saved through childbearing" complicates things for everyone who believes people are saved by faith alone.) References to Adam and Eve certainly give a line of argumentation a universal feel.

But when first-century rabbis like Jesus and Paul allude to the stories of the Torah, including the creation accounts, they are not participating in "straight exegesis" as we would understand it today. Rather, their creative interpretations of the text are influenced by the hermeneutical conventions of Second Temple Judaism, which allow for quite a bit of "play" with the narrative texts. According to Peter Enns, Paul often uses Adam and Eve as a way of "appropriating an ancient story to address pressing concerns of the moment."

I've heard all sorts of explanations about what Paul meant with these few sentences—that he was countering teachings from the Roman cults that the gender order should be reversed, that he had simply accepted the widely held belief that women are more easily deceived than men and responsible for the Fall, that "saved through childbearing" refers to Christ's arrival through Mary, that "saved through childbearing" is meant to discourage women from engaging in the anti-children activities of the cults, that childbearing has a special redemptive effect, and so on. (I have a hard time with that last one seeing as how Jesus consistently praised singleness and celibacy as an option for committed Christians, as did Paul in 1 and 2 Corinthians.)

No one seems to know for sure what this passages means, and frankly, I've just about given up on figuring out exactly what's going on with it. But here's the thing: Anyone who says that Paul's instructions regarding the women at Ephesus are universally binding because he appeals to the creation narrative to make his point can be consistent in that position only if they also require women in their church to cover their heads, as Paul uses a very similar line of argumentation to advocate that. (See 1 Corinthians 11:1–16.)

WHAT ABOUT WOMEN TODAY?

So what about women today? Can we really compare women who have devoted their lives to studying Scripture, many with seminary degrees and years of experience, to the promiscuous, first-century Roman widows mooching off the church and spreading idle tales from door to door?

Obviously, Paul didn't have a problem with women teaching in general.* He honored Priscilla, a teacher to the apostle Apollos, and praised Timothy's mother and grandmother for teaching Timothy all he knew about faith. He recognized Junia as an apostle, Phoebe as a deacon, and Euodia and Syntyche as church planters.

In fact, these days, women in the pulpit are more highly educated than their male counterparts. While over three-quarters of female pastors (77 percent) hold seminary degrees, less than two-thirds of male pastors (63 percent) can say the same.† It continues to amaze me that some evangelicals believe that Fred Phelps of Westboro Baptist Church, who was ordained at seventeen without a seminary degree, is more qualified by virtue of being a man to speak to the church than someone like my friend Jackie Roese, who received top honors at her seminary and is now a pastor at Irving Bible Church in Dallas, or Catherine Hamlin, who devoted her life to caring for fistula patients in Africa, or Sarah Coakley, who is one of Christianity's most influential theologians and philosophers, currently working on a four-volume systematic theology.

Something needs to change.

WHERE DO WE DRAW THE LINE?

With all these bright, trained women running around, it's no wonder complementarians have a difficult time applying their own restrictions on the roles of women in the church.‡ For example,

---

* Rachel Held Evans, "Who's Who Among Biblical Women Leaders," Rachel Held Evans Blog, June 6, 2012, https://rachelheldevans.com/blog/mutuality-women-leaders.
† "20 Years of Surveys Show Key Differences in the Faith of America's Men and Women," *Barna*, August 1, 2011, https://www.barna.com/research/20-years-of-surveys-show-key-differences-in-the-faith-of-americas-men-and-women/.
‡ Rachel Held Evans, "Complementarians Are Selective, Too," Rachel Held Evans

John Piper was once asked by a man, "Is it wrong for me to listen to Beth Moore?"*

"No," Piper said, "unless you begin to become dependent on her as your shepherd-pastor. This is the way I feel about women speaking occasionally in Sunday school. We don't need to be picky on this. The Bible is clear that women shouldn't teach and have authority over men. In context, I think this means that women shouldn't be the authoritative teachers of the church—they shouldn't be elders." He went on to say that women like Beth Moore and Elisabeth Elliot should be free to speak, to write, and to teach.

In other words, it's okay to learn from women . . . just not too much.

Piper appears to consider the first half of 1 Timothy 2:12 ("a woman should not have authority") as universally applicable, but disregards the second half ("she must be quiet") by encouraging women like Moore to continue speaking. If the first half of 1 Timothy 2 is so crucial to the complementarian hierarchal construct, why is the second half (along with the silence command in 1 Corinthians 14:34) essentially ignored? Why is it that complementarian women are forbidden from assuming leadership in churches, and yet permitted to speak? Nowhere does the Bible spell out this distinction between teaching and speaking or between leader and "shepherd-pastor," and yet Piper seems seriously committed to it.

I've spent far more time than I care to admit combing through complementarian literature, reading debates about whether women can read Scripture aloud in church, whether female missionaries should be permitted to give presentations on Sunday evenings,

---

Blog, September 12, 2011, https://rachelheldevans.com/blog/complementarians-are-selective-too.

* John Piper, "Is It Wrong for Men to Listen to Female Speakers? An Interview with John Piper," Desiring God, July 31, 2010, https://www.desiringgod.org/interviews/is-it-wrong-for-men-to-listen-to-female-speakers.

what age groups women should be allowed to teach in Sunday school, whether women can speak in small group Bible studies, what titles to bestow upon worship leaders and children's ministry coordinators so that they don't appear too authoritative, and on and on and on. If you really want to give yourself a headache, check out Wayne Grudem's article "But What *Should* Women Do in the Church?"* in which he painstakingly lists eighty-three church ministries in "decreasing order of authority and influence" to help churches decide which ministries are appropriate for women. I confess that when I read this list, the first image to come to my mind is that of a man straining gnats and swallowing camels.

Scot McKnight himself changed his position on women and teaching when he realized that his favorite Bible professor, the one from whom he'd learned the most about interpreting and applying Scripture, was a woman. "Anyone who thinks it is wrong for a woman to teach in church can be consistent with that point of view only if they refuse to read and learn from women scholars," he concluded. "This means not reading their books lest they become teachers."

And as one commenter noted yesterday, many complementarians don't seem to have a problem with women assuming leadership and teaching roles as missionaries in developing countries, "because if it's happening 'over there,' 'somewhere else,' in some primitive place where lifestyles aren't quite as sophisticated, and buildings aren't quite so solid, and people are presumed to be simpler, then it's as if it isn't really happening . . . I'm thinking of the modern Junias like Lottie Moon, Jackie Pullinger, Mary Slessor, Amy Carmichael, Marie Monsen, Gladys Aylward, etc."

I've been told by some complementarians that women are

---

* Wayne Grudem, "But What *Should* Women Do in the Church?" *CBMW News*, Vol. 1, No. 2 (November 1995): 1, 3–7, https://cbmw.org/wp-content/uploads/2024/11/1-2.pdf.

permitted to teach in such circumstances because "desperate times call for desperate measures." *But anyone who doesn't see the entire world as desperate for the gospel isn't paying much attention. Those who think the urgency of Pentecost has passed, that the world doesn't need every trained and passionate advocate for the gospel it can get, "have eyes to see but do not see and ears to hear but do not hear"* [Ezekiel 12:2, NIV].

WHAT SHOULD WE DO FOR THE SAKE OF THE GOSPEL?

I can't know for sure, but I believe that Paul's instructions to Timothy regarding the women at Ephesus were intended to protect the gospel from untrained teachers and to ensure that the church remain distinct from the cults of the surrounding culture. And I believe that, just as he celebrated Junia and Priscilla and Phoebe, he would celebrate and affirm the many trained, gifted, and passionate women who are preaching the gospel from behind pulpits, in darkened slums, in front of classrooms, in busy homes, and before crowds of people longing to encounter God.

It has been pointed out that as long as Christians remain embroiled in endless debates about what women can and cannot do for Jesus, we are only utilizing *half the church*. Women have so much to bring to Christianity—so many gifts, so many insights, so many new ways of looking at things, expressing things, enacting things, and questioning things. I am convinced that the gospel will only benefit from more women preaching it.

What a tragic and agonizing irony that instructions once delivered for the purpose of avoiding needless offense are now invoked in ways that needlessly offend, that words once meant to help draw people to the gospel now repel them! Research shows that the overall number of women attending church has dropped by 11 percent in the last twenty years.* I suspect that part of this has to do with the fact that when female executives, entrepreneurs, academics, and creatives are told that they have to check their gifts at the church door, many turn away for good. In a more egalitarian culture, where women are assumed to have the same value as men, restricting women's roles based on their gender is unnecessarily offensive. It drives people *away* from the gospel—and not because of the cost of discipleship.

And while our sisters around the world continue to suffer from trafficking, exploitation, violence, neglect, maternal mortality, and discrimination, those of us who are perhaps most equipped to respond with prophetic words and actions—women of faith—are being systematically silenced by our own faith communities.

Scot McKnight has wisely asked: "Do you think Paul would have put women 'behind the pulpit' if it would have been advantageous 'for the sake of the gospel'?"

Or, put another way: Do you think Paul would have prevented women from speaking if he knew it would hurt the gospel?

The answer to that question should be a lot simpler than it has become.

Originally posted on June 7, 2012.

---

* "20 Years of Surveys Show Key Differences in the Faith of America's Men and Women," *Barna*, August 1, 2011, https://www.barna.com/research/20-years-of-surveys-show-key-differences-in-the-faith-of-americas-men-and-women/.

"... Your Daughters Will Prophesy"

> Whoever welcomes a prophet as a prophet will receive a prophet's reward, and whoever welcomes a righteous person as a righteous person will receive a righteous person's reward. (Jesus, Matthew 10:41)

Josiah became king of Israel when he was just eight years old.

Described as Israel's last good king, he reigned for thirty-one years during a final period of peace before the Babylonian exile. About halfway through his reign, Josiah learns that the long-lost Book of the Law—the Torah—has been discovered in the temple. Upon hearing the words of the Torah read aloud, Josiah tears his robes in repentance and summons a prophet, for he sees how far Israel has strayed from God's ways.

Contemporaries of Josiah included the famed prophets Jeremiah, Zephaniah, Nahum, and Habakkuk—all of whom have books of the Bible named after them. But Josiah did not choose any of those men. Instead he chose Huldah, a woman and prophet who lived in Jerusalem. "Huldah is not chosen because no men were available," writes Scot McKnight. "She is chosen because she is truly exceptional among the prophets."

Huldah first confirms the scroll's authenticity and then tells Josiah that the disobedience of Israel will indeed lead to its destruction, but that Josiah himself would die in peace. Thus, Huldah not only interpreted but also authorized the document that would become the core of Jewish and Christian scripture. Her prophecy was fulfilled thirty-five years later (2 Kings 22).

The Bible identifies ten such female prophets in the Old and New Testaments: Miriam, Deborah, Huldah, Noadiah, Isaiah's wife, Anna, and the four daughters of Philip. In addition, women like Rachel, Hannah, Abigail, Elisabeth, and Mary are described as having prophetic visions about the future of their children, the destiny of nations, and the coming Messiah.

When the Holy Spirit descended upon the first Christians at Pentecost, Peter draws from the words of the prophet Joel to describe what has happened:

> *Your sons and daughters will prophesy,* your young men will see visions, your old men will dream dreams. Even on my servants, *both men and women,* I will pour out my Spirit in those days, and they will prophesy. (Acts 2:17–18; italics added)

The breaking in of the new creation after Christ's resurrection unleashed a cacophony of new prophetic voices, and apparently, prophesying among women was such a common activity in the early church that Paul had to remind women to cover their heads when they did it. While some may try to downplay biblical examples of female disciples, deacons, preachers, leaders, and apostles, no one can deny the Bible's long tradition of prophetic feminine vision.

I believe that right now, we need that prophetic vision more than ever.

Right now, thirty thousand children die every day from preventable disease.*

Right now, women and girls account for 71 percent of modern slavery victims.†

Right now, a woman dies in childbirth every two minutes.‡

Right now, women ages fifteen to forty-four are more likely to be maimed or to die from male violence than from cancer, malaria, traffic accidents, and war combined.§

Meanwhile, the evangelical church has busied itself with endless debates about the "appropriate roles" of women in the church and complaints about the supposed "feminization of the church," as if women are no longer needed for the Kingdom, as if we've stepped outside our bounds. Meanwhile, churches are spending years debating whether a female missionary should be allowed to speak on a Sunday morning, whether students older than ten should have female Sunday school teachers, whether women should be allowed to read from Scripture in a church service, whether girls should be encouraged to attend seminary, whether women should be permitted to collect the offering or write the church newsletter or make an announcement. Those of us who are perhaps most equipped to

---

* "Child Survival Act Would Save the Lives of 30,000 Children Daily," ONE Campaign, May 10, 2007, https://www.one.org/us/press/child-survival-act-would-save-the-lives-of-30000-children-daily/.

† *Global Estimates of Modern Slavery: Forced Labour and Forced Marriage* (International Labour Organization and Walk Free Foundation, 2017), https://www.ilo.org/sites/default/files/wcmsp5/groups/public/@dgreports/@dcomm/documents/publication/wcms_575479.pdf.

‡ "Every Two Minutes a Woman Dies in Pregnancy and Childbirth: Tackling a Global Maternal Health Crisis," United Nations Population Fund, April 7, 2025, https://www.unfpa.org/news/every-two-minutes-woman-dies-pregnancy-and-childbirth-tackling-global-maternal-health-crisis#:~:text=UNITED%20NATIONS%2C%20New%20York%20%E2%80%93%20An,for%20which%20we%20have%20estimates.

§ "The Secretary-General's Campaign to End Violence Against Women," UN Department of Public Information, November 2008, http://unis.unvienna.org/pdf/violence_against_women_backgrounder_2008.pdf.

speak and act prophetically in response to the violence, poverty, and inequality that plague our sisters around the world are being silenced ourselves.

Folks who see the leadership of women like Huldah and Junia as special exceptions for times of great need are oblivious to the world in which we live. Those who think the urgency of Pentecost has passed are deluding themselves. They "have eyes to see but do not see and ears to hear but do not hear."

Women around the world need the voices of all their sisters to cry out in one accord.

I'm with Sarah on this one.* *We cannot afford to wait for permission to make change; women themselves must be the change.*

So, ladies—speak out.

Preach.

Prophecy.

Stand with your sisters.

Change the world.

And if a man ever tries to use the Bible as a weapon against you to keep you from speaking the truth, just throw on a head covering and tell him that you're prophesying, just like the Bible says you can do.

To those who will not accept us as preachers, we will have to become prophets.

Originally posted on December 13, 2011.

---

* Here, Rachel linked to fellow blogger and writer Sarah Bessey (also your editor here, hi). The post is no longer available on the internet but some portions found their way into my first book, *Jesus Feminist*.

The Troubler

A REFLECTION BY REV. DR. SCOT McKNIGHT

Years ago, Rachel Held Evans wrote a post that is more true today—as I write this, we are enduring a crushing defeat in the recent presidential vote as a past president becomes the next president—than it was when Rachel penned her prophetic words. Her post finished with this: "To those who will not accept us [women] as preachers, we will have to become prophets." These words follow from a post in which she details the name of ten women prophets in the Bible, along with the liberating words on Pentecost that "your sons and DAUGHTERS will prophesy" (Acts 2:17, emphasis added).

Too many girls, young women, and older women have participated in churches that have been complementarian, even if as "so-called soft complementarians." Too many were deprived of a vision for their calling; too many were not provided a path to walk into that calling; and too many now languish in less-than callings. Rachel paved the way for such women to exercise their voices and their agency.

When Rachel wrote her first book, *Evolving in Monkey Town: How a Girl Who Knew All the Answers Learned to Ask the Questions*, I was sent a copy, and I loved it. I encouraged a biologist colleague to blog about her book because I wanted the science of her book to be backed by someone who knew biology, evolution, and human genome research. She took her world on at not only one of its most inflexible points (creation science, anti-evolution), but she knew the implications it would have for her own life.

What I admired in Rachel—over and over, and I mean weekly on her blog and various platforms—was her courage, her clear-window prose, her defense of Jesus while exposing the hypocrisies and injustices of the generally evangelical church in the USA. I did not meet Rachel until we were together at the Austin Presbyterian seminary. With many others, when I met her I felt like I was meeting an old friend. I had walked with her writings for years by that time. Her address that day—call it a sermon, an address, a lecture, or a prophetic word—proved to me that she was a gifted speaker, theologian, and prophet for our day.

When my wife Kris and I followed her illness and death, we were stunned. We grieve her loss. We lost her courage and her voice as a "troubler" for the conservative church of the USA.

We are not Rachels today, but we can echo that glorious voice she had.

Is God a Man? A Brief Response to CBMW's Accusation of Heresy

Some time ago, I wrote a post for Holy Week about Mary's experience during the crucifixion.* At the end of the post, I refer to God as *she*. I believe it's the only time in any of my published writing I have done so, as I typically avoid gendered pronouns when writing about God or simply refer to God as *he*.

Well today Owen Strachan, president of the Council on Biblical Manhood and Womanhood [CBMW], took to Twitter to declare the post heresy.† (It's unclear to me why it's only just now coming up.) It's no small thing to be named a heretic by someone in a position of Christian leadership, and the tweet has already given rise to all sorts of crazy rumors, so I figured a brief response might be warranted.

---

* Rachel Held Evans, "Women of the Passion, Part 2: Mary's Heart Is Pierced (Again)," Rachel Held Evans Blog, April 6, 2012, https://rachelheldevans.com/blog/women-of-the-passion-mary-pierced-heart.

† It was a common occurrence in the blogosphere of the time for people to respond publicly to blog posts, treating Twitter as a public square for airing opinions and building connections. Owen Strachan, then-president of the Council of Biblical Manhood and Womanhood, was a frequent sparring partner of Rachel's on that platform. His original critique, from May 16, 2014, is still available at https://x.com/ostrachan/status/467378592347729920. In it he wrote: "Let's stop pretending like all's okay. @rachelheldevans called God a she: 'God Herself.' . . . This is heresy, straight up."

First, I wholeheartedly affirm the Apostle's and Nicene Creeds and I believe Scripture to be inspired by God and authoritative in the Christian life. Like Owen, I believe in the good news that Jesus Christ is Lord and would gladly join him in proclaiming the great mystery of the faith—that Christ has died, Christ has risen, and Christ will come again. I disagree with Owen that differences in theology regarding gender are matters of orthodoxy, particularly given the number of faithful Christians who have disagreed on these issues through the centuries, and I'm disappointed he resorted to charges of heresy when we should be able to discuss these differences with gentleness and respect.

Second, I believe Scripture teaches that both men and women are created in the image of God (Genesis 1:27), which means both masculinity and femininity are—at some level—part of God's nature. Scripture often uses feminine imagery to describe God as a mother, nurse, seamstress, midwife, etc. (Ruth 2:12, Psalm 17:8, Matthew 23:37, Isaiah 46:3–4, Job 38:29, Hosea 11:3–4, Psalm 22:9, Luke 13:20–21, Luke 15:8–9), and while God is often referred to as Father, and Jesus was certainly a man, the Hebrew word for Holy Spirit is a feminine noun. And in the New Testament, the Spirit is frequently connected with images of childbirth and nursing (John 3:5; cf. John 1:13; 1 John 4:7; 5:1, 4, 18).

Mimi Haddad of Christians for Biblical Equality does a really fine job unpacking these images in her article on the topic, "Is God Male?"*

Finally (and as Mimi points out), the self-naming of God in Scripture is "I AM WHO I AM"—a name without gender. I suspect that's because, though God is a person, God is not a human being like us. The people of Israel received a strong warning from

---

* Mimi Haddad, "Is God Male?", CBE International, September 5, 2012, https://www.cbeinternational.org/resource/presidents-message-god-male/.

God about this in Deuteronomy 4:15–17: *"You saw no form of any kind the day the* LORD *spoke to you at Horeb out of the fire. Therefore watch yourselves very carefully, so that you do not become corrupt and make for yourselves an idol, an image of any shape, whether formed like a man or a woman, or like any animal on earth or any bird that flies in the air . . ."*

I believe that when we declare God to be exclusively male, we flirt with idolatry, for we re-create God in a human image. And the fact that some people find the notion of a feminine God so repulsive reveals the degree to which this type of idolatry has snuck into the church and the degree to which women in our society are still seen as lesser beings than men.

That said, I use the feminine pronoun for God very sparingly in my writing. Usually, I either avoid using a gendered pronoun altogether or I use the word *he* to avert unnecessary controversy (much to the chagrin of my more progressive readers!). I don't have a problem referring to God as *Father*, or as *he*. Scripture does this often. To insist on referring to God only as *she* would be to commit the same error. As Mimi puts it: "God is self-revealed in terms we can understand through our own experiences, using metaphors which are, at times, feminine. We should not, however, make these metaphors—these implicit comparisons—absolutes. When we do, we are making God in our image, whether male or female. God is not limited by gender because God is Spirit. It is idolatry to make God male or female. God is no more female or goddess than God is male, and males have no priority over women in the New Covenant community because of gender (Gal 3:27–29)."

To say that God is *not* a man is not the same as saying God *is* a woman. It is saying that God transcends gender categories.

On the very rare occasion that I refer to God as *she*, I do it with a lot of intentionality and with the goal of reminding myself and my readers that God is not merely some elevated, deified version of ourselves. God is not a man. God is not white. God is not American. God might not even be a Bama fan. *(Too far?)*

And as a woman, referring to God as *she* or as *Mother* serves as an important, liberating reminder that I am indeed created in the image of God, not as some lesser being who exists in perpetual subordination to men, but as an expression of God's very self.

If that makes me a heretic, guilty as charged.

Originally posted on May 16, 2014.

If Men Got the Titus 2 Treatment . . .

Every evangelical woman knows what it's like to get the Titus 2 Treatment.

This happens whenever a woman is presented with a universal statement about the "biblical" role of women in the world, which is typically extrapolated from a single biblical text without regard to literary or historical context and followed by a parenthetical string of additional unrelated and out-of-context Bible verses for support.

For example, in an article that characterizes a man who takes responsibility for the laundry as a "man fail," Owen Strachan of the Council on Biblical Manhood and Womanhood writes: "The curse bore down upon Eve's primary activity, childbearing, showing that her intended sphere of labor and dominion-taking was the home (Genesis 3:16). This is true of the virtuous woman of Proverbs 31 as well, who though something of a whirling dervish of godly femininity was not, like her husband, by the city gates with the elders (Proverbs 31:23), but working tirelessly to bless her family and manage her home for God's glory."*

Classic. Root feminine identity in the curse rather than the

---

* Owen Strachan, "The 'Dad Mom' and the 'Man Fail,'" Patheos, "Thought Life," last updated November 2, 2011, https://www.patheos.com/blogs/thoughtlife/2011/11/the-dad-mom-and-the-man-fail/.

redemptive work of Christ and then make the argument that because the ancient Near Eastern woman of Proverbs 31 is not described as consulting with the elders, then all women everywhere for all of time are restricted to the realm of the home and therefore responsible for the laundry.

I call this the "Titus 2 Treatment" because Titus 2:5 is one of the most commonly abused passages in this regard. It's a verse in which women are instructed to be "busy at home," (as opposed to being idle at home, not, as some claim, as opposed to working outside of the home),[*] and I've seen it cited in support of all sorts of statements about how domestic duties such as washing the dishes or doing the laundry fall exclusively to women and how mothers who have careers outside of the home are shirking their God-ordained roles.

So I thought it might be fun to give guys a sense of what it's like to get the Titus 2 treatment with this little piece. (Don't take it too seriously):

THE CRISIS OF BIBLICAL MASCULINITY IN THE CHURCH

A Reflection by Roberta Heard Ellis[†]

It has come to my attention that we are facing a crisis of biblical masculinity in the church today. An increasing number of men are neglecting the roles God clearly outlined for them in Scripture (Genesis 3:19, 1 Thessalonians 5:26, 1 Timothy 2:8) in favor of blatant cultural capitulation. I'd like to focus on three biblical principles that many modern men, out of total disregard for Scripture, continue to ignore: sweating, kissing, and hand-raising.

---

[*] Here, Rachel linked to a CBE International article called "Busy at Home?" That article has moved since posting and can now be found here; https://www.cbeinternational.org/resource/busy-home/.

[†] This is a clear nom de plume for snark purposes.

1. Sweating

Take a look around our culture and you will see millions of men who earn a living by working in climate-controlled office buildings. Such work may be mentally strenuous, but far too often, it can be accomplished without even breaking a sweat.

The curse of Genesis 3 clearly describes man's primary activity as difficult physical labor. "By the sweat of your brow you will eat your food until you return to the ground," God declares in Genesis 3:19.

David, who is described as a "man after my [God's] own heart" (Acts 13:22) was a shepherd (1 Samuel 16:11), who clubbed wild animals to death (1 Samuel 17:35–36). He was also a warrior (1 Samuel 18:27) and a king (2 Samuel 12:30).

The men of Scripture—Abraham, Isaac, Sampson, Daniel, Jesus, Peter, Paul—are men of action whose occupations centered around physical labor like farming, shepherding, carpentry, tent-making, and fighting animals with their bare hands. (Note: Any exceptions to this trend should be immediately discounted as irrelevant anomalies.) Nowhere in Scripture is a man of God described as sitting at a desk in an office building from nine to five. Nowhere.

So men who wish to honor God with their lives and humbly submit to his will should make physical labor their primary occupation, and resist the urge to give in to our culture's glorification of "white-collar" work, which is a departure from biblical principles of masculinity.

Now, some men will say they find office work more stimulating and rewarding than manual labor, or that it provides more financial security in their particular situation, but these men are more interested in pursuing selfish ambitions and wealth than submitting themselves to the Word of God. Our culture's rampant obesity epidemic among men can be clearly traced to this departure from God's perfect design. And it threatens to undo our whole society, negatively affecting our children and generations to come.

2. Kissing

It may surprise many men to learn that one of the most common instructions found in New Testament Scripture is for Christians to "greet one another with a holy kiss" (Romans 16:16, 1 Corinthians 16:20, 2 Corinthians 13:12, 1 Thessalonians 5:26, 1 Peter 5:14). In 1 Thessalonians 5:26, Paul specifically instructs men to do this.

Yet despite the fact that this is one of the most repeated directives of Scripture, one is hard-pressed to find men kissing one another on the check in churches today. This is because those who do not take the Bible seriously claim these clear teachings of Scripture have a "cultural" component.

But let us not forget that God's word does not change or pass away (Malachi 3:6, Mark 13:31) and also that studying the Greco-Roman cultural context of the New Testament is kind of a pain. We are therefore obligated to take God at his word, whether these instructions make sense in our culture or not.

3. Hand-Raising

First Timothy 2 stipulates the responsibilities of men and women in worship.

Thankfully, 1 Timothy 2:12—"I do not permit a woman to teach or to assume authority over a man"—continues to be rigidly applied in many churches today without regard to its original context or intended audience. However, the instructions of 1 Timothy 2:8—"I want the men EVERYWHERE to pray, lifting up holy hands without anger or disputing" (emphasis mine)—is taken as a sort of suggestion that need not be directly enforced in the modern church.

Often I have been to churches where women are properly silenced, but men do not even bother to lift their hands during prayer! Furthermore, some of these men are known to engage in public disputes around theology—often on their blogs—which this passage clearly condemns.

And it's not just the rules for worship in 1 Timothy 2 that men have chosen to disregard. These days, little attention is paid to 1 Corinthians 11:14—"Does not the very nature of things teach you that if a man has long hair, it is a disgrace to him"—even though the language used here is the same used in Romans 1:26, which many Christians are quite fond of citing when condemning other people.

In summary, if staying true to the Word of God means applying its instructions to women literally, without regard to their cultural contexts or original intended audiences, then faithfulness requires we do the same for men.

It's only fair.

It seems funny, bizarre even, to subject men to the "Titus 2 Treatment." But don't forget that every day, there are very real Christian women who are discouraged from pursuing ministry positions, dream jobs, or equal partnerships with their spouses because of how the Bible is used to manage and regulate women.

Originally posted on February 12, 2014.

Donald Trump and a Tale of Two Gospels

As it becomes clear Donald Trump's candidacy for president will be more than a sideshow this year, the probable Republican nominee is making his pitch to Christian voters.

You would think it would be a hard sell given the fact that the real estate mogul and reality star has boasted about his extramarital affairs, profited off casinos and strip clubs, said he doesn't need to ask God for forgiveness, called for targeting innocent civilians in war, mocked a reporter with a disability, threatened the religious liberty of minority groups in the US, and gained wide support among white nationalists for consistently lying about and demeaning Blacks, Mexican immigrants, Muslims, and Syrian refugees.

But polls show that despite all of this, Trump remains favored among evangelical voters. After speaking at Liberty University last week, Trump scored an important endorsement from Jerry Falwell Jr., a prominent leader of the Religious Right who, to the applause of thousands, compared Trump to Jesus and Martin Luther King Jr.

Despite what the polls say, I personally don't know a single evangelical Christian who considers Trump a model Christian. His scant church attendance and clumsiness at citing Scripture have not gone unnoticed here in the Bible Belt. Russell Moore of the Ethics and Religious Liberty Commission of the Southern Baptist Convention has been an outspoken voice against evangelical alignment with Trump, and I've found his righteous incredulity over Trump's religious pandering refreshing.

Yet Falwell's support is hardly isolated, and I suspect if Trump is the nominee, he will continue to find even more of it from the Religious Right (which I designate as a subset of a broader and more diverse evangelicalism). Despite about a million think-pieces on the topic, the reasons are not that mysterious. Racism and xenophobia remain powerful forces in our country, as does celebrity worship, and white Christians aren't as immune from these influences as they like to think.

Indeed, a quick study of history shows the origins of Liberty University and the Religious Right lie not in their opposition to abortion (that came later), but rather in their opposition to racial integration.* Trump's message mirrors several postures that have characterized the Religious Right from the beginning:

1. A glorified nostalgia for the past (*"make America great again!" "America was once a Christian nation!"*) that minimizes the historical suffering of women and minority groups in this country,

2. an overwrought persecution complex that confuses sharing civil rights with others with being persecuted by them, and

3. a persistent fear of the perceived "other"—Muslims, LGBT people, immigrants, refugees, etc.—that results in culture wars meant to "take back" the public square. Trump's promise that

---

* Stephen Prothero, "When Donald Trump Goes to Liberty U.," CNN, last updated January 17, 2016, https://www.cnn.com/2016/01/16/opinions/prothero-trump-liberty/.

"everyone will say Merry Christmas" when he's president appeals to those who think being wished "happy holidays" by a store clerk is a form of religious oppression (and who apparently remain unconcerned about how Trump's mandate will be enforced upon those of other faiths). Both the Trump campaign and the Religious Right movement begin with the assumption that things were better in this country when the culture was dominated by white Christian men and that things will get better if white Christian men are freed from the burden of "political correctness" and restored to dominance once again.

But perhaps the most tantalizing of Trump's pitches to the Religious Right, and the one with broadest appeal, is his promise to protect their power.

"I'll tell you one thing," he told a crowd in Sioux Center, Iowa, "I get elected president, we're going to be saying 'merry Christmas' again . . . And by the way, Christianity will have power . . . because if I'm there, you're going to have somebody representing you very, very well."

This is the gospel of Donald Trump, his "good news" to Christian voters: Stick with me and you'll be a winner. Stick with me and I'll give you power, protection, prestige.

It's also the very thing Satan promised Jesus when he tempted him in the desert.

"I will give you power and authority over all the kingdoms of the world," Satan said, "for it has been given to me and I can give it to anyone I want to."

While Jesus resisted the allure of power and privilege, it has long been a snare to his followers, and the Religious Right sold its soul long ago. Its support of Trump proves once again it will do anything to protect its power, even if it means baptizing as anointed a candidate whose rhetoric and actions contradict any sane understanding of what Christianity is about.

Trump's sloppy citations of Scripture are accepted by many at Liberty University because, as an arm of the Religious Right, the school's primary function is political, not religious. The Bible is harvested for a few conservative sound bites, Jesus reduced to an object of veneration whose death saves but whose life and teachings remain inconsequential. When power is the end game, faithfulness bows to political expediency.

ANOTHER GOSPEL . . .

After his pep rally at Liberty, Trump was flying high, claiming with his usual hyperbolic flourish that Christians just *LOVE* him.

. . . And then he made the critical mistake of actually walking into a church.

Last Sunday, Trump took a break from the campaign trail to surprise the congregation of First Presbyterian Church in Muscatine, Iowa, with a visit to their regular morning service.*

Now understand, as a liturgical Mainline Protestant congregation, First Presbyterian Church follows the Revised Common Lectionary, which means the Scriptural passages for the service and sermon are determined years in advance. Had Trump wandered into my church—St. Luke's Episcopal Church in Cleveland, Tennessee—that morning, he would have encountered the very same texts. Thousands of congregations around the world—from Lutherans to Anglicans, to Presbyterians, to members of the United Church of Christ and other denominations—stick with

---

* Jack Jenkins, "Donald Trump Accidentally Sat Through a Sermon About Welcoming Immigrants," ThinkProgress, January 25, 2016, https://archive.thinkprogress.org/donald-trump-accidentally-sat-through-a-sermon-about-welcoming-immigrants-175857c57c52/.

this calendar as a way of pulling the days' focus around a common theme. Nothing about the service would have changed just because Trump walked through the door (well except maybe the tension in the room!).

The first Scripture reading that morning came from 1 Corinthians 12, and at First Presbyterian Church Muscatine it was read from *The Message*, an idiomatic translation by Eugene Peterson:

> But I also want you to think about how this keeps your significance from getting blown up into self-importance. For no matter how significant you are, it is only because of what you are a part of. An enormous eye or a gigantic hand wouldn't be a body, but a monster. What we have is one body with many parts, each its proper size and in its proper place. No part is important on its own. Can you imagine Eye telling Hand, "Get lost; I don't need you"? Or, Head telling Foot, "You're fired; your job has been phased out"?

Then came the sermon, which was based on one of the most important passages of the New Testament, the one where Jesus teaches at the synagogue in Nazareth and explains exactly what his ministry is all about: "The Spirit of the Lord is upon me, because he has anointed me to bring good news to the poor. He has sent me to proclaim release to the captives and recovery of sight to the blind, to let the oppressed go free, to proclaim the year of the Lord's favor."

This passage from Luke 4 is a declaration of the nature and aim of the gospel—the good news—and as the next verse reveals, it nearly got Jesus thrown off a cliff. As it turns out, the kind of people Donald Trump and the Religious Right deem acceptable collateral damage in their quest for power—the poor, the oppressed, the marginalized, the hated minorities—are the very people Jesus prioritized. His life and ministry started with them, and his Kingdom will ultimately be realized through them. The gospel isn't about protecting power and privilege, but rather about surrendering them until God's vision of justice is fulfilled.

As Rev. Dr. Pam Saturnia put it: "Jesus has come to proclaim freedom and healing to those who are the most unloved, who are the most discriminated against, the most forgotten in our community and in our world. Jesus has come to proclaim the year of the Lord's favor on the teenagers who are homeless, on the Syrian refugees, on the Mexican migrants, and the people who find themselves prisoners of addiction and their families, on the poorest of the poor in Haiti—Jesus has come for them."

After the service, Trump seemed a little defensive, wondering aloud to the press if the Corinthians passage was directed at him ("I have more humility than people think," he said) and arguing, "I want to take care of all people but with Syrians, we just can't do it here."

But contrary to Trump's prevailing worldview, this event had not in fact been orchestrated around him. The man had simply stepped into a big ole' pile of actual gospel and immediately realized it contradicted everything he stands for.

In contrast to Liberty University's convocation service, this church was a place where Scripture was quoted at length and in context, where the words of Jesus were honored and heeded, and where the vanities of a racist billionaire were challenged rather than coddled for the sake of financial and political gain. Kudos to Rev. Saturnia for sticking with the prophetic word God had given for that day and not cowering or compromising because it might offend one of the most powerful men in the world.

Donald Trump had an encounter with the gospel of Jesus Christ and rather than propping him up, it made him uncomfortable . . . as tends to happen with anyone who is actually paying attention, myself included.

When I left evangelicalism for a Mainline church, I was teased by some evangelicals who informed me I'd picked the losing team. They reminded me that Mainline churches like my Episcopal church in Tennessee and First Presbyterian Church in Muscatine, Iowa, are losing members at faster rates than evangelical churches are losing them. I'd jumped the evangelical ship, the said, for nothing but a capsizing lifeboat.

They aren't entirely wrong. We Mainliners don't fill many megachurch buildings these days, and our pastors don't typically write bestselling "biblical diet" books or get quoted on CNN. But what these critics fail to understand is I don't go to church to be with a bunch of "winners." I go to church to be with the people of God, people transformed by the gospel of Jesus Christ.

Sure, the "good news" of safety, popularity, and political power is more appealing to the masses, but it's not the good news Jesus preached. Not by a long shot. No one ever said the fruit of the Spirit is money, success, or political power. Rather, the fruit of the Spirit is love, joy, peace, patience, kindness, goodness, faithfulness, and self-control—qualities that can be found in all types of communities be they conservative or liberal, evangelical or Mainline Protestant, big or small. Getting lots of people to go to church (or to attend a convocation/political rally) isn't the same as making disciples of Jesus Christ, and Christian leaders would do well to remember the difference.

As Rev. Saturnia said, the words of Jesus tend to "comfort the afflicted and afflict the comfortable."

Last Sunday, those words were enough to make one of the most powerful men in the country squirm. How's that for being politically incorrect?

Originally posted on January 28, 2016.

A Perversion of the Gospel

A REFLECTION BY SHANE CLAIBORNE

I miss Rachel Held Evans. Okay, now that I got that out there, let me say this: I am honored to be part of this project. It gave me an excuse to reread the dozens of marvelous, witty, and insightful articles Rachel wrote online. And while I was at it, I scrolled through a few of our exchanges I saved on my phone, which all left me grateful for her, wishing we were able to have her around a little longer, and immensely thankful to be a part of this cloud of witnesses putting our voices together alongside hers to share some love and hope and joy at this critical moment in history.

As I write this, Donald Trump has been reelected as the forty-seventh president of the United States. And once again it was with the vote of 81 percent of white evangelical Christians, the same number that supported him back when Rachel wrote this in 2016.[*]

Help us, Lord. And pray for us, Rachel.

In the New Testament's Letter of Paul to the Galatians, the apostle Paul wrote: "I am astonished that you are so quickly deserting the one who called you to live in the grace of Christ and are turning to a different Gospel—which is really no gospel at all. Evidently some

---

[*] Harriet Sherwood, "White Evangelical Christians Stick by Trump Again, Exit Polls Show," *The Guardian*, November 6, 2020, https://www.theguardian.com/us-news/2020/nov/06/white-evangelical-christians-supported-trump.

people are throwing you into confusion and are trying to pervert the gospel of Christ" (Galatians 1:6–7, niv).

Imagine that—people creating confusion and trying to pervert the gospel of Christ . . .

The word *gospel* was an imperial word that Jesus snatched from the empire's lexicon and flipped on its head. It is true to say that there have always been two "gospels"—the gospel of Jesus and Caesar's gospel of empire. In fact, there was a saying in 6 BCE (inscribed on a government building in Asia Minor), a decade before Christ, declaring that Caesar was the savior of the world, the alpha and omega, the restorer of everything, and it says that literally the birthday of Augustus Caesar is the beginning of the "gospel."

It's also worth noting that the word *gospel* means "good news" despite the bad news we see evident in many "gospel" preachers and churches, which is why Rachel's words are so piercing as she distinguishes between the gospel of Trump and the gospel of Jesus.

An apple tree doesn't need a sign to tell you what it is. You can tell by the fruit. We know who Donald Trump is . . . he has shown us, over and over, by the vulgarities and bullying and slander. He has made a vocation out of the seven deadly sins and a mockery out of the fruits of the Spirit.

Over and over, Rachel and many of us essentially keep saying, "Yes, we are troubled by Trump, but we are even more troubled by the 'Christians' who support him."

The election of Donald Trump is bigger than Donald Trump. He represents a disturbing vision for America and a distorted version of the Christian faith. And when so many folks professing to follow Jesus continue to defend Trump, this becomes a spiritual crisis, a discipleship crisis. Leaders like Franklin Graham, Robert Jeffress, and Sean Feucht forfeited their spiritual and moral authority for the pursuit of power, as Rachel says, succumbing to the very temptations Jesus faced in the desert.

It is as if many Christian leaders and evangelists have never heard the words of our Savior, "What good will it be for someone to gain the whole world, and forfeit their soul?" (Matthew 16:26, niv).

One of the things I love about Rachel Held Evans is how she kept pointing us back to Jesus. The real Jesus—the brown-skinned, Palestinian, Jewish, refugee, homeless, born-in-a-manger-because-there-was-no-room-in-the-inn Jesus. The Jesus who came from a neighborhood people said from which "nothing good could come." The Jesus who was executed on the empire's cross but died with love on his lips. The one who exposed the powers and triumphed over them with love, and forgiveness, and an empty tomb. That Jesus.

So let us stand strong, even as some seek to pervert the gospel of Christ. May we reject the false gospel of empire, and Trump, and embrace the gospel of Jesus, which is always good news to the poor and the most vulnerable. Let us proclaim the good news of Jesus with our lives and with our lips—as Rachel did.

For the Sake of the Gospel, Drop the Persecution Complex

Did you hear about the pastor who was arrested for not marrying a same-sex couple? What about the publisher that got sued for refusing to censor antigay verses from the Bible?

Both of these stories have been exposed as fakes of course, but that didn't keep hundreds of thousands of conservative Christians from sharing them online this week.* When I pointed out to a friend that the story he had just shared on social media wasn't true, he replied, *"Well, it might as well be. Christians in this country are under attack."*

It has become a familiar refrain. We hear it every Christmas when an unsuspecting store clerk wishes the wrong Christian "happy holidays" instead of "Merry Christmas." We hear it whenever a high school drops its traditional prefootball game prayer out of respect for those students who may be Jewish or Muslim or nonreligious. An entire industry of books and films has blossomed in the red soil of the American Christian persecution complex, with

---

* Ed Stetzer, "An Embarrassing Week for Christians Sharing Fake News," *Christianity Today*, July 13, 2015, no longer available online.

the first "God's Not Dead" installment caricaturing and vilifying atheists and the second set to expose liberal efforts to "expel God from the classroom once and for all."

Now, most of the time, this phenomenon falls into the frustrating but relatively harmless category of culture war posturing, but lately, as the apocalyptic, fear-based rhetoric continues to ratchet up in the wake of the Supreme Court's decision regarding same-sex marriage, and as that rhetoric continues to target and demonize LGBT people, it's been doing some real harm. Just last week I received at least a dozen messages from friends and readers who told me the response from Christians to the Supreme Court ruling confirmed for them what they've known in their hearts for a while: They don't want anything to do with Christianity anymore, not if this is what it's all about.

So what I'd like to suggest to my fellow Christians is that perhaps taking up the cross means laying down the persecution complex. A spirit of fear and entitlement does more to obscure the gospel than elucidate it. Here are some reasons why: **The persecution complex is not based in reality.** Not only do American Christians experience complete religious freedom in this country, we also enjoy tremendous privilege. More than 70 percent of the population identifies as Christian, as do the majority of our representatives to congress and every single US president. Our churches, whose steeples dot every cityscape and small town in the land, are exempt from paying taxes, and unlike many people of other faiths, we don't have to worry about fighting with our employers to take time off to celebrate our religious holidays as they are largely taken for granted.

In spite of all this, many Christians like to imagine themselves as the scrappy underdogs, bullied and oppressed for their faith yet bravely standing for their beliefs. Former pastor Mark Driscoll made news a few years ago by accusing the Orange County City Council of religious discrimination for not allowing him to convert a building in the area into a church. It was later revealed he knew from the beginning the building wasn't zoned for a church but was using the American Christian persecution complex to try and garner support for bending the rules.

Neil Carter, who was actually fired from his teaching job for being an atheist, suggests that Christians create fictions like these because "real life does not sufficiently validate people's persecution complexes. . . . [Christians] are manufacturing conflicts in order to have something to rally behind," he writes. "It makes them feel more in touch with the early Church's tumultuous beginnings. But it takes a lot of smoke in mirrors to make it look like the people with the most privilege in a region (like Christians in the Bible Belt) are being mistreated by the people who run things. Where I live, all the judges, jurors, and attorneys are devout Christians. So are the teachers, the principal, and almost all of the parents."*

The persecution complex blinds Christians to our own privilege, which then blinds us to the challenges faced by the genuinely underprivileged in this country. We get so focused on ourselves and our own concerns we forget the admonition of the apostle Paul to "not merely look out for your own personal interests, but also for the interests of others" (Philippians 2:4).

And if you think the SCOTUS ruling did anything to alter this privilege, a few reality checkers are in order:

Reality Check #1: No one lost any rights in the Supreme Court decision. What happened was a minority group that had previously been denied a civil right the rest of us take for granted was

---

* Neil Carter, "The Sequel to God's Not Dead Happened in My Classroom, But in Reverse," Godless in Dixie, July 15, 2015, no longer available online.

given access to that right. Sharing civil rights with other people is not the same as being persecuted by them. In fact, I see the decision as a victory for religious freedom in the sense that people whose religion supports and encourages same-sex unions will no longer be prohibited from practicing that important religious value simply because some of their neighbors hold a different view. I have yet to see a shred of evidence to suggest that the presence of a marriage license in the home of a gay couple has any power to negatively affect the marriage of the straight couple down the street.

Reality Check #2: Contrary to what you may have read on Facebook, pastors and priests will not be forced to marry same-sex couples or be fined for refusing to . . . just as they are not presently forced to marry interfaith couples if their tradition opposes it, or cohabitating couples if their tradition opposes it, or divorcees if their tradition opposes it, or interracial couples if their tradition opposes it. That religious freedom has, and very likely will, be preserved. Just take interracial marriage, for example. It's been forty-eight years since the Supreme Court ruled that the laws in sixteen states prohibiting interracial marriage were unconstitutional. At the time, only about 25 percent of the American public supported interracial marriage, with many citing religious reasons for opposing it.* While public opinion has (thankfully) changed, the right of a clergy member to refuse to marry an interracial couple hasn't. Just as a pastor can still refuse to marry an interracial couple, he can still refuse to marry a same-sex couple without fear of government intervention. There is no indication whatsoever this will change.

---

* Frank Newport, "In U.S., 87% Approve of Black-White Marriage, vs. 4% in 1958," Gallup, July 25, 2013, https://news.gallup.com/poll/163697/approve-marriage-blacks-whites.aspx.

Reality Check #3: Facing disagreement is not the same as facing persecution. Conservative Christians are right about one thing: public opinion has shifted on same-sex marriage (particularly within the church), and this means they are more likely to encounter pushback when they insist same-sex marriage ought to be illegal. Facebook friends may argue with them. Comedians may satirize them. Bloggers may write posts like these disagreeing with them. But to conflate such disagreement with the sort of persecution Jesus warned his disciples about is not only myopic, but also a slap in the face to those Christians who face very real persecution around the world. Living in a pluralistic society that also grants freedom and civil rights protection to those with whom one disagrees is not the same as religious persecution. And crying persecution every time one doesn't get one's way is an insult to the very real religious persecution happening in the world today. It's no way to be a good citizen and certainly no way to advance the gospel in the world.

Which brings me to my second point . . .

THE PERSECUTION COMPLEX MINIMIZES THE VERY REAL SUFFERING OF OTHERS.

If Dan and I walk the streets of downtown Dayton, Tennessee, holding hands, it will not even occur to us to fear for our safety or worry about harassment because of it. I'm afraid the same cannot be said for a gay couple engaging in the same activity. (It should be noted that in 2004, our county commission attempted to criminalize homosexuality.)* That's because in spite of shifting views on same-sex marriage, gay, lesbian, bisexual, and transgender people

---

* Associated Press, "Tenn. County Officials Seek to Ban Gays," Fox News, last updated January 14, 2015, https://www.foxnews.com/story/tenn-county-officials-seek-to-ban-gays.

continue to face incredible hostility here in the US and around the world, often at the hands of Christians.

Here in the US, homeless and suicide rates among LGBTQ+ youth remain shockingly high, in part because conservative Christian leaders like John MacArthur instruct parents of gay children to "hand them over to Satan" and refuse to associate with them.* Half of gay males experience a negative reaction from parents when they come out, and in 26 percent of those cases, the gay child is thrown out of the home. Studies suggest that between 25 percent and 50 percent of homeless youth are on the street because of their sexual orientation or gender identity. Those whose families reject them are five times more likely to attempt suicide than those whose families support them.† In most states, people can still be fired from their (secular) jobs just for being gay, or thrown out of their homes if their landlord doesn't like LGBTQ+ people. Many LGBTQ+ people recall getting bullied mercilessly in school, and I've heard from several who report that they learned their first antigay slur in their church youth group.

For years, conservative Christians pushed for so-called reparative therapy efforts to change people's sexual orientation from homosexual to heterosexual, which proved so traumatizing and dangerous to LGBTQ+ people and their parents that even the head of the most popular "ex-gay" organization, Exodus International, apologized for the damage done by those efforts and shut the organization down.‡

---

* J. T. Eberhard, "Pastor John MacArthur: You Must Alienate Gay Kids and Turn Them over to Satan," no longer available online.
† Statistics are from PFLAG NYC, no longer available online; and "Facts About Suicide," Trevor Project, July 16, 2021, https://www.thetrevorproject.org/resources/article/facts-about-suicide/.
‡ John Burnett, "Group That Claimed to 'Cure' Gays Disbands, Leader Apologizes," NPR, "All Things Considered," June 20, 2013, https://www.npr.org/2013/06/20/193965227/group-that-claimed-to-cure-gays-disbands-leader-apologizes.

Christian leaders have blamed gay and lesbian people for the attacks on 9/11, Hurricane Katrina, and all sorts of natural and man-made disasters. The myth that gay and lesbian people are child molesters often goes unchallenged when spread from the pulpit, and in the '80s and '90s, many Christians refused to support efforts to curb the HIV/AIDS crisis as they believed it to be a "curse from God" that gay people deserved.[*] Among Gospel Coalition participants alone, it has been suggested recently that LGBTQ+ people are so disgusting they ought to induce a gag reflex and that supporting same-sex marriage is worse than supporting slavery.[†] I have several friends who were so traumatized by their experiences with Christians they cannot even walk through the doors of a church without suffering a physical reaction similar to PTSD—uncontrolled shaking, sweating, and panic. And I have cried with parents of LGBTQ+ kids who were stripped of membership in their beloved churches simply because they wouldn't publicly denounce their children.[‡]

And this is just what LGBTQ+ people face here in the US. Influenced by evangelical missionaries to the continent, many African nations have adopted legislation in which people can be thrown in jail or executed for being gay. (Just this week, John Piper tweeted his support of Kenya's criminalization of homosexuality.)[§] There are seventy-nine countries in which homosexuality is ille-

---

[*] Mae Elise Cannon, Lisa Sharon Harper, Troy Jackson, and Soong-Chan Rah, *Forgive Us: Confessions of a Compromised Faith* (Zondervan, 2014), 140.
[†] Rachel Held Evans, "Responding to Homophobia in the Christian Community," Rachel Held Evans Blog, August 23, 2013, https://rachelheldevans.com/blog/homophobia-christians-gag-reflex-gospel-coalition; Douglas Wilson, "Time for a Little Q&A," *Blog & Mablog: Theology That Bites Back*, July 3, 2015, https://dougwils.com/s7-engaging-the-culture/time-for-a-little-q-a.html.
[‡] Rachel Held Evans, "The Parents," Rachel Held Evans Blog, January 5, 2015, https://rachelheldevans.com/blog/parents-lgbt.
[§] Thaddeus Baklinski, "Kenyan Leaders to Obama: Don't Lecture Us on Gay 'Marriage,'" LifeSite, July 8, 2015, https://www.lifesitenews.com/news/kenyan-leaders-to-obama-dont-lecture-us-on-gay-marriage.

gal and many more in which LGBTQ+ people are advised not to travel because they may be violently threatened and harassed.

When it comes to opposition to gay rights, conservative Christians have been on the front lines, opposing measures that would give people in same-sex relationships the right to visit their partners in the hospital, file taxes jointly, adopt children, share insurance, and rent apartments without fear of unjust eviction. Routinely, fundamentalist Christians compare people in same-sex relationships to pedophiles and demand an explanation for how their most important relationships are any different from people having sex with dogs. Antigay bullying, discrimination, and hate speech often go unchallenged by Christians, and are far too often perpetuated by them.

So when Kevin DeYoung laments at the Gospel Coalition that Christians who opposed same-sex marriage are "worried about social ostracism and cultural marginalization" and asks that supporters of LGBTQ+ equality stick up for Christians when "their jobs, their reputations, and their freedoms are threatened," it's hard to blame anyone for balking with righteous incredulity.*

Where is the concern for gay kids getting kicked out of their homes to live on the streets? Where is the opposition to LGBTQ+ bullying and housing discrimination? Why remain silent when Christian leaders speak in crude and hateful terms about LGBT people or support the criminalization of homosexuality overseas?

What the persecution complex suggests is that conservative Christians only care about bullying, oppression, and discrimination when it happens to them. If it happens to LGBTQ+ people, or to people in other religious minority groups, it is of little concern (or is tacitly supported). Compassion and advocacy are

---

* Kevin DeYoung, "40 Questions for Christians Now Waving Rainbow Flags," TGC: The Gospel Coalition, July 1, 2015, https://www.thegospelcoalition.org/blogs/kevindeyoung/2015/07/01/40-questions-for-christians-now-waving-rainbow-flags/.

rooted in self-interest alone and Christian privilege is guarded ruthlessly, even if it comes at the expense of others.

Furthermore, when Christian leaders predict God's impending judgment on the US in the wake of the Supreme Court decision, arguing "our country's foundations are being destroyed," it suggests that slavery, genocide, extreme gender inequity, and Jim Crow weren't serious enough to warrant a response from God, but now that our gay neighbors can get marriage licenses, all hell is sure to break loose. This reveals a profound ignorance regarding the suffering of other minority groups, both historically and presently. When white conservative Christians obsess over their own perceived oppression, it becomes incredibly difficult to engage in important conversations about religious, racial, and gender privilege that are necessary for creating a more just society. How can we begin to recognize our own privilege and the harm it can cause when it remains unchecked if we believe ourselves to be an oppressed minority?

The discomfort of conservative Christians whose views on gender and sexuality are being challenged more than they once were is nothing compared to the suffering faced by LGBTQ+ people and religious and ethnic minorities in this country. We would all do well to remember that.

THE PERSECUTION COMPLEX VILIFIES LGBTQ+ PEOPLE AND IGNORES INTERSECTING IDENTITIES.

In addition to minimizing the suffering of LGBTQ+ people and other minority groups, the persecution complex caricatures them as evil villains out to destroy Christians, which is a tried and true way of making an already marginalized group appear more powerful than they actually are in order to turn public opinion against them. When

Christian leaders blame LGBTQ+ people for natural disasters or warn they are going to "come after" Christians, it's hard not to be reminded of what was often said about Jews in Europe to justify centuries of prejudice against them. This sort of rhetoric dehumanizes our neighbors and prevents us from loving them well.

There is an inconsistency, too, in the justification of discrimination against LGBTQ+ people that points to a special animus against them. County clerks who cite their Christian values when refusing to issue marriage licenses to same-sex couples don't also refuse licenses to cohabitating couples, or divorcees, or interfaith couples (also frowned upon in conservative Christian circles), nor do the bakers and restaurant owners who refuse to serve LGBTQ+ people refuse to serve other perceived "sinners."

And perhaps most important, the "gays vs. Christians" narrative ignores the fact that 42 percent of gay Americans identify as Christians.* The majority of my gay, lesbian, bisexual, and transgender friends are devoted followers of Jesus whose faith in the midst of near-constant attack puts my own faith to shame. Obviously, LGBTQ+ people aren't interested in persecuting themselves! But framing this as a culture war between Christians and LGBTQ+ people suggests that they have to choose and further marginalizes LGBT Christians by denying them their very identity. It says, "You say you're a Christian, but you really aren't," which, if you've ever had that accusation thrown your way, you know is incredibly condescending and painful.

In a wise and grace-filled post entitled "We're Not Out to Get You," Andrew Holubeck writes "[Most LGBTQ+ people] are not actually out to take away anyone's freedom to worship, preach, and

---

* "A Survey of LGBT Americans: Chapter 6: Religion," Pew Research Center, June 13, 2013, https://www.pewresearch.org/social-trends/2013/06/13/chapter-6-religion/.

teach as they please. I know it's rather convenient and comforting to believe that we are, to see us as 'the bad guys' out to destroy you, because then you don't have to deal with the messy idea that good people can still significantly disagree on very important issues. We certainly do the same thing to you all, and for the same reasons. But I think it would do us all a world of good if both sides worked harder to resist the temptation to vilify the other."*

THE PERSECUTION COMPLEX OBSCURES THE GOSPEL OF JESUS CHRIST.

You know who was actually persecuted for their religious beliefs?

Jews under Roman occupation in the first century.

And you know what Jesus told those Jews to do?

Pay your taxes. Give to those who ask. Do not turn people away. Love your neighbors. Love even your enemies.

When Jesus spoke of "walking the second mile," he was referring to an oppressive Roman law that allowed a traveling Roman solider to demand that a stranger carry his pack for up to one mile. No doubt some of Jesus's first listeners had been forced to do just that, to drop their farming equipment, fishing nets, or carpentry tools and carry a heavy pack, losing hours of work in the process. The law allowed the soldier to demand from them a mile, no more. Jesus told his followers to walk two.

"If anyone slaps you on the right cheek, turn to them the other cheek also," he said. "And if anyone wants to sue you and take your shirt, hand over your coat as well. If anyone forces you to go one mile, go with them two miles. Give to the one

---

* "We're Not Out to Get You," From the Desk of Helen Lovejoy, July 3, 2015, https://mylutheranfriend.wordpress.com/2015/07/03/were-not-out-to-get-you/.

who asks you, and do not turn away from the one who wants to borrow from you . . . Love your enemies and pray for those who persecute you, that you may be children of your Father in heaven . . . If you love those who love you, what reward will you get? Are not even the tax collectors doing that? And if you greet only your own people, what are you doing more than others? Do not even pagans do that? Be perfect, therefore, as your heavenly Father is perfect."

As Christians, our most "deeply held religious belief" is that Jesus Christ died on the cross for sinful people, and that in imitation of that, we are called to love God, to love our neighbors, and to love even our enemies to the point of death. And yet right now, the prevailing perception of American Christians is that baking a cake for a gay couple is too much to ask.

As I've made it clear in the past, I support marriage equality and affirm my gay and lesbian friends who want to commit themselves to another person for life. But over and beyond my beliefs regarding homosexuality is my most deeply held conviction that I am called to love my neighbor as myself . . . even if it costs me something, even if it means walking a second mile. And I know many of my fellow Christians who hold a more conservative view of sexuality share that conviction too.

I've been watching people with golden crosses around their necks and on their lapels shout at the TV about how serving gay and lesbian people is a violation of their "sincerely held religious beliefs." And I can't help but laugh at the sad irony of it. Two-thousand years ago, Jesus hung from that cross, looked out on the people who put him there, and said, "Father, forgive them." Jesus served sinners all the way to the cross.

If conservative Christians continue to treat LGBTQ+ people as second-class citizens and cry persecution every time they don't get their way, they will lose far more than the culture wars. They will lose the Christian identity. We've obscured the gospel when the "right to refuse" service has become a more widely known Christian value than the impulse to give it.

Lord, have mercy on us and show us a new way.

Originally posted on July 15, 2015.

Christians, MLK Day, and Historical Amnesia

On the second day of Martin Luther King Jr.'s imprisonment in a Birmingham jail, a guard slipped him a copy of the morning paper. By the dim light of his cell, King read the tall black letters that headlined the second page: WHITE CLERGYMEN URGE LOCAL NEGROES TO WITHDRAW FROM DEMONSTRATIONS.

Eight Alabama pastors had penned a statement entitled "A Call for Unity" in which they expressed basic agreement with King regarding integration and Jim Crow, but took issue with his methods, arguing protests and sit-ins represented the sort of "extreme measures" that only incited racial tensions.* This appeal to Christian unity and "law and order and common sense" found resonance among many of Birmingham's white Christians.

In response, Martin Luther King wrote his famous "Letter from a Birmingham Jail," which has become a standard entry in freshman writing and rhetoric classes.† His words are as relevant today as they were in 1963:

---

* "Public Statement by Eight Alabama Clergymen, Denouncing Martin Luther King Jr.'s Efforts," Mass Resistance, accessed April 5, 2025, https://www.massresistance.org/docs/gen/09a/mlk_day/statement.html.
† "Letter from a Birmingham Jail," African Studies Center, University of Pennsylvania, accessed April 5, 2025, https://www.africa.upenn.edu/Articles_Gen/Letter_Birmingham.html.

> I have almost reached the regrettable conclusion that the Negro's great stumbling block in his stride toward freedom is not . . . the Ku Klux Klanner, but the white moderate, who is more devoted to "order" than to justice; who prefers a negative peace, which is the absence of tension, to a positive peace, which is the presence of justice; who constantly says, "I agree with you in the goal you seek, but I cannot agree with your methods of direct action." . . . Shallow understanding from people of good will is more frustrating than absolute misunderstanding from people of ill will. Lukewarm acceptance is much more bewildering than outright rejection. . . . We will have to repent in this generation not merely for the hateful words and actions of the bad people but for the appalling silence of the good people.

People in schools and churches across the country will pay homage to Martin Luther King Jr. today, and many will read "Letter from a Birmingham Jail," which is right and good.

But few will read "A Call for Unity" or any of the thousands of editorials, letters, articles, and sermons composed by American whites—most of them Christians—in opposition to King's work. We forget that just as our most heated discussions on social media emerge from the context of a cultural conversation, so too did the treatises of theologians and activists past. When we familiarize ourselves with only one side of the debate (typically the side ultimately found to be just), we miss the full depth of the argument and, worse yet, slip into a sort of historical amnesia that allows us to believe we too would have chosen the side of good on account of its seemingly obvious virtue.

Everyone does this of course, but today I want to focus on how we Christians in particular tend to whitewash history, a phenomenon recently explored by blogger Neil Carter in a post engaging Tim Keller's book *The Reason for God*.* Keller argues that Christians have served on the front lines of nearly every social movement toward morality and justice in modern Western civilization, including the abolition of slavery and the Civil Rights Movement in America, which is certainly true given the religious demographics of Western and American culture. But as Carter rightly notes, there's no denying the reality that these Christians faced their most adamant (and violent) opposition, not from atheists or Muslims or Hindus . . . but from other Christians. Reducing the struggles of the past to conflict between "the Christians" and "the culture" disregards the fact that slavery, Jim Crow, Native American removal, and all sorts of racial and gender inequalities have all flourished in a supposedly *Christian* culture.

Of course it is just as erroneous when (some) atheists claim religion serves only as an impediment to social justice. After all, Dr. King was a devout Christian who masterfully appealed to Scripture to comfort the oppressed and challenge their oppressors. To downplay the sincerity of his faith, and the faith of many who have worked for justice and compassion through the centuries, dishonors their legacy in another way.

But it cannot be forgotten that Christian ministers wrote nearly half of all defenses of slavery in the buildup to the Civil War, and that many segregationists cited religious freedom to justify their opposition to integrating private Christian schools. Dr. King was not as universally beloved at the time of his assassination as he is now and in 1966 carried a 63 percent disapproval rating.[†] It seems it's

---

* Neil Carter, "Setting the Record Straight," *Godless in Dixie*, no longer available online.
† Frank Newport, "Martin Luther King Jr.: Revered More After Death Than Before," Gallup, January 16, 2006, https://www.gallup.com/poll/20920/martin-luther-king-jr-revered-more-after-death-than-before.aspx.

much easier for white people to sing the praises of Martin Luther King Jr., Rosa Parks, and other civil rights leaders when they are dead than when they are alive and making us uncomfortable.

This is why I believe it's so important to study both historical religious arguments supporting the abolition of slavery and historical religious arguments opposing the abolition of slavery,* as well as historical religious arguments supporting desegregation and historical religious arguments opposing desegregation—not because I believe both sides are equal, but because the patterns of argumentation that emerge are so unnervingly familiar:

> The Bible is declared "clear" on a matter to oppose any challenge to the status quo.†
> Those disrupting social norms are said to be threatening the peace and Christian unity.
> Sympathy may be expressed for the plight of the oppressed, but their methods of protest are criticized as "disruptive" or "uncivil."
> Civil rights are opposed on the grounds of religious freedom.
> Those calling attention to systemic injustice are accused of inciting tensions rather than simply calling them out.
> Deaths are justified because the dead brought it on themselves by committing some infraction. (I'm thinking here of the similarity between justifications for lynchings in the past and justifications for police brutality in the present.)

---

* Rachel Held Evans, "Is Abolition Biblical?," Rachel Held Evans Blog, February 28, 2013, https://rachelheldevans.com/blog/is-abolition-biblical.
† See "The Bible Was 'Clear' . . . ," elsewhere in this book.

And on and on it goes.

It's easy to comfort ourselves with the thought that Christians of the past were only *using* religion and Scripture to support their oppression, but in truth those Christians rarely saw it that way. Often the difference between *using* Scripture to justify injustice and *appealing* to Scripture to support the truth proves clearest in hindsight. Pride, privilege, and confirmation bias are formidable adversaries on the path to justice, which is why we must familiarize ourselves with past justifications for oppression or inaction lest we make the same mistakes again.

We see all of this play out today as Liberty University observes MLK Day by hosting Donald Trump as its convocation speaker. Trump has enjoyed wide support from white supremacist groups on account of his hateful rhetoric regarding Muslims and immigrants, and the Republican frontrunner has shared bogus crime statistics from white nationalist websites to oppose the #BlackLivesMatter movement and stir up fear of Black people.*

When protestors questioned Liberty's timing, officials responded by saying they plan to honor Martin Luther King Jr. as they do every year with a short tribute video.†

It would be funny if it weren't so insulting. (Note: Some Liberty students plan to hold a protest outside the event.)‡

---

* Ben Schreckinger, "White Supremacist Groups See Trump Bump," *Politico*, December 10, 2015, https://www.politico.com/story/2015/12/donald-trump-white-supremacists-216620; Eric Bradner, "Trump Retweets Fake, Racially Charged Crime Data from Non-Existent Group," CNN, updated November 23, 2015, https://www.cnn.com/2015/11/22/politics/donald-trump-black-crime-police-retweet/.

† Michael Walsh, "He Has a Dream: Liberty University Defends Choice of Trump as MLK Day Speaker," Yahoo! News, January 14, 2016, https://www.yahoo.com/politics/he-has-a-dream-liberty-university-defends-choice-224222438.html.

‡ Selena Hill, "Liberty University Students to Hold Protest Against Decision to Select Donald Trump as MLK Speaker," Latin Post, updated January 16, 2016, https://www.latinpost.com/articles/109169/20160116/liberty-university-students-to-hold-protest-against-decision-to-select-donald-trump-as-mlk-speaker.html.

I suspect that missing from the tribute video will be any acknowledgment of the fact that the founder of Liberty University, Jerry Falwell, vehemently opposed the work of Martin Luther King Jr., publicly condemned him as a communist, and delivered an impassioned sermon the day after King's march to Selma opposing civil rights marchers as "left wing leaders" whose only aim was to stir up racial tensions and violence. Missing also will be any mention of the fact that Falwell and other conservative evangelicals fought tooth and nail against the 1978 ruling that stripped tax-exempt status from all-white private schools formed in reaction to integration, calling it a violation of their religious freedom.*

Inviting a white supremacist to speak on MLK Day and then supposing that a short tribute video will make up for it shows just how real and pervasive the "shallow understanding" and "lukewarm acceptance" King warned about remains a part of white Christian culture.

So, white folks, before you share that MLK quote on Facebook or join in a service project today, ask yourself:

> Would I have disobeyed the instructions of my pastor and walked alongside Black protestors in Birmingham?
> Would I have risked being seen as a troublemaker by friends and family for joining a movement that landed many of its participants in jail?
> Would I have been willing to sacrifice my reputation as a "Bible-believing Christian" by rejecting biblical

---

* Stephen Prothero, "When Donald Trump Goes to Liberty U.," CNN, updated January 17, 2016, https://www.cnn.com/2016/01/16/opinions/prothero-trump-liberty/.

arguments used to support segregation and oppose civil disobedience? Am I ready to consider how I might be complicit in similar injustices today?

I wish I could be more certain my own answer would be yes.*

Originally posted on January 17, 2016.

---

* Rachel shared links to these resources: *Birmingham Revolution: Martin Luther King Jr.'s Epic Challenge to the Church*, by Edward Gilbreath; *Forgive Us: Confessions of a Compromised Faith*, by Mae Elise Cannon, Lisa Sharon Harper, Troy Jackson, and Soong-Chan Rah; *The Civil War as a Theological Crisis*, by Mark Noll; *The Cross and the Lynching Tree*, by James Cone; and *The New Jim Crow: Mass Incarceration in an Age of Colorblindness*, by Michelle Alexander.

The Other Lie
By Lisa Sharon Harper

Editor's note: Rachel was known for being generous with her platform, often inviting other writers to guest-post on her blog. This is an excerpt of one such example, written by activist Lisa Sharon Harper marking one month since the shooting death of Michael Brown in Ferguson, Missouri.

He stood. Nervous; he shifted his weight from left to right, then leaned left again, as if asking the wall to hold him up. He looked at me, unsure.

I nodded as if to say, "It's okay to say it."

The tall, dirty-blond, clean-cut, forty-something ministry leader stood before about twenty evangelical pastors and ministry leaders from across St. Louis, Missouri. They were squeezed around two long tables in a slightly raised and sectioned-off area of the dining room. The general public sat on ground level within earshot of our "private" conversation.

This dialogue at Three Kings Public House, a Washington University–area bar and grill, was convened to help St. Louis's evangelical clergy begin to process their responses to the explosive conflict taking place only twenty minutes away in Ferguson.

Moments before the forty-something stood, I had shared about the biblical concept of shalom. White, Black, and Asian American leaders of evangelical churches, networks, and ministries considered the implications of three spiritual truths:

1. Every human being on the face of the earth—every person in this restaurant, every person on the street, and every single person in Ferguson—is made in the image of God.

2. That means, all things being equal, every single person on earth was created with the command and the capacity to exercise Genesis 1:26–27 dominion, which means to steward, or in modern terms, to exercise agency or lead.

3. To diminish the ability of humans to exercise dominion is to diminish the image of God in them—and to diminish God's image on earth. And the fastest and surest way to diminish the ability of humans to exercise agency, to lead, is through poverty or oppression.

The pastors reflected on how it made them feel (in their gut) to imagine being led by the residents of Ferguson. For Isaiah 61 says, our society's healing will come from their leadership.

The forty-something leaned against the wall, then stood straight, looked at the group, and spoke the words:

"As a white man," he said, "I have been taught that I was created to lead everyone else."

Another St. Louis faith leader stood and confessed: "It never even occurred to me that I would be led by the people of Ferguson. It never entered my mind as a possibility.". . . .

Now, imagine this: What would it look like for the people of God to cultivate the image of God in every corner of our nation?

And what if we did this through just investing, through disciplined consumption, and by legislating toward a world where governance affirms the truth (not the lie) that all humanity is created in God's image and therefore has capacity to lead?

There is no supreme humanity. There is only humanity.

Originally posted on September 9, 2014.

She Did That

A REFLECTION BY LISA SHARON HARPER

Prophetic blogger and author Rachel Held Evans was not supposed to change the world, but she did. With cutting wit Rachel penned six books over a period of nine years. With each one she clarified further the evangelical conundrum. But even before her books, Rachel blogged. She invited millennial evangelicals to follow her epic journey as she defied the tyranny of certainty that had taped the mouths and shackled the movements of generations of evangelicals before.

Born in 1981, in Birmingham, Alabama, Rachel Evans entered the world in Southern transition space between the fire hoses and slobbering dogs of Bull Conner's reign of terror and the 1980s rise of the Religious Right. Then, when she was fourteen, her family moved to Dayton, Tennessee, home of the infamous 1925 Scopes Monkey Trial. John Scopes, the defendant, fought and won the right to teach evolution in public schools despite the fundamentalists who rose up to squash the teaching and ended up knee-deep in monkey shit.

Sprung from the well of white evangelical culture wars, Rachel's writing could have gone another direction entirely. She could have found her writing home in the prolific women's devotional guides that discipled a generation of white women within conservative religion. She could have turned to her humor and written about raising children, finding hobbies, and being kind—playing the game like so many famous white women writers of the era. But she didn't.

Rachel wielded her humor like a sword aimed at the invisible web of white male hegemony over evangelical faith. I mean, who actually lives an entire year according to the biblical mandates of womanhood? Rachel did. That was genius!

So, when I met this short, unassuming, bob-cut, white woman wearing a silk scarf wrap at a White House function, circa 2014, I didn't realize the subversive countercultural warrior I was encountering. I hadn't followed her journey out of evangelicalism like the throngs of white evangelicals whose own journeys had been altered by following hers. I only knew what I picked up in our conversation. Somehow, this young, Southern white woman was aware of her whiteness and the whiteness of her world—and she invited partnership to slay the beast of white patriarchy.

Later that year, Michael Brown was shot down by Officer Darren Wilson on Canfield Avenue in Ferguson, Missouri. I was invited to help organize multiethnic evangelical churches in St. Louis to support the Hands Up Don't Shoot movement. *Christianity Today* asked me to write a reflection on my time there. So, I wrote about "The Lie" that I encountered there—that Black people are not fully human and therefore not worthy of full protection of the law.* Rachel read that piece and contacted me to ask if I would write a follow-up piece for her blog.

Of all the pieces on her blog, this is the one that I remember the most—not because of the writing, but because of Rachel's action—the act of sharing her platform. She was among the first true white women allies I knew. She didn't ask me to write as a charitable

---

* Lisa Sharon Harper, "It's Time to Listen: 'The Lie,'" *The Exchange*: A Blog by Ed Stetzer, *Christianity Today*, no longer available online.

gesture. Rather, she wanted to expose her audience to voices and perspectives they might otherwise never get to hear.

Before she died, Rachel joined me in the 2018 "Call to Pause" initiative. Thirty-five evangelical leaders called evangelicals to pause and consider the reverberating repercussions of the hasty appointment of culture warrior Brett Kavanaugh to the Supreme Court.

Rachel Held Evans was an ally, not only through her words, but also through her actions—to the end. Her blog documents her path to that prophetic space. That is why I have chosen this blog as my favorite.

Calling Your Reps and Planting Onions: A Plan for Faithful Resistance

What's happening in America right now is not normal. This is not the routine ebb and flow of liberal and conservative shifts in power. It's not merely the heated aftermath of a contentious election. What we're facing in this country is an administration characterized by unprecedented levels of authoritarianism, dishonesty, incompetence, and corruption, and a legislative branch unwilling to hold the president accountable.

Influenced by advisors whose white nationalist views are well-known, the president has waged a propaganda war against ethnic and religious minorities, stoking fear and hate by lying about crime rates, terrorist attacks, and voter fraud and by issuing executive orders that have already hurt many thousands of people around the world, including desperate refugee families.* Muslims, including lifelong US citizens, are being detained at airports for

---

* Paul Waldman, "Steve Bannon Is the Most Powerful Person in the Trump White House. That Should Terrify Us," *Washington Post*, February 1, 2017, https://www.washingtonpost.com/blogs/plum-line/wp/2017/02/01/steve-bannon-is-the-most-powerful-person-in-the-trump-white-house-that-should-terrify-us/?utm_term=.0f9dff583761; Michelle Ye Hee Lee, Glenn Kessler, and Leslie Shapiro, "100 Days of Trump Claims," *Washington Post*, February 21, 2017, https://www.washingtonpost.com/graphics/politics/trump-claims/.

no other reason than their faith, and law enforcement officials report a surge in hate crimes against them.* When challenged by the facts or with the law, the administration responds with attempts to undermine the free press and the judiciary, even going so far as to call the free press "an enemy of the people."

To make matters worse, with some important exceptions, the white conservative church has largely supported the president, shrugging off his rampant dishonesty, self-aggrandizement, racism, misogyny, and bullying. My inbox is filled with messages from young evangelicals who feel angered and betrayed as they watch their religious community align itself with values they don't recognize.

It's been hard for me write about all this, I confess. For one thing, I have what the parenting books refer to as an "active toddler"—a little hurricane of distraction, full of joy and fury and stale Cheerios. I'm also finishing up my fourth book, which like every other book I've written, is proving the hardest EVER. But most of all, like many other writers and artists with whom I've spoken, I'm struggling a bit to process what's happening. When every day brings with it another startling act of authoritarianism or oppression, it's hard to catch your breath long enough to think of something worthwhile to say. These times call for good words, certainly, but more importantly they call for creative, concrete action.

So, since many of you have asked me what sort of practical steps you can take to combat the abuses of this administration and help those most affected by it, I thought I'd share my own personal plan

---

* Cindy Boren, "Muslim American Olympian Ibtihaj Muhammad Says She Was Detained by U.S. Customs," *Washington Post*, February 9, 2017, https://www.washingtonpost.com/news/early-lead/wp/2017/02/09/muslim-american-olympian-ibtihaj-muhammad-says-she-was-detained-by-u-s-customs/?utm_term=.d528a066c968; Eric Lichtblau, "US Hate Crimes Surge 6%, Fueled by Attacks on Muslims," *New York Times*, November 14, 2016, https://www.nytimes.com/2016/11/15/us/politics/fbi-hate-crimes-muslims.html.

of action in hopes it might prove useful to others. I'm the kind of person who tends to get passionate about something, overcommit, and then burn out, so I purposefully made these plans manageable. This is not a weeks-long protest; this is a years-long countermovement that has to be sustainable to be effective. So with that in mind, here are six ideas:

1. IDENTIFY WHERE YOU HAVE THE MOST INFLUENCE LOCALLY AND NATIONALLY, AND LEAD THERE.

Knowing I have something of a national platform, I've been thinking a lot about how to use it more effectively—perhaps by focusing my best op-ed writing on one or two [issues] and using the rest of my influence to amplify those church leaders, activists, and artists doing the good work of justice all around the world. I've also been freshly convicted about the importance of strengthening my relationships with schools, nonprofits, and community organizations here in East Tennessee, and am considering new ways to volunteer/contribute that will work for our family over the long haul.

Perhaps you're on the PTA at your kids' school. What might you do to help encourage and equip teachers to combat what's been called the "Trump effect"—an increase in bullying, particularly against children of color and religious minorities? What questions can you ask to ensure your school is teaching kids how to think critically about media and discern the truth amidst competing sources? It might be a good time to follow through on that longtime desire to volunteer as a coach or tutor and to familiarize yourself with federal laws protecting the rights of students with disabilities so you can speak up if they are threatened. Have the parents of vulnerable kids in your community organized? How can you lend your support?

Or maybe you lead a small group at church. What about introducing some justice-themed books into your weekly or monthly discussions? They don't have to be overtly political; something like *The Myth of a Christian Nation* by Greg Boyd or *Forgive Us* by Lisa Sharon Harper, Troy Jackson, Mae Elise Cannon, and Soong-Chan Rah might be a good start. If you're an elder, or deacon, or on the vestry, consider proposing that your church sponsor a refugee family through a local resettlement organization, or partner with a local mosque or synagogue to engage in interfaith conversations and activities that are mutually supportive. Incorporate lament and confession into your worship and confront the sins of racism and white supremacy with boldness. Don't be afraid your actions will be considered "political." Remember, silence in this climate is a political statement too.

Maybe you're just good at getting friends together and planning social events. How about rallying the troops for a weekend protest, or organizing an informal fundraiser for World Relief? Or maybe you're the quiet, steady one your friends respect and come to for advice. Speaking up on behalf of immigrants or LGBT kids will mean a lot coming from you, so have courage and say something when the Spirit nudges. Don't let a racist, homophobic, or misogynistic comment slide. For too long white folks have tolerated that nonsense, and it's one reason we have the president we do.

2. IDENTIFY THE ORGANIZATIONS, ARTISTS, AND LEADERS FROM MARGINALIZED COMMUNITIES WORKING FOR JUSTICE AND SUPPORT THEM/FOLLOW THEIR LEAD.

Many thousands of citizens, including many Christians, have been working for social justice for years—through nonprofit organizations, community organizing efforts, and justice-oriented churches.

As tempting as it may be to try and start something new on your own, it is far wiser to identify these groups, at the local and national levels, and lend your support.

For example, most cities have refugee resettlement organizations that assist families fleeing war-torn countries with housing, education, and employment. Ours in Chattanooga/Knoxville is called Bridge Refugee Services. Attend a fundraiser, volunteer a little time each week to help newcomers with errands, or partner with some friends to furnish a family's home.

If voting rights are a concern to you (and they should be, especially if you live in North Carolina), consider connecting with Rev. William J. Barber II of the North Carolina NAACP as he leads protests and organizing efforts around voting rights and other important causes. Find out if your community has a local chapter of Black Lives Matter or attend the next Gay Christian Network conference or Reformation Project gathering. If you're unsure of where to start, you can find a long list of faith-based community organizations through the PICO network.

Nationally, this is a good time to donate to the ACLU, the National Immigration Law Center, and organizations that protect reporters and a free press. If you're like me, you've probably already "rage subscribed" to every newspaper or magazine the administration deems "an enemy of the people" for reporting the facts. Keep speaking up for a free press, and be sure and offer an encouraging word to any journalists you know.

Of course, there are many, many more that could be mentioned, which is why, through the forty days of Lent, I'll be using my social media feeds to offer "40 Days of Support" featuring forty individuals, organizations, and initiatives whose work is crucial during these times.

The important thing here is to follow the lead of those people who have been working within marginalized communities for years. They don't need you to be their voice. They just need you to listen, to learn, and to offer support.

3. GET POLITICAL.

This president cannot continue to abuse his power at the expense of the vulnerable without the support of Congress, which means it is our duty to hold them accountable and demand change. I know some Christians are uncomfortable with that, preferring not to "mix" faith and politics (as if we can compartmentalize), but as Aaron Niequist put it the other day, "if we want to love our neighbor, we will naturally get involved in building the systems that lead to flourishing, and fighting to change the unjust systems that target the poor, weak, and marginalized. We can't pretend to love our neighbor while we ignore the realities that hurt them."*

The gospel may not be partisan, but it is certainly political, and it's as appropriate as ever for Christians to ask that the people who represent them represent the concerns of the poor, the sick, the marginalized, and the strangers whom Jesus loves. It's appropriate, too, to expect Republicans in Congress to hold this administration accountable to basic ethical standards, and to vote them out of office if they refuse to do so out of party loyalty.

Everyone I know who works in Washington tells me that calling your representatives is one of the most effective strategies for waging public protest. This year I added the phone numbers of my representatives to the contact list in my phone, and I try to call at least three times a week. (It might help to set an alarm on your phone if you're busy or forgetful.) As one who struggles with a touch of phone phobia, I've benefited from scripts you can find

---

* Instagram Post by Aaron Niequist, accessed April 17, 2025, www.instagram.com/p/BQ0caHlA9Ws/

online, which I adjust to reflect my own personal concerns. It also helps to ask questions—*"Has Senator Corker spoken against Steve Bannon's position on the National Security Council? Is he aware of Bannon's white nationalist views?"* And since all of my representatives claim to be Christians, I usually try to appeal to Christian values to find some common ground. Here's how I see it: In the time it takes me to scroll angrily through Twitter for five minutes, I can write a script and make a call.

In addition to calling your representatives, consider attending a town hall, writing letters to the editor of your local paper, connecting with the local Democratic Party to help with voter registration efforts and to challenge voter suppression/gerrymandering, and (because it's becoming painfully obvious that progressives have ceded local politics to the extreme right for too long) running for office or helping a better candidate get the job. If, like me, you live in what seems like a hopelessly red district, you might want to check out Swing Left, which helps you locate the closest "swing district" that will decide the majority in Congress and join a team working to elect democrats, who won't give this president a free pass, to those seats.

4. GROUND YOURSELF IN COMMUNITY AND CONTEMPLATION.

I had the privilege a few years ago of meeting Dr. Cornel West, a man who has been engaged in activism and justice work for decades. As others will certainly tell you, the most immediate impression you get of Dr. West when in his presence is that this is a person of deep, seemingly limitless joy. Dr. West is no fool. He hasn't got his head in the sand. Few people are as aware of the inequities that persist in our nation and as committed to prophetically calling them out. And yet Dr. West brings such a sense of hope and peace to his work, it's contagious. "I cannot be an optimist," he says, "but I am a prisoner of hope."

These are trying times, and sometimes just keeping up with the latest news tempts one to despair. Dr. West reminds us that the only way to work for justice in a sustainable way is to be rooted in the nourishing soil of contemplation and community.

By contemplation, I mean spiritual practices of rest, prayer, and devotion that connect us to God in a way that unburdens. For some, this means beginning and ending each day in prayer and mediation. For others, it means taking a Sabbath away from all the noise of social media to hike or cook or read. For extroverts I suppose it means finding some friends with whom to verbally process . . . like, at a bar . . . or something? (Sorry. I don't really understand your world.)

It's also important to stay connected with community. I know a lot of folks want nothing to do with the church right now, and I get that. If your faith community is actively working to support the systems of white supremacy and patriarchy that are enabling this administration, you may need to take a break, or leave. (There are plenty of other churches actively working in the other direction, believe me!) But whether you go to church on Sunday mornings or not, try to stay tethered to a larger community in which you have an investment and which has an investment in you—maybe it's a small group that gets together for pizza and conversations on Thursday nights, or maybe it's the local chapter of a community organization, or maybe it's the people in your neighborhood. Community keeps us accountable and compassionate. It prevents us from thinking too highly of ourselves and taking too much on. It reminds us that we need one another, that we're not alone, and that we have a great cloud of witnesses spanning thousands of years and hundreds of cultures from which to draw strength.

5. CREATE OPPORTUNITIES FOR MEANINGFUL (BUT NOT NECESSARILY "POLITE") DIALOG.

Probably the most common question I'm asked on the road these days is, *"How can I talk to family, friends, and fellow churchgoers with whom I disagree politically?"* I feel a bit hypocritical admonishing my readers toward kindness and understanding when I too have been avoiding such conversations like the plague, but I do think healthy, constructive dialog is possible, and that it's best tackled around a shared table, over steaming plates of mashed potatoes and green beans, amidst the laughter and grace that emerges organically from deep, trusted relationships.

That said, we shouldn't avoid talking about injustice because we're afraid of making things uncomfortable or offending someone. Having lived down South my whole life I know exactly what it feels like to smile through racism and xenophobia in order to maintain that false, sticky-sweet sense of decorum. But a recent enlightening article from a German writer about how Americans are far too timid when confronting prejudice—*"at the dinner table, I've noticed, what Germans call a discussion, Americans call an argument"*—reminds us that this fear of confrontation is exactly what preserves the status quo, often with disastrous consequences.* Now's not the time to play it safe. If someone in your Bible study repeats a lie about Muslims, call it out. If your Grandma makes a racist remark, tell her it's not okay. We're stuck with this president in large part because white people are so worried about hurting other white people's feelings [that] we won't name the sin racism. (Here it's important to note that telling oppressed people they

---

* Sabine Heinlein, "Take It from a German: Americans Are Too Timid in Confronting Hate," *Daily Beast*, January 1, 2017, https://www.thedailybeast.com/articles/2017/01/01/take-it-from-a-german-americans-are-too-timid-in-confronting-hate.html.

need gracefully engage their oppressors is unhelpful. Let them make the call on how, and with whom, they engage.)

As far as creating opportunities for dialog within your faith communities, I'd recommend starting with a book club, perhaps around a book like *Trouble I've Seen* by Drew Hart, or *The New Jim Crow* by Michelle Alexander, or *Assimilate or Go Home* by D. L. Mayfield, or *Forgive Us* by the authors mentioned above—something that's not directly about this election or this presidency, but that addresses issues related to justice. (If your conversation partners are more conservative, you can take turns picking the title.) This creates the opportunity for conversation without setting it up as a debate.

6. PLANT ONIONS.

In revisiting Madeleine L'Engle's Genesis Trilogy, I've been struck by how forthcoming the author is about her own fears around raising children during the Cold War. She writes of one particularly worrisome season: "Planting onions that spring was an act of faith in the future, for I was very fearful for our planet."*

"Planting onions" has come to signify for me the importance of remaining committed to those slow-growing, long-term investments in my family, my community, and the world, no matter what happens over the next four years. Right now it may seem like an afternoon of changing diapers and wiping noses has little to do with "the resistance," but raising decent, compassionate kids, and being faithful to the call to love them exactly as they are in exactly this moment, is the good work of the Kingdom, in any

---

* Madeleine L'Engle, *And It Was Good: Reflections on Beginnings* (Convergent Books, 2017), 10.

age. There have been times when I've wondered if all the hours I'm pouring into this next book, a book about the Bible, will be relevant when all anyone's talking about these days is politics, but then I remember that this is the creative ground I've been called to cultivate, so I will trust my Maker with the yield.

Those after-school tutoring sessions may strike you as low-impact when you survey the great needs of the world, but the investment of your time and care may alter the trajectory of a kid's life forever. Pastors, I know many of you are struggling with how to shepherd a politically diverse community through these tumultuous times, but please know those relationships you're navigating one visit, one meal, and one awkward coffee hour at a time matter more than any political speech delivered by a celebrity.

We are bound to get discouraged, certainly, but we won't become useless until we abandon our onion patches, those little pieces of earth where we cultivate our greatest hopes and dreams for the world.

So, resist. Speak out. Call your representatives and get behind the people and organizations working for change. But don't neglect your gardens—of both the literal and the metaphorical type. Plant like the rain will come.

Originally posted on March 1, 2017.

Postelection Thoughts on Rachel and Feminist Solidarity

A REFLECTION BY CANDICE MARIE BENBOW

If Rachel were here, she would've told white women about themselves (again) after the 2024 election. I know this because it mattered to her to use her privilege, as a white woman, to amplify the work and voices of women who weren't white. She did it for me. The number of editors who reached out to me, at her behest, introduced my writing and work in spaces that had otherwise been closed. I met the agent who breathed life back into my writing career and got to publish my first book because Rachel thought it not robbery to extend her community and network toward me. One of one, she was.

. . . or is she? In so many ways, Rachel was doing all she could to ensure that women, white women especially, understood the assignment—which is to smash the patriarchy that is within us. In another essay, called "We Need Feminism . . . ," Rachel laid out the case for the necessity of feminism in the world. With pointed simplicity, she outlined the harm girls and women experience around the world and how our commitment to equality—which is what feminism is—would eradicate that harm. Written in 2014 for the #WomenAgainstFeminism campaign, the piece could have been written yesterday. Girls are still going missing at alarming rates, and though nobody eats at Hardee's anymore, fast food chains still seem to objectify women to sell us a spicy chicken sandwich.

I write this days after Kamala Harris lost the presidential election to Donald Trump. He was found liable of sexual abuse in civil court, found guilty of thirty-four felonies, impeached twice, and then won in a landslide victory with 52 percent of white women voting for him. I also write this ten years after Rachel wrote her case for feminism, and my heart is broken because it's clear that not enough white women read it.

Like many, I met Rachel on Twitter (now known as X). Following the election, I became part of the mass exodus of people leaving the platform and grieving what it has become. Purchased by the Trump and Hitler-idolizing billionaire Elon Musk, it's not the space where we would watch Rachel gather those who intentionally misrepresented her work and words. She held up the light for so many of us, believing God calls us all to make this world better. And she is right: We need feminism.

We need feminism because Black women need to experience the same kind of allyship, with more white women, that I shared with Rachel. We need feminism because we are much stronger for this fight when we are united. Rachel knew that. She told us then, and if she could, she would tell us now. Yet her words from ten years ago still ring true. *She* that hath an ear . . .

Repenting of "Colorblindness"

> They dress the wound of my people
> as though it were not serious.
> "Peace, peace," they say,
> when there is no peace.
> . . . .
> No, they have no shame at all;
> they do not even know how to blush. (Jeremiah 6:14, NIV)

In her groundbreaking book *The New Jim Crow: Mass Incarceration in the Age of Colorblindness*, Michelle Alexander notes that "racial caste systems do not require racial hostility or overt bigotry to thrive. They need only racial indifference." Or, as Martin Luther King Jr. put it, they need only "sincere ignorance and conscientious stupidity."*

I ran headlong into my own "sincere ignorance and conscientious stupidity" just two weeks ago when I gave a lecture for a writers conference at Princeton Theological Seminary and in reference to Jesus's parable of the vineyard workers described God

---

* Michelle Alexander, *The New Jim Crow: Mass Incarceration in the Age of Colorblindness* (New Press: 2010), 17; Martin Luther King Jr., *Strength to Love* (Fortress, 2010), 39.

as a "generous master" whom we serve with our faithful work. Afterward, a Black woman approached me and with far more grace than I deserved, reminded me that to African American listeners like her the image of God as a cosmic master is not only discomforting but frightening and oppressive.

It seemed so obvious the moment she said it, but in all my preparation, it simply hadn't occurred to me to reconsider my phraseology because privilege had rendered the word *master* neutral in my mind. (After all, the landowner in that parable had paid his workers, right?) Had I been more aware of how people of color view the world, had I spent just a little more time listening well and considering context, I would have known better and avoided a hurtful error.

In this case, and in so many other cases, the problem is that being white in America means I get to be oblivious. I get to be ignorant. I get to be "colorblind" when it suits me, and that luxury is exactly what keeps me and so many other well-intentioned white people from doing more to confront, repent of, and combat white supremacy and racial injustice in America.

See, many of us have spent years believing that we combat gender inequity by raising awareness and calling it out, we combat human trafficking by raising awareness and calling it out, we combat corruption by raising awareness and calling it out, and we combat racism by not breathing a word. The goal with race, we've been taught, is to "not see color," to treat everyone exactly the same, to avoid the topic altogether like it's the imaginary lava in a children's game.

But as Alexander puts it, "the colorblind public consensus that prevails in America today—i.e., the widespread belief that race no longer matters—has blinded us to the realities of race in our society and facilitated the emergence of a new caste system . . . Seeing race is not the problem. Refusing to care for the people we see is the problem. We should hope not for a colorblind society but instead for a world in which we can see each other fully, learn from each other, and do what we can to respond to each other with love."*

It think it's this misguided notion of "colorblindness" (which isn't even supported by science)† that leads people to say things like:

> "Why do they [people of color] have to make this about race? They're being oversensitive."
>
> "This murder/excessive force/mass shooting/act of discrimination/imprisonment was an isolated incident and not indicative of a larger cultural problem. We need to get all the facts before we start talking about race."
>
> "I'm not a racist. I don't even see color."
>
> "The Confederate flag is about heritage, not hate."
>
> "We need to return to the days when America was a Christian nation."

Like my reference to God as "master," such statements don't necessarily arise out of overt hostility or hate (though of course sometimes they do), but rather out of ignorance regarding the historical and cultural context from which recent race-related events have emerged. It's a failure to connect the Charleston shooting with the hundreds of other church fires and bombings that have terrorized Black churchgoers for centuries, or the violent breakup of a pool party by police with memories of segregated pools, gunned-down teenagers, and brutalization against Black women. It's thinking the

---

* Alexander, *New Jim Crow*, 14.
† Chris Mooney, "The Science of Why Cops Shoot Young Black Men," *Mother Jones*, December 1, 2014, https://www.motherjones.com/politics/2014/12/science-of-racism-prejudice/.

deaths of Trayvon Martin, Eric Garner, and Freddie Gray are just "isolated incidents" when every statistic and study under the sun suggests the justice system is rigged against Black men. It's the notion that Black people have "made this about race" when it was white people who, convinced their own race was superior, captured, enslaved, raped, lynched, and discriminated against an entire group of people because of the color of their skin.

This selective "colorblindness" is a mighty convenient approach to race in America for white people, for it allows us to paper over America's troubled (and decidedly anti-Christian) history, to discount racism as a thing of the past for which we are no longer responsible, and to ignore persistent racial injustices like mass incarceration, police brutality, voting rights issues, white flight, and economic inequality, all while consistently benefiting from an oppressive system we claim we cannot even see. "Colorblindness" means I can attend a Christian conference with all white speakers and not even notice or consider that a problem. It means I can be shocked by use of the n-word because it's never been inappropriately directed at me. It means my default is to consider police heroes because, unlike my Black friends, I don't get pulled over at least once or twice a year. It means I can describe God as my master without even flinching.

Meanwhile, "colorblindness" is a luxury people of color in America simply cannot afford. Black mothers don't get to opt out of seeing color, for example, when they sit their ten-year-olds down for "the talk" about how to avoid getting shot by police. Our Black and Native American brothers and sisters don't get to join white pastors and politicians in uncritically celebrating America's "Christian heritage" when that heritage meant rape, enslavement, genocide, lynching, and discrimination against their families. Theologians of color don't benefit from "colorblindness" when their perspectives are discounted as "contextual" while those of white, Western theologians are considered the objective default.

"Colorblindness," rather than being a goal for which to aim, ought to be a sin from which to repent. God doesn't want us to close our eyes to injustice. We are not called to be neutral. God wants us to see—even if it makes us uncomfortable, even if we're not exactly sure what to do. Yes, the apostle Paul spoke about how there is "neither male nor female, slave nor free, Jew nor Gentile" in the family of God, but he was also quick to acknowledge those same categories when he saw one group oppressing the other. Listening to, believing, and standing in solidarity with those who are crying out in pain strengthens Christian unity not weakens it.

Originally posted on June 26, 2015.

"Why Are You All Writing About Me?"
A REFLECTION BY KATHY KHANG

I can almost hear Rachel laughing, "Why are you all writing about me?" She was humble and genuinely curious, which is why she is missed. It is why I miss her and her voice.

We should not impose a specific theological shift or assume Rachel would've sided with "us," but as she shifted into something different from white evangelicalism, she was still a white Christian female thought leader managing her influence and platform in a way I can only hope would've been less influencer and more influenced by the many voices that she was listening to.

Mine included.

Many years ago, in a completely different season of faith and belief, she and I met in person at a women's conference. We were both speakers, and I was feeling very much out of my league. It was a larger, whiter platform than my voice would've attracted, so I asked the conference planners why they reached out to me and how we were connected.

"Rachel Held Evans gave us your name and suggested we reach out. She said you were someone we should listen to."

And that was Rachel. I reached out to her and thanked her for the referral, and essentially she said that I was doing the participants a favor.

I was late to the RHE game. I had never heard of her in my small multiethnic evangelical world. She had blogged a few words about a book I coauthored with several other Asian American women, *More Than Serving Tea*, and that was how I learned about Rachel Held Evans.

That was her humility and curiosity, that she should not be in a space without others she was still learning from and with. That she should not use her influence and platform for just her own thoughts and ideas but to share what she was learning from and with others.

And then she became just Rachel. Not an influencer. Not a big name author. She was and is Rachel—a loving and imperfect wife and mother who stayed down-to-earth, humble, and curious about God and the people who believed or maybe weren't sure about belief. She listened and asked questions, sharing her observations, even as they were shifting and changing with the church's own shifts.

As I reflect on not just her writing but also her being and way of moving in the world, I miss her. I miss her humility and curiosity that can sometimes be difficult to find in all the spaces of faith. I'm writing about Rachel so that we, so that I, can be reminded by her and by the Spirit who guided her, to be humble and curious.

Editor's note: The following essays require a bit of background. In 2014, it became public that World Vision US, an evangelical relief organization, had an employment policy that allowed the hiring of LGBTQ+ persons, particularly those legally married to someone of the same sex. The ensuing backlash from evangelicals was swift and fierce.

Rachel and many other progressive Christian leaders leaped to World Vision USA's defense. Rachel not only personally supported a sponsored child, she had participated in what was then known as a "blogger trip," traveling to Bolivia in 2011 with a team of fellow bloggers in support of the work of World Vision before this decision. She had recommended the charity to her readers and often referenced that experience as a transformative one in her life.

However, two days later, in the face of relentless criticism and cancellations of child sponsorships by outraged evangelicals, World Vision reversed that policy, confirming that it would no longer be hiring Christians in same-sex marriages. This experience profoundly impacted Rachel, and it shaped her work moving forward. As she wrote, as a direct consequence of that decision, "I'm done fighting for a seat at the evangelical table, done trying to force that culture to change."

On the World Vision Reaction: Some Bad News, Some Good News, and Some Ideas

So here's what happened . . .*

On Monday afternoon, Richard Stearns, president of the Christian humanitarian organization World Vision, announced that his organization would not be taking a position on the divisive issue of same-sex marriage. The charity would, however, permit the employment of gay Christians in legal same-sex marriages.

Stearns told *Christianity Today*: "It's easy to read a lot more into this decision than is really there. This is not an endorsement of same-sex marriage. We have decided we are not going to get into that debate. Nor is this a rejection of traditional marriage, which we affirm and support. . . . It is us deferring to the authority of churches and denominations on theological issues. We're an op-

---

* Rachel later updated this post with the following addendum: "So it may have been a mistake to post this when feelings were still so raw. I'm concerned that the article has failed to generate healthy dialog—and I take full responsibility for that—so I'm going to close the comment thread. I'm thrilled that so many people have decided to sponsor children or make a donation through World Vision, so I'll leave the post up. Perhaps we can revisit the conversation after we've had some time to reflect. Thanks!" Of course, things would change in this story before then.

erational arm of the global church, we're not a theological arm of the church."*

Across the web, many evangelicals responded by declaring their intentions to pull their financial support from World Vision over the matter. Denny Burk of Southern Baptist Theological Seminary tweeted "Farewell, World Vision." Trevin Wax at the Gospel Coalition wrote a blog post placing all the blame for pulled child sponsorships on gay and lesbian people and their supporters, saying he "grieves for the children" who will lose access to basic necessities over the issue, before including single parents and divorcees among those who are destroying the lives of children around the world.† He posted a picture of a crying Black child at the top of his post for effect, reinforcing his message that it's the fault of *those sinners over there*" that evangelicals have been forced to deprive that hungry child of food.

Let me repeat that sequence of events:

1. World Vision announces it will not take a position on debates around gay marriage, but will employ people in same-sex marriages in its US offices.

2. In protest, some evangelicals threaten to halt their current funding for food, water, clothing, and shelter to children and communities sponsored by World Vision.

3. Evangelical spokespeople say they "weep for the children" who will suffer as a result of pulled sponsorships, and blame gay and

---

* Celeste Gracey and Jeremy Weber, "World Vision: Why We're Hiring Gay Christians in Same Sex Marriages," *Christianity Today*, March 24, 2014, https://www.christianitytoday.com/2014/03/world-vision-why-hiring-gay-christians-same-sex-marriage/.
† Trevin Wax, "World Vision and Why We Grieve for the Children," TGC: The Gospel Coalition, March 25, 2014, https://thegospelcoalition.org/blogs/trevin wax/2014/03/24/grieving-for-the-children/.

lesbian people (and divorcees and single parents) *for the actions of evangelicals.*

It's as ridiculous as it sounds.

And it puts into stark, unsettling relief just how out-of-control the evangelical obsession with homosexuality has become. Organizations don't get "farewelled" for hiring divorcees. People don't get kicked out of their churches for struggling with pride or for not wearing head coverings when they pray. But when it comes to homosexuality, Trevin Wax and many others have decided "the gospel is at stake."

I have to ask: *Since when?* Since when has the reality that Christ has died, Christ has risen, and Christ will come again ever been threatened by two men committing their lives to one another? Since when have the historic Christian creeds, recognized for centuries as the theological articulation of Orthodoxy, included a word about the issue of gay marriage? Since when have my gay and lesbian friends—many of whom are committed Christians—ever kept me from loving God with all my heart, soul, mind, and strength and loving my neighbor as myself? Since when has a single interpretation of the biblical passages in question here been deemed the only one faithful Christians can have?

The gospel is at stake only insofar as we make one's position on same-sex marriage a part of it. The gospel is threatened, not by gay people getting married, but by Christians saying support of or opposition to gay marriage is an essential part of the gospel when it's not.

Furthermore, the notion that the way to "punish" World Vision is to withdraw support from its efforts to feed, clothe, heal, comfort, rescue, and shelter "the least of these" is so contrary to the teachings of Jesus—particularly Matthew 25:31–46—it's hard to know where to start.

I'm a longtime World Vision supporter and I've seen firsthand the effectiveness of its work, particularly child sponsorships. I beg Christians not to drop their sponsorships or monthly giving to World Vision because they don't like the idea of gay people working for the organization. (If you're having second thoughts about that, just imagine writing a letter to your sponsored child explaining exactly why you can't help him or his community anymore.)

I'm always careful not to equate opposition to gay marriage with hate. But the singling out and scapegoating of gay and lesbian people that's happening here is deeply troubling to me. When Christians declare that they would rather withhold aid from people who need it than serve alongside gay and lesbian people helping to provide that aid, something's very, very wrong. It might not be hate, but it is a nefarious sort of stigmatizing, and it's wrong.

Finally, all this overdramatic "farewelling" over nonessential issues is getting tiresome. It's shutting the door of the Kingdom in people's faces. It's tying up heavy burdens and placing them on people's backs. It's straining gnats and swallowing camels. It's playing the gatekeeper with smug, self-righteous pride when it is *God* who decides who comes to the table, *God* who makes the guest list, *God* who opens the doors to the Kingdom.

Perhaps the greatest irony of all is that in rejecting the poor, the hungry, the marginalized, the outcast, and "the least of these," these brothers and sisters have essentially "farewelled" Christ himself. What a lonely world they have created!

But now, the good news . . .

The good news is that the gospel isn't a coalition to delineate and defend, but an expansive, worldwide movement that knows no political or geographic boundaries. It is a like a tree that is growing toward the sky, with enough branches for all the birds of the air to find a place to nest. It's like a hidden pearl, like wheat growing among tares, like mustard seeds splitting beneath the soil. It's alive and it's growing and it won't be stopped.

The good news is that God makes the guest list to the heavenly banquet—not you, not me, not Denny Burk, not John Piper.

The good news is that thousands of World Vision staff from around the world will continue their good work today—building wells, providing life-saving vaccinations, caring for Syrian refugees, partnering with communities to develop business and agricultural opportunities, lifting families out of poverty, and feeding, clothing, and sheltering vulnerable children.

The good news—and I want those of you who are discouraged to hear this—is that things are changing. As loud as these legalistic voices may seem right now, you will notice that they are often the *same voices*, over and over again. What I hear every day on the road and in my office is something different. It's a freedom song, and it's coming from thousands of pastors, writers, parents, teachers, and Christ-followers from all walks of life from all around the country and world. My desk is cluttered with books arguing for a more compassionate and inclusive way forward. Where I once scoured the internet for articles in support of women's equality and LGBT equality, they are now plentiful, overwhelming. Letters detailing changed hearts and minds clog up my inbox. Things are changing. Hearts are softening. People are listening to their gay and lesbian brothers and sisters and engaging Scripture in fresh, yet faithful, ways. And even when we disagree, there is a growing desire to drop our weapons, stop waging war, and start washing feet.

Originally posted on March 25, 2014.

World Vision Update

After intense financial pressure from evangelicals, World Vision has decided to reverse its decision regarding employment of gay and lesbian people.

I don't know what to say. I really don't.

For those of you who donated, thank you. That money will be put to good use, I assure you. But I am deeply, profoundly sorry that I inadvertently rallied these fundraising efforts in response to the fallout from a decision that would ultimately be reversed. Though I certainly hope everyone who sponsored a child or made a donation will continue to support World Vision, I can see how this effort would make you feel betrayed, as though it were launched under false pretense. And I'm so, so sorry for that. I'm as surprised by all this as you are.

This whole situation has left me feeling frustrated, heartbroken, and lost. I don't think I've ever been more angry at the church, particularly the evangelical culture in which I was raised and with which I for so long identified. I confess I had not realized the true extent of the disdain many evangelicals have toward LGBT people, nor had I expected World Vision to yield to that disdain by reversing its decision under financial pressure.

Honestly, it feels like a betrayal from every side.

Something has to change. And I'm as committed as ever to being a part of that change.

But not today.

Today, I don't know what else to do but grieve with everyone else who feels like a religious refugee today. This sucks, and I'm so, so sorry.

I hope you take some comfort in the fact that perhaps, as a result of our petty warring, some kids were sponsored today.

*Originally posted on March 26, 2014,
just hours after the previous post as the news broke
about the reversal of the decision.*

What Now?

Twenty minutes after World Vision announced that in response to financial pressure from evangelicals it would reverse its decision to employ Christians in same-sex relationships, I climbed into the giant SUV of a Baptist minister, where bags of Chick-fil-A were waiting to be consumed by a group of hungry college students, and cried.

I try so hard to be professional when I'm out on the road speaking, but this had been such a blow I was shaking with anger.

"I'm so sorry," my host said when I told him what happened. "This was wrong. This was ugly and wrong."

(It's amazing how, in certain moments, a simple acknowledgment of pain can be such a gift of grace.)

"You know what?" I said after a few minutes of quiet. "I'm done. I'm done with this whole conversation. I'm starting a cereal blog. That's always been my backup plan anyway."

"You mean. . . . like breakfast cereal?"

"Yeah, like breakfast cereal. I'm kind of an expert on it."

"Oh . . . well, that sounds fascinating!"

(Say what you will about Baptists, but they are consistently, sometimes inconceivably, nice.)

"I know, right? And the only controversy would be between Cinnamon Toast Crunch people and Golden Graham people.

Maybe I could work on getting those two sides to talk to each other."

"Well, with God all things are possible."

"Indeed."

Within minutes I was laughing and eating chicken nuggets with a bunch of bright, engaged Christian students at Wingate University, remembering once again that the church is bigger and more beautiful than its ugliest moments.

After what happened last week, I hear a lot of people asking, "What now? What do we do after this?"

The response to World Vision revealed some major fault lines in the church, and many of us who grew up evangelical interpreted all the gleeful "farewelling" from evangelical leaders as our final kick out the door.

As I talked to the Baptist minister about this, he said, "Seems like you've been wanting to leave evangelicalism for a while but can't quite let go."

"Exactly," I said. "When people at progressive conferences dis on evangelicalism, I'm the first to jump in and defend it. I identify myself as evangelical in interviews with the press because I want people to know that evangelicalism is a broad and diverse movement with a common spirit, but not necessarily uniform theological or political beliefs. And I speak up when a few vocal evangelical leaders say hateful things about LGBT people or encourage bullying or condone misogyny because I feel like I have this investment in the community and it's important for those invested in the community to speak up when its leaders are hurting our witness to the world . . . But I'm not sure I can do that anymore. I'm not sure I can defend a label when the label has come to mean something in our culture that isn't worth defending anymore and when it's been made abundantly clear that I'm not welcome at the table anyway."

"It seems to me," he responded, "that for you, evangelicalism is like the ex you broke up with a while ago but still stalk a little bit on Facebook."

(I'm telling you, the dude is like a prophet.)

"That's exactly what it is!" I said.

"Maybe it's time to pull the plug," he said, "for you own health and happiness."

"Maybe it is."

Don't worry. I'm not starting a cereal blog, nor am I pulling the plug.

But I'm done fighting for a seat at the evangelical table, done trying to force that culture to change.

For many years, I felt that part of my call as a writer and blogger of faith was to be a different sort of evangelical, to advocate for things like gender equality, respect for LGBTQ+ people, and acceptance of science and biblical scholarship within my community. But I think that perhaps I became more invested in trying to "fix" evangelicalism (to my standards! oh the hubris!) than in growing the Kingdom. And as helpful as I know that work has been for so many of you, I think it's time to take a slightly different approach.

So rather than wearing out my voice in calling for an end to evangelicalism's culture wars, I think it's time to focus on finding and creating church among its many refugees—women called to ministry, our LGBTQ+ brother and sisters, science-lovers, doubters, dreamers, misfits, abuse survivors, those who refuse to choose between their intellectual integrity and their faith or their compassion and their religion, those who have, for whatever reason, been "farewelled."

Instead of fighting for a seat at the evangelical table, I want to prepare tables in the wilderness, where everyone is welcome and where we can go on discussing (and debating!) the Bible, science, sexuality, gender, racial reconciliation, justice, church, and faith, but without labels, without wars.

I want this little online community to be like Kathy Escobar's beautiful church in Denver, the Refuge, "where everyone is safe but no one is comfortable." I want it to be a place where we can tell our stories, confess our sins, discuss Scripture, ask questions, disagree with grace, grieve, heal, create, follow Jesus, and rally together to do justice and love mercy—not just with our words, but with our actions. I want it to be a community that partners with people and organizations serving those on the margins. I want it to be a community led by people like Jeff Chu, Ben Moberg, and Christena Cleveland who exhibited more grace and patience last week than I knew was possible. I want it to feature and celebrate the voices of those speaking prophetically from the margins. I want us to continue to advocate for "the least of these."

I want this community to be a place where the churched and un-churched, Republicans and Democrats, American citizens and people from around the world, can come together to dream big dreams for the future. I want it to be a place where those who are tired and worn out from religion can find rest . . . not more fighting, not more judgment . . . just rest and peace for weary souls. I want us to be a community where we "learn the unforced rhythms of grace" together.

I certainly hope we create a community here where everyone—those leaving evangelicalism, those staying, and those just trying to figure it out—is welcome to the table, so long as it is approached with peace.

Finally, you can take the girl out of evangelicalism, but you can never take evangelicalism out of the girl. And that's fine by me.

I will forever be grateful for all the beautiful gifts evangelicalism gave me—a high esteem for and knowledge of Scripture, a heart for activism, and a deeply personal experience and expression of faith. It was, after all, evangelicals who baptized me, evangelicals who taught me to read and pray and cook. It was evangelicals who first called me a Christian, evangelicals who first told me I was beloved by God. And it was evangelicals (my parents) who let me sob in their arms yesterday, evangelicals who risked their reputations to reach out in peace last week.

Evangelicalism has been and always will be home. I suspect a part of me will always miss it.

But there's something strangely liberating about standing in the middle of this scorched earth terrain with the resolution to stop fighting, the resolution to give up. I am reminded of the one thing all we Christians have in common, whether we're Evangelical, Roman Catholic, Pentecostal, Presbyterian, Greek Orthodox, Seventh-Day Adventist, Anabaptist, Quaker, or something in between: We are Resurrection people.

Our God is in the business of bringing dead things back to life, so if we want in on God's business, we better prepare to follow God to all the rock-bottom, scorched-earth, dead-on-arrival corners of this world—including those in our own hearts—because that's where God works, that's where God gardens. There's no ladder to holiness to climb, no self-improvement plan to follow. It's just death and resurrection, over and over again, day after day, as God reaches down into our deepest graves and with the same power that raised Jesus from the dead wrests us from our pride, our apathy, our fear, our prejudice, our anger, our hurt, and our despair.

Most days I don't know which is harder for me to believe: that God reanimated the brain functions of a man three days dead, or that God can bring back to life all the beautiful things we have killed. Both seem pretty unlikely to me.

This never-ending winter has felt like one long Easter Saturday. But Sunday's coming . . . I can feel it.

Originally posted on April 1, 2014.

Life After Evangelicalism

This is for everyone who stayed home from church yesterday—for every mom of a disabled kid, every survivor of sexual assault, every Black or brown body in a predominantly white community, every son or daughter of an immigrant, every defender of the marginalized who just couldn't bring yourself to stand and sing "Great Is Thy Faithfulness" alongside the people you feel sold you out this week, the Christians who supported Donald Trump in this election.

Please hear me:

You are not alone.

You are not alone in your grief.

You are not alone in your anger.

You are not alone in your doubt, frustration, and fear.

The community that introduced you to Jesus—that baptized you and named you a beloved child of God—has aligned itself with values you don't recognize, powers that oppress.

It's an enormous blow, and it'll knock the wind right out of you.

Your disillusionment with the church may seem like a petty wound to nurse right now, with Latino children getting taunted by their classmates, Muslim communities facing religious persecution, and Black families grappling with a world in which white nationalism has been validated and emboldened, but grief is grief.

And your grief is real and justified.

The stark reality is that most white Christians, including more than 80 percent of white evangelical Christians, supported Donald Trump for president, despite his evident immorality, bigotry, and disregard for the dignity of women (not to mention complete lack of qualification or competency). We're about to witness firsthand what happens when the established church compromises its moral authority for the promise of power, and it won't be pretty. I predict millennials in particular will continue to drop out of religious life, and the ethnic divides within American Christianity, which many sought to heal with a quick-fix approach to "racial reconciliation" that bypassed repentance and justice, will only widen.

There's an op-ed out every minute urging the bewildered to get out of their bubbles and get to know some Trump supporters, but you don't need to do that, do you?

These are the people you worship with each week, the people whose kids hang out with your kids, the people who brought you a chicken casserole when you had surgery, the people you call with good news, the people you're now wishing you'd spoken with more bluntly, more honestly.

They aren't strangers to you, are they? But suddenly, you are a stranger among them.

And that's a lonely place to be.

I know because I've been there. I've stood in a sanctuary singing songs I didn't feel like singing, pretending to agree with a political ideology I no longer agreed with, praying to a God I wasn't sure I believed in anymore. It whittles down your spirit, a little at a time, until one day you realize it's not you going to church anymore, but some ghost of you, some cardboard cutout you send out to maintain the status quo, to keep up appearances. The sense of isolation is profound, palpable.

You have some decisions up ahead, the most pressing of which is to stay or to go.

I'm not going to tell you what to do about that.

When writing about her troubled marriage, author Glennon Doyle wisely avoids telling other women what to do, and instead puts the choice this way: "Does a Love Warrior Go? YES. If that's what her deepest wisdom tells her to do. Does a Love Warrior Stay? YES. If that's what her deepest wisdom tells her to do. Both roads are hard. And both roads can lead to redemption."*

The same is true for church. There is no single road to redemption. And there is certainly not a straight one. As novelist Marilynne Robinson has said, "grace is not so poor a thing that it cannot present itself in any number of ways."†

Perhaps you will stay and work for reform. Perhaps you will leave to join a new community, another tradition. Perhaps you won't know for a while.

But I think we both know something has to change.

I eventually left evangelicalism when it became clear that the fight was wearing me down, with little promise of change, especially as it concerned my LGBTQ+ friends and neighbors. After a few years of wilderness wandering (you should expect that, by the way—look for the manna; look for the water from rock), I found myself in the Episcopal Church, which is no less riddled with conflict and shortcomings than any other Christian tradition, but which introduced me to the sacraments that have managed to sustain my ever-complicated, ever-faltering faith.

---

* Originally found at Glennon Doyle's Momastery blog at "This Is What I Believe About Marriage, Infidelity, Divorce & Redemption," Momastery, accessed April 17, 2025, https://momastery.com/blog/2016/02/29/marriage-divorce-and-redemption/. It can also be found at this Facebook post: https://www.facebook.com/glennondoyle/posts/after-walking-through-sisters-divorce-and-remarriage-my-own-separation-and-recon/10153942358549710/.

† Marilynne Robinson, *Gilead* (Farrar, Straus and Giroux, 2004), 240.

I'm telling you this because I want you to know there is life after evangelicalism.

Perhaps you've been told for as long as you can remember that the rest of the world is dark and evil, and that progressive Christianity is full of faithless, lukewarm liberals. But that's not true. Not by a long shot.

You see those churches on TV getting defaced by swastikas and racial slurs? Why do you think they've been targeted?

Because those churches are inclusive and diverse. Because the love inside is so magnetic, so real, so threatening to powers and principalities, even the Devil knows it.

The church universal is so much bigger than white American evangelicalism, and that's going to become ever more apparent in the months and years to come.

The good news is that Jesus is already on the margins. Jesus is already present among the very people and places our president-elect despises as weak. When we stand in solidarity with the despised and the suffering, Jesus stands with us. We don't have to abandon Jesus to abandon the unholy marriage between Donald Trump and the white American church. In these troubled times, a prophetic resistance will certainly emerge, made up of clergy, activists, artists, humorists, liturgists, parents, teachers, and volunteers committed to partnering with and defending "the least of these." I found my faith again in the margins—through the Gay Christian Network, for example, and among fellow doubters and dreamers who limp from their wrestling with God—and I'll be amplifying and supporting these efforts even more as they face potential new threats under this administration. I hope you will join us.

But you should know that as you take those first shaky steps toward something new, grief will stalk along, catching you by surprise.

Losing your first faith is like losing a dear family member or friend, and as with any other death, you sense its absence most profoundly in those everyday moments when it used to be present—in a beloved hymn, in a Bible verse or prayer, in a strained relationship that used to be so easy.

Certainly many are suffering right now, and your crisis of faith may pale in comparison. There are a lot of other things I want to write about and advocate for now, but I wanted to say this first:

You are not alone.

There is life after this. There is faith after this.

Hold on.

Originally posted on November 14, 2016.

Faith in God, Even in Disillusionment
A REFLECTION BY KELSEY HANSON WOODRUFF

Many women throughout history have been inspired by the evangelical tradition, which has recognized the work of the Holy Spirit in laypeople. In early evangelical revivals, in the progressive-era reform movements, and in twenty-first-century digital formats, women without formal theological education or institutional titles have heeded the call of God to raise their voices in public. Armed with a degree in literature and a sharp mind, Rachel imbibed theology, history, and biblical studies, synthesizing many sources in approachable writing that resonated with her readers. She was an unusually gifted writer, and as a believer, she felt compelled to use this gift to reach others. Rachel felt it was her responsibility to use her platform to amplify other voices and to encourage other writers, especially women. Rachel was a key node in a network of progressive Christian women authors, many of whom are included in this volume, who asserted their right to exegete Scripture, to theologize, and to publicly wonder about and proclaim their faith.

Rachel was also one of many evangelical women who ultimately felt they no longer belonged in the tradition of their youth. In "Life After Evangelicalism," she reflects on her disappointment with conservative evangelicalism, though notably she writes in the second person, beginning with, "You are not alone." Like so many of her posts, Rachel wrote this not for her own catharsis, but for readers who shared her heartbreak. You can sense her pain when she writes that "the community that introduced you to Jesus—that baptized you and named you a beloved child of God" had betrayed cherished values. Evangelicalism had baptized Rachel, showed her the love of God, encouraged her to read the Scriptures, imbued her with the value of treating others as she would want to be treated. And yet, as she wrote in a blog post the year before, it was also evangelicalism that told her that being a woman limited her leadership, that science should be distrusted, and that "democrats and gay people and Episcopalians" were her enemies.

"Life After Evangelicalism" went live just days after the first election of Donald Trump, declaring that Rachel's faith tradition of origin had turned its back on the very things she still treasured. For Rachel and so many of her readers, Trump's election was a turning point in their relationship with evangelicalism. Her prediction that many of her fellow millennials would leave religious life because of evangelicals' support of Trump would indeed come to pass. Yet, Rachel believed Christianity was wider than one particular stream. She had already left an evangelical church to find belonging in a mainline Protestant tradition, and many of her readers would follow, finding alternative communities in which to live out their faith in Jesus.

During the eleven and a half years that Rachel posted on her blog, white evangelical Christianity in America was undergoing a transformation. The readers who gathered there demonstrated one outcome of this transformation: the digital communities that formed at the margins of evangelicalism. In Rachel's blog and social media threads, readers found comfort that they were not alone in their discomfort with the direction of evangelicalism. They rejected the growing Christian nationalism, the dominance of patriarchy, the intolerance of other religions, and white supremacy.

Rachel wanted her readers to know that their faith in God could persist even in their disillusionment. She encouraged her readers to "hold on" to their hope for a faith that better embodied the ethic of Jesus, who stands at the margins caring for the least of these. Though Rachel would be accused by conservatives of abandoning her faith, she considered herself to be doing the opposite. The evangelical tradition had taught her to model her life on Jesus's, and she did not plan to stop.

PART THREE

CASSEROLES, EVANGELICALISM, AND THE KINGDOM OF THE HUNGRY

Essays on the Church

15 Reasons I Left Church

Eight million twenty-somethings have left the church, and it seems like everyone is trying to figure out why.

Last week, writer Christian Piatt offered seven reasons, and then four more reasons.* Researcher David Kinnaman recently authored a book entitled *You Lost Me*, which details the findings of Barna researchers who interviewed hundreds of eighteen- to twenty-nine-year-olds about why they left the church.†

I left the church when I was twenty-seven. I am now thirty, and after trying unsuccessfully to start a house church, my husband and I are struggling to find a faith community in which we feel we belong. I've been reluctant to write about this search in the past, but it seems like such a common experience, I think it's time to open up, especially now that I've had some time to process. But let's begin with fifteen reasons why I left:

---

* Christian Piatt, "Seven Reasons Why Young Adults Quit Church," Red Letter Christians, March 14, 2012, https://redletterchristians.org/2012/03/14/seven-reasons-why-young-adults-quit-church/; Christian Piatt, "Four More (BIG) Reasons Young Adults Quit Church," Red Letter Christians, March 18, 2012, https://redletterchristians.org/2012/03/18/four-more-big-reasons-young-adults-quit-church/.

† David Kinnaman, *You Lost Me: Why Young Christians Are Leaving Church . . . and Rethinking Faith* (Baker, 2011).

1. I left the church because I'm better at planning Bible studies than baby showers . . . but they only wanted me to plan baby showers.

2. I left the church because when we talked about sin, we mostly talked about sex.

3. I left the church because my questions were seen as liabilities.

4. I left the church because sometimes it felt like a cult, or a country club, and I wasn't sure which was worse.

5. I left the church because I believe the earth is 4.5 billion years old and that humans share a common ancestor with apes, which I was told was incompatible with my faith.

6. I left the church because sometimes I doubt, and church can be the worst place to doubt.

7. I left the church because I didn't want to be anyone's "project."

8. I left the church because it was often assumed that everyone in the congregation voted for Republicans.

9. I left the church because I felt like I was the only one troubled by stories of violence and misogyny and genocide found in the Bible, and I was tired of people telling me not to worry about it because "God's ways are higher than our ways."

10. I left the church because of my own selfishness and pride.

11. I left the church because I knew I would never see a woman behind the pulpit, at least not in the congregation in which I grew up.

12. I left the church because I wanted to help people in my community without feeling pressure to convert them to Christianity.

13. I left the church because I had learned more from Oprah about addressing poverty and injustice than I had learned from twenty-five years of Sunday school.

14. I left the church because there are days when I'm not sure I believe in God, and no one told me that "dark nights of the soul" can be part of the faith experience.

15. I left the church because one day, they put signs out in the church lawn that said "Marriage = 1 Man + 1 Woman: Vote Yes on Prop 1," and I knew the moment I saw them that I never wanted to come back.*

"We aren't looking for a faith that provides all the answers; we're looking for one in which we are free to ask the questions."†

Originally posted on March 20, 2012.

---

* Prop 1 was the Tennessee Marriage Protection Amendment (2006), a state constitutional amendment banning same-sex unions; it was approved by 81 percent of voters.
† Rachel Held Evans, *Evolving in Monkey Town: How a Girl Who Knew All the Answers Learned to Ask the Questions* (Zondervan, 2010), 270.

15 Reasons I Returned to the Church

So yesterday's post, "15 Reasons I Left Church," generated a massive response, which I was not expecting. (Must have struck a nerve.) Thank you so much for your comments. They were honest, encouraging, challenging, and true.*

As I mentioned in that post, I left church when I was twenty-seven, and for a couple of years, I really struggled with my faith. But as many of you pointed out, sometimes leaving church is the best way to find the Church—with a capital-C, and that's exactly what has happened as I've encountered the goodness and grace of God's people at the Catholic church down the street, at the local church that rallied to bring food to my mom during her cancer treatments, through our quirky, grace-filled (but sadly now defunct) church plant, among friends and neighbors and fellow searchers, and, of course, with you.

Dan and I are still in search of a faith community that feels like home, but at the risk of sounding cliché, "not all who wander are lost."

So in that spirit, here are fifteen reasons I've returned to the Church:

---

* Rachel often wrote new blog posts in response to the conversation that previous posts elicited, as part of her ongoing conversation with her readers.

1. Jesus

2. *The Book of Common Prayer*

3. The fact that when somebody gets sick or dies or has a baby or loses their job, it's the church ladies who are the first to show up at the front door with a casserole and a hug

4. Anne Lamott

5. Communion

6. Connecting with other searchers who may not be part of a church, but are part of The Church (this includes many of you!)

7. The first sermon I ever heard from a woman

8. Sucking up my pride and embracing the fact that, like it or not, I need community . . . and real community isn't about surrounding myself with people just like me

9. Liturgy that reads like poetry

10. Madeleine L'Engle

11. My parents, who, though we don't always agree on all the political or theological details, have modeled Christian compassion and grace better than anyone I know and who have supported me through every "evolution" of faith

12. The BioLogos Foundation, and especially Karl Giberson, who was the first to reach out to me and tell me that I didn't have to choose between my intellectual integrity and my faith

13. The Mission (our church plant), which even though it failed on paper, changed my life and gave me hope for the future of the Church*

14. Friends with whom we gather each week for movies, food, conversations about God, and the occasional (slightly awkward) church visit

15. Grace, grace, grace, grace, grace, grace, grace

Originally posted on March 21, 2012.

---

* Later, Rachel would go on to write the *New York Times* bestseller *Searching for Sunday*, which chronicles her journey within the church in general, along with that church plant in particular.

So Our Church Plant Failed...

Easter Sunday will be the last time we meet together as The Mission. We're throwing a little send-off party for our pastor and his family, who made the difficult decision to move to south Florida where a new youth ministry position awaits.

There were no big arguments, no dramatic exits, no taking sides. We just couldn't sustain the church financially.

Yep. It's that boring . . . and it's that sad.

On the one hand, I'm thankful . . .

I'm thankful that we managed to end in the same way we began—unified, of the same mind, with grace, and in love. Too often the dissolution of a church is messy business, with hurt feelings, accusations, and blame circling around the whole affair like hungry vultures. I'm so grateful that we were a part of a church that did things differently, even if it was just for a time.

I'm thankful for the friends we made. Many of the relationships we built through The Mission have become integral and enriching parts of our lives. Dan and I agreed that if all we take from this experience is our new friends, then it was totally worth it.

I'm thankful that, at least for a short time, we created an environment in which those who had been wounded by the church felt safe. As we were talking Sunday, one such participant confessed that The Mission had helped her soften toward those who had hurt her in the past, that she felt more prepared to worship alongside those whose faith looks different from her own because The Mission had provided a place of rest in which she could be herself. As much as I wish we could continue to provide that safe place for her (and for ourselves), maybe it's more important that we helped her feel at home in her own skin, regardless of where she worships.

I'm thankful that we did what we said we would do. We reached out to the community by volunteering and giving. We gathered together a group that was theologically and politically diverse. We refused to draw lines in the sand when it came to nonessential doctrines. We humbly confessed our doubts, our shortcomings, our fears, and our questions. We focused our study and our efforts on joining God's mission of reconciliation, and together we loved God and one another well.

I'm thankful that for the first time in my life, my gifts as a teacher were encouraged and celebrated in the church, even though I am a woman. I wasn't turned away or talked about because of what I write about on the blog and in my books. Whereas most churches have treated me as a liability, this one treated me as an asset.

I'm thankful that our pastor consistently devoted himself to extensive study, research, and good teaching, even when he was often speaking to just ten or twelve people. That says a lot about his character.

I'm thankful that instead of simply complaining about church in the Bible Belt, Dan and I took a risk and got our hands dirty in an effort to "be the change." We knew that this was a risk and that failure was a possibility. But we did it anyway, and I'm proud of that.

But I'm also really sad . . .

I'm sad because it sucks to invest your time, money, hopes, and dreams into something that doesn't work out.

I'm sad because I will miss my pastor, his wife, and their two beautiful daughters.

I'm sad because I feel guilty for not generating more time, more money, and more energy to building this church. Sometimes I worry that the reason we didn't succeed was because of my reputation. Maybe people didn't come because they knew that "the girl who believes in evolution" was in attendance.

I'm sad . . . no, I'm angry . . . because I know there are people in this community who will be delighted to hear that we failed.

I'm sad because I feel that our failure only confirms my fears that a church like this one—in which all are welcome, in which women can lead, in which politics don't get in the way of fellowship, in which questions are encouraged, in which a diversity of opinions is celebrated, in which gossip is kept to a minimum—simply cannot make it in Dayton.

And I'm sad because the prospect of searching for another church leaves me feeling so exhausted, so bitter, so cynical, and so lonely I just can't imagine climbing out of bed on Sunday mornings ever again.

So I guess this season of life is shaping up to be one big Holy Saturday.

We are disappointed.

We are thankful.

We are confused.

We are waiting.

Right now it's hard to imagine a Resurrection Sunday around the corner, but I suppose that if the same spirit that raised Christ from the dead lives in us today, anything is possible.

Originally posted on April 20, 2011.

Sunday Morning

In the summertime, the light darts through the slits in the blinds all gold and sudden—no gentle fade through purple and blue and gray to get you used to the idea of another day. I wake and listen to Dan breathe next to me. We stopped setting an alarm a long time ago.

Somewhere between 8 and 9, when the songbirds have settled down, I formulate my excuse:

Too far to the Orthodox Church.
Too late for the Episcopal Church.
Too liberal for the Baptist Church.
Too conservative for the Mainline Church.
Too protestant for the Catholic Church.
Too catholic for the Bible Church.

No one asks anymore, but I was raised to be ready with an answer. So the excuses are part of the routine now—like finally kicking off the covers, like my dark roast coffee with cream, like checking email, like morning prayer:

> "Lord God, almighty and everlasting Father, you have brought me in safety to the beginning of this day. Preserve me with your mighty power, that I may not fall into sin, nor be overcome by adversity; and in all I do, direct

me to the fulfilling of your purposes; through Jesus Christ my Lord."*

Have I fallen into sin?

Who will bring casseroles when I have a baby?

What I feel these days is not guilt, but something far more nefarious: dull resignation. There are nearly two hundred churches near my small, Southern town, and hundreds more if we make the long drive to Chattanooga, so the fact that I can't seem to make it through a single service without questioning the existence of God says a lot more about me than it does about church, now doesn't it?

Do I want a church that fits me, or a me that fits the church?

God makes sense to me under the trees, and God makes sense to me in poetry and prayer, and God makes sense to me in Eucharist and Baptism and community and even creeds . . . but not in the offering plate, not in the building campaign, not in the pastor-who-shall-not-be-questioned, not in the politics, not in the assumptions about what a good Christian girl ought to be.

Gentle, quiet.

Am I selfish for wanting more?

And who will bring casseroles when I have a baby?

I don't know how to explain it—to my family, to my readers, to myself—that, despite the fact that I know these good people would love me unconditionally, I don't want to go back. I don't want to be the change. I don't want to try anymore.

It's 10:30 a.m., and I'm still tired—

still tired from our failed church plant,

still tired from the local gossip,

still tired of being seen as a project and a prayer request because

---

* *The Book of Common Prayer* (Seabury, 1979), 137.

I believe the earth is more than six thousand years old and that Anne Frank didn't go to hell,

stiff tired of patriarchy,

still tired of feeling farther away from myself when I am in church than when I am anywhere else in the world.

I don't know how to explain it—to my family, to my readers, to myself—how, when my gay friends aren't welcome at the Table and my sisters aren't welcome at the pulpit, somehow I'm not welcome there either. I feel at once pride and guilt.

But who will bring casseroles when I have a baby?

> "Lord God, almighty and everlasting Father, you have brought me in safety to the beginning of this day. Preserve me with your mighty power, that I may not fall into sin, nor be overcome by adversity; and in all I do, direct me to the fulfilling of your purposes; through Jesus Christ my Lord."

The sun has now lit the whole house, and I pray regardless of whether the prayer feels right.

And hope that someday the same spirit will carry me back to church.

Originally posted on July 2, 2012.

On Casseroles and Finding Community

A REFLECTION BY KRISTEN HOWERTON

I grew up going to church twice on Sundays and on Wednesday nights. My childhood was spent playing in the vestibule or doing cartwheels with friends in the fellowship hall while we waited for our parents to finally stop talking and take us to lunch at Golden Corral. The running joke was that the church should give my mom her own set of keys to lock up, since we were usually the last to leave. Church was our spiritual home, our social network, our safety net, and our third space.

It's no surprise I married a pastor and joined these same rhythms in adulthood. I was a dutiful pastor's wife. I volunteered in youth group, sang on the worship team, and ran the church missions program. We did have keys and we often did lock up because we were the last to leave. The church was where I felt most at home, where I believed my purpose was rooted.

But over time, things began to shift. There was a subtle but unmistakable transition as my church began to align more overtly with conservative ideologies, especially on issues around gay rights, immigration, and national politics. The church's stance on gender, sexuality, and leadership began to clash with my own evolving beliefs. Then, a longtime friend was fired from the church staff when he came out as gay. My values, which had always been centered on compassion, justice, and inclusion, were increasingly out of step with my own church.

And yet the thought of leaving was terrifying. How could I leave behind something that was so integral to my sense of identity and belonging? And yet, how could I stay at a place where that very belonging was not extended to everyone?

Then I discovered other Christians on a similar journey. When Rachel wrote, "Who will bring casseroles when I have a baby?" I immediately knew what she meant. Rachel articulated so well a shared fear of losing community, and spoke for so many of us. She understood that community was not just about the physical space we occupy but the emotional safety and support that surrounds us. She gave voice to our own fears of isolation and loss.

Rachel and I spent the better part of the past decade in a friend group of postevangelical misfits. It was a community of people who had grown up in a faith they had then deconstructed and put back together. We were sometimes cynical and irreverent and oftentimes silly. We updated each other on our kids, our faith crises, our personal and public failures, and sent each other some of the most hilarious photos that surely would make our mothers blush. But most of all, we were ardent supporters of one another.

Eventually, both Rachel and I left our churches, but we never gave up on community.

Rachel wanted to create community for others, and she did. Alongside Sarah Bessey and Jeff Chu, Rachel built a sanctuary in Evolving Faith. The conferences became a gathering ground for those of us struggling with the dissonance between our personal convictions and the practice of Christianity. Here, we found a space to wrestle with our beliefs openly and to reclaim the parts of our faith that felt steadfast. Between the Evolving Faith community and her writing, Rachel gave us the permission we needed to let go of what no longer served us, showing us how to live out our values with courage and kindness. She made it possible for those of us who felt like "outsiders" in our own faith to feel seen and understood. And for so many of us, this community became a reminder that there is indeed room for all of us at the table. Belonging isn't defined by where we gather but by the grace we extend to ourselves and each other along the way.

What I wish I could tell Rachel is that when she died, an entire community did show up with casseroles, both literally and figuratively. The very community she helped build, with her words and with her unflinching honesty, rallied together to surround her family in love and care. It was a testament to the lasting impact of Rachel's life.

Blessed Are the Un-Cool

People sometimes assume that because I'm a progressive thirty-year-old who enjoys Mumford & Sons and has no children, I must want a super-hip church—you know, the kind that's called "Thrive" or "Be" and that boasts "an awesome worship experience," a fair-trade coffee bar, its own iPhone app, and a pastor who looks like a Jonas Brother.

While none of these features are inherently wrong (and can, of course, be used by good people to do good things), these days I find myself longing for a church with a cool factor of about zero.

That's right.

I want a church that includes fussy kids, old liturgy, bad sound, weird congregants, and . . . *brace yourself* . . . painfully amateur "special music" now and then.

Why?

Well, for one thing, when the gospel story is accompanied by a fog machine and light show, I always get this creeped-out feeling like someone's trying to sell me something. It's as though we're all compensating for the fact that Christianity's not good enough to stand on its own so we're adding snacks.

But more importantly, I want to be part of an un-cool church because I want to be part of a community that shares the reputation of Jesus, and like it or not, Jesus's favorite people in the world were not cool. They were mostly sinners, misfits, outcasts, weirdoes, poor people, sick people, and crazy people.

Cool congregations can get so wrapped up in the "performance" of church that they forget to actually be the church, a phenomenon painfully illustrated by the story of the child with cerebral palsy who was escorted from the Easter service at Elevation Church for being a "distraction."*

Really?

It seems to me that this congregation was distracted long before this little boy showed up! In their self-proclaimed quest for "an explosive, phenomenal movement of God—something you have to see to believe," they missed Jesus when he was right under their nose.†

Was the paralytic man lowered from the rooftop in the middle of a sermon a distraction?

Was the Canaanite woman who harassed Jesus and his disciples about healing her daughter a distraction?

Were the blind men from Jericho who annoyed the crowd with their relentless cries a distraction?

Jesus didn't think so. In fact, he seemed to think that they were the point.

Jesus taught us that when we throw a banquet or a party, our invitation list should include the ones our society overlooks and marginalizes. So why do our church marketing teams target the young, the hip, the healthy, and the resourced?

In her book *Bossypants*, Tina Fey describes working for the

---

* "NC Boy with Cerebral Palsy Asked to Leave an Easter Service at the Megachurch Elevation Church," WFMY News, no longer available online.
† The quote was on the Elevation Church website at the time. It has since been removed.

YMCA in Chicago soon after graduating from college. This particular YMCA included "a great mix of high-end yuppie fitness facility, a wonderful community resource for families, and an old-school residence for disenfranchised men," so Fey shares a host of funny stories about working the front desk. One such story involves one of the residents forgetting to take his meds, bumping into a young mom on her way to a workout session, and saying something wildly inappropriate (and very funny—you should definitely go out and get this book). Fey writes, *"The young mother was beside herself. That's the kind of trouble you get when diverse groups of people actually cross paths with one another. That's why many of the worst things in the world happen in and around Starbucks bathrooms."**

Church can be a lot like the Y . . . or a Starbucks bathroom.

We have one place for the un-cool people (our ministries) and another place for the cool people (our church services). When we actually bump into one another, things can get awkward, so we try to avoid it.

It's easy to pick on Elevation Church in this case, but the truth is we're all guilty of thinking we're too cool for the least of these. Our elitism shows up when we forbid others from contributing art and music because we deem it unworthy of glorifying God, or when we scoot our family an extra foot or two down the pew when an autistic guy sits down. Having helped start a church, I remember hoping that our hip guests wouldn't be turned off by our less-than-hip guests. For a second I forgot that in church, of all places, those distinctions should disappear.

Some of us wear our brokenness on the inside, others on the outside.

---

* Tina Fey, *Bossypants* (Little, Brown, 2011), 78.

But we're all broken.
We're all un-cool.
We're all in need of a Savior.

So let's cut the crap, pull the plug, and have us some distracting church services . . . the kind where Jesus would fit right in.

Originally posted on June 15, 2011.

Rachel Didn't Just Write About Including the Un-Cool, She Befriended Us

A REFLECTION BY SHANNON DINGLE

Rachel didn't try to be cool. That made her endearing, especially to people like me who were decidedly un-cool. When we talked, her realness came through, and she welcomed me to be authentic too.

I'm autistic, physically disabled, and chronically ill, and I live with PTSD and ADHD. My kids have a wide range of diagnoses as well, and use supportive braces, a motorized wheelchair, and lots of medications. We can never show up somewhere without being conspicuous.

And church is often the hardest place to show up. In the US, where we live, churches are one of the only public spaces exempt from the legal requirement to be accessible to disabled people by the Americans with Disabilities Act (or ADA). Even more, evangelical churches fought for that exemption, actively working to prevent families like mine from being welcome in their communities.

I miss Rachel deeply, but never more than when I wish she could be a sounding board for some concern challenging me. I wanted to send her a message the other day, as our church still lacks accessibility in our new-to-us building, so my daughter can't get to the kids' area down two stairs in her wheelchair. They've been "working on it" for a couple years now, with no discernible progress.

Rachel would have wept angry tears with me, as this is surely not earth as it is in heaven. Rachel would have accepted my now-bitter words, as she'd agree that injustice isn't okay. And Rachel would probably have helped me find better words to advocate for our family and others like us as we stay at our un-cool church, because Rachel didn't care about going with the flow in any direction Jesus wouldn't have gone.

Rachel didn't just write about including the un-cool; she befriended us. She made sure we belonged as much as she belonged. I miss my friend, and I long for more of her hospitality in the church and the world.

On "Outgrowing" American Christianity

Every now and then a blog post or article will make the rounds in which the author claims to have "outgrown" church or religion or, in this case, American Christianity.*

I remember having similar feelings of emancipation, of starting over from scratch when I first began to realize the evangelical faith I had inherited was not the only kind of faith there was. And perhaps such feelings are a necessary and unavoidable part of growing up, of making that important distinction between oneself and one's parents.

And yet, when it came time to write a book about church (which, like every book, began with the rather rigorous and uncomfortable exercise of confronting my own bullshit),† I couldn't deny the reality that, as much as I may dream of it, there's no starting from scratch . . . for any of us. Our culture, our past, our biases, our experiences, our communities, our wounds, our healing—this isn't the baggage we carry; it's the skin we wear. We can't just slough it off.

---

* John Pavlovitz, "My Emancipation from American Christianity," *Huffington Post*, updated December 4, 2016, https://www.huffpost.com/entry/my-emancipation-from-american-christianity_b_8718400. Rachel noted: "I agree with many of the points of his post. My aim here is less to critique and more to add a slightly different perspective. This isn't a call-out, just a conversation."

† Here, Rachel is referencing her own book, *Searching for Sunday: Loving, Leaving, and Finding the Church*.

Sure, it would be easier to tell the story of my emancipation from the evil ways of those Christians who identify as conservative, evangelical, American. But it wouldn't have been a true story . . . at least not for me. While my disagreements with many in that community are important and real, those Christians were, and continue to be, my friends. They were often the first to show up at my front door with a casserole when the family was down with the flu. They taught me to love and memorize Scripture, to change a diaper, to rejoice with those who rejoice and weep with those who weep, and to think critically enough to deconstruct and reassess some of their own teachings. Most importantly, they were the first people to introduce me to Jesus, something I never want to take for granted.

Certainly others bear much deeper scars, but even the most painful religious experiences cannot simply be discarded. They must be confronted, molded, repurposed. It's a messy, sacred process. This is why, in the wake of my last book release, I so strongly disliked headlines about my "leaving evangelicalism for the Episcopal Church." While I'm happy to acknowledge that I've switched denominational affiliation, there is much about evangelicalism that I joyfully bring with me through the doors of St. Luke's Episcopal Church and which the people there joyfully receive. Very little of my faith has involved leaving and arriving. The vast majority of it has involved wrestling, meandering, stretching, struggling. As the saying goes, it's a work in progress. My spiritual GPS has yet to chirp, "You have arrived."

I suspect all these claims of having left empty religion to find the true faith are ubiquitous in both evangelical and progressive Christian publishing culture precisely because they stem from the same illusion—that we are each a blank slate, that we have the ability to start over. But the idea that an American can just stop being an American, or that a Christian can just stop being religious, strikes me as naïve at best, arrogant at worst. It's no better than the Bible reader who insists he's not interpreting the text, just reading it, or the white male theologian who insists his theological views are the objective default, while those of women, African Americans, or Christians from the global South and East are contextual. It presumes that progressive Christians, unlike those conservative Christians, are totally unaffected by the trappings of American culture. If only it were that easy.

Let's be real, folks: If you're reading the Bible, you're interpreting it. If you identify as a Christian, you're part of a religion. If you're an American citizen living in America, you can deliberately surround yourself with global perspectives (a good idea!) but you can't just opt out of American Christianity. It's far better to acknowledge the fact that our contexts, privileges, affiliations, and blind spots affect our worldview than it is to announce we've managed to finally overcome or outgrown them. I find it odd that so many who claim to have a postmodern view of Christianity seem so entrenched in modern, Enlightenment-based ideas of objectivity and progress.

Perhaps real maturity is exhibited not in thinking myself above other Christians and organized religion, but in humbly recognizing the reality that I can't escape my own cultural situation and life experiences, nor do I want to escape the good gift of my (dysfunctional, beautiful, necessary) global faith community. This consideration made the writing process infinitely more difficult and infinitely more rewarding. I suspect it had the same effect on my faith.

The truth is, I am a Christian, which means I am religious. And I am an American, which means my Christianity is affected by privilege, by Western philosophy, by seventeenth-century Puritanism, and by Psalty the Singing Songbook. My American Christian heritage includes both Martin Luther King Jr. and the white segregationists who opposed him—a reality that is both empowering and uncomfortable, but one I can't escape, one I want to look squarely in the eyes.

Loving the church means both critiquing it and celebrating it. We don't have to choose between those two things. But those of us who remain Christian cannot imagine ourselves to be so far above the church—including the American church—that we are not a part of it.

Yes, we are called to grow and mature, and yes, our convictions and denominational affiliations will likely change, but I've found I'm a better writer—and a better person—when I'm more focused on outgrowing the old me than I am on outgrowing other people in my community.

After all, this is Kingdom growth. There aren't ladders, only trellises.

Originally posted on December 5, 2015.

Why a Seminary Degree Doesn't Have to Make You a Jerk

Not too long ago, I was at a dinner party and was asked by the hostess if I'd been embroiled in any intense writing projects lately. (I suspect my slightly dazed, what-is-this-thing-called-sunshine? look was something of a giveaway.) I laughed and told the group about *Searching for Sunday*—perhaps the most challenging and rewarding creative project of my life—which at the time was a mere ten thousand words away from completion.

Barely had the familiar elevator pitch, "it's a book about a doubter's search for church, arranged around seven sacraments," left my lips when a young, seminary-trained man at the table interrupted me and launched into a fifteen-minute lecture on sacramental theology, suggesting I Google Alexander Schmemann (whose book, *For the Life of the World*, I'd already read three times) before "attempting a popular treatment" of the sacraments.

I received several apologetic glances from the hostess, who finally managed to wrangle the conversation away from the young Calvinist and turn it to the topic of asparagus, which, miraculously, he did not seem to have an opinion about. We never returned to the sacraments, whose beauty and power had been lighting up my imagination for the last fourteen months.

The truth is, my lack of seminary training is something I'm deeply insecure about. Every writer struggles with self-doubt, and the refrain most commonly caught in a loop in my brain is: *Who do you think you are? What do you know about God or faith or church? You haven't even been to seminary! What could you possibly teach anyone?*

This insecurity gets reinforced by people like my dinner companion, who seem especially perturbed that an undereducated woman like me has built a platform from which to write and speak about faith.

Regardless of how well they know me or my work, these guys tend to approach our conversations with a paternalistic familiarity that makes me uncomfortable, immediately rendering me the student and them the teacher. I am not criticized; I am "lovingly corrected." We do not discuss where we agree or disagree; I am informed of what I got right and what I got wrong. It's not a peer-to-peer conversation; it's a session of "pastoral counseling," initiated by a man who is not, in fact, my pastor.

What they don't realize, of course, is that I am intensely aware of my lack of theological qualifications, which is precisely why I read a lot, cite my sources, ask questions, listen, apologize when I get stuff wrong, and refuse to fake my way through Q&A sessions when the honest "A" is "I don't know." It's also why I invite comments and critiques from faithful collaborators—pastors, scholars, artists, scientists, doctors, parents, blog commenters, and editors—who often know more about a given topic than I and whose insights improve my writing by miles. My gifts and training are in creative writing. My interests are in matters of faith. I know I am not entitled to respect, but on my better days, I am of the conviction that regular people can talk about God too, and perhaps even prophesy.

It would be easy to turn this post into a rant against the much-maligned phenomenon "mansplaining," which is certainly real, though perhaps too liberally invoked on social media. What I'd rather do is tell you about the alternative, about just a few of the people who treat me and nearly everyone they encounter with respect, openness, and humble teachability, even as they carry around an armful of credentials.

A seminary degree doesn't have to make you a jerk. You can be an expert on ancient Hebrew without fancying yourself an expert on everything. In fact, the people who have taught me the most in life do not view themselves as teachers, but rather as perpetual students, always eager to learn more and always open to changing their minds.

Perhaps the closest example of this in my life is Dan, an insatiable and avid learner who has as one of his life's mottos, "Always assume there's someone in the room who knows more about the topic at hand than you do." He says he learned much of this from his sister-in-law, Maki, who is smart, curious, entrepreneurial, and who will "listen your mouth off" if you let her. Like Maki, Dan responds with the delight of a child whenever he encounters some new and interesting idea, and like Maki, Dan is no respecter of persons when it comes to seeking out teachers—whether it's the grocery bagger, a theoretical physicist, or an eleven-year-old nephew. Dan doesn't have to prove himself an expert on everything because he's secure enough in what he knows and what he doesn't know to engage other people as peers. As we were talking about this post today he said to me: "Tell them that if they're in a conversation where they are the expert, they ought to change the subject. Because what fun is that?"

When it comes to matters of faith, my father is like this too—open, curious, and humble. As a kid I believed his degree from Dallas Seminary made him an all-knowing expert on Jesus and the Bible and I bragged to my friends that he was a "Master of Divinity." But when my questions evolved into the kind without easy answers, Dad refused to respond with empty platitudes or weak apologetics, and instead simply took my hand, walked with me through all the pain and anger and fear that accompanies religious doubt, and said, "I don't know, Rachel. Let's find out together."

I've been fortunate, too, to have pastors who respect the people in their congregations as peers rather than sheep in perpetual need of guidance. In *Searching for Sunday*, I write about Brian Ward, who even as a youth pastor at a church that forbade women from teaching and leading was the first to tell me I had gifts for teaching and leading. Just a few months ago, I met with the rector of our new church who, though he sat in an office lined with heavy commentaries and some of his own published work, said, "We're so glad you're a part of this community. You have so much to teach us!"

And then there are the people with whom I've had the pleasure to converse and collaborate as a result of my writing, people with big brains and fancy degrees who have every right to shrug off the musings of a small-town author, but who instead engage me with enthusiasm, interest, and mutual respect . . . even if we don't always agree and even if they offer useful, critical feedback.

Richard Beck is one such person. The man is one of the smartest, most well-read people I know, armed with a PhD in experimental psychology and years of researching and writing. But Richard is also one of the kindest, most encouraging people I know. He's someone who engages in conversation in such a way that you walk away feeling both smarter and more confident, like you've both learned and contributed. Richard will recount with enthusiasm and specificity all the things he's learned from me, from other bloggers, from his students, from his wife Jana, from the Bible study he leads with fifty inmates at a maximum security prison each week. The world is his lab and he's a joyful, engaged observer, taking notes on it all.

The same could be said of credentialed people like Peter Enns,

Scot McKnight, and Walter Brueggemann, who have graciously offered their encouragement and insight to me through the years, and of course to the many credentialed women—Nadia Bolz-Weber, Christena Cleveland, Lauren Winner—who have done the same.

Brueggemann recently displayed his trademark humility in acknowledging: "Until the middle of the twentieth century Scripture study was essentially white males. And white males—including myself—always walked under the flag of objectivity. 'We are objective scholars!' Now what we are discovering in the presence of many other voices is that what we thought was objectivity is simply white-male experience."*

Even Walter Brueggemann . . . WALTER BRUEGGEMANN, PEOPLE . . . knows he doesn't know everything. Even Walter Brueggemann values the insights and perspectives of other people, especially those whose gender, race, or socioeconomic status means they see Scripture differently than he.

Whenever I catch myself looking down my nose at a first-time author with a new book or a blogger who has yet to learn the term *intersectionality*, I think about people like Walter B., my dad, Dan, Richard Beck, Maki, and Nadia, people who aren't so quick to let on how much they know, people who delight in learning from others, even from me. And I pray that I become more like them—curious, humble, awestruck, and kind. I pray I grow secure enough to listen and learn as a student of the world.

Originally posted on May 1, 2015.

---

* Trinity Church Boston, "A Year of the Bible: Brueggemann on Prophetic Tradition of the Hebrew Bible," YouTube, Trinity Church Boston, April 4, 2014, https://www.youtube.com/watch?v=WItkRx8xCoo.

When Twitter Was Fun: Remembering RHE's Online Work

A REFLECTION BY REV. EMMY KEGLER

Like so many people, I first met Rachel through Twitter, sometime around 2013. This was the Before Times: before COVID, before Musk, before "parasocial relationship" was a commonplace expression. Twitter was where a lot of people like me were gathering—voracious readers, theology nerds, religious types who didn't quite fit with their in-person versions of the church but weren't ready to give up on Jesus, not just yet. Everyone had their own reasons. Like thousands of other digital nomads, I was looking for iterations of Christianity that took the Bible seriously but not hatefully. Rachel was, too.

What I knew when I first started reading her blog was that she was earnest and thoughtful, endlessly kind, and willing to be a little sarcastic in the face of any foolishness that tried to prevent others from hearing the good news. I trusted her implicitly, an increasingly unusual act for me as I began to realize just how deep cruelty toward queer people like me still ran in God's supposed church. I knew Rachel to be a safe person, not because she had a rainbow emoji in her bio, but because her words and actions embodied compassionate protection.

For all these reasons I dared, one day in 2014, to push back on an assertion she was making. In the wake of an evangelical conference called "The Gospel, Homosexuality, and the Future of Marriage" where not a single LGBTQ+ person spoke (not even a celibate one!), Rachel tweeted that a more expansive alternative was available at the Gay Christian Network. I knew enough about GCN to know it included queer people who were celibate, which made me distrustful of the whole scheme; I was worried it would be another version of "all are welcome just kidding, only if you promise to be alone forever."

I openly said that I was anxious about walking into a space where celibacy was presented as an option, based on years of being told it was the only option. Rachel responded with grace, as she always did, but then added to it: She mentioned fellow bloggers (kids, that's what we used to call content creators) who could attest to it being a wide space for many ways of being faithful and queer. She didn't send me the video of her GCN talk from the year before, but rather sent me in the direction of other people who'd had the same worries I had. She didn't try to convince me. She didn't need to be right. She, as she so often did, let others' stories speak.

In the years after, in which I became lucky to call Rachel a supporter and a friend, I saw her do the same thing over and over again. She was a remarkable writer, thinker, theologian (even if she humbly resisted the label), and speaker, but she also continually passed the microphone and centered others' voices. What Rachel knew—by good instincts or wise discernment—was that the work of good news in a changing church did not begin or end with her. She was one thread in the rich quilt spreading backward and forward in time and place, stitching the body of Christ together. She knew when to get out of her own way and let the Spirit pick up the weaving.

Five Things You Don't Have to Leave Behind When You Leave Fundamentalism

. . . although sometimes you have to rediscover them.

1. LOVE FOR THE BIBLE

Fundamentalists often treat the Bible as a set of propositional statements designed to conform to modern, Enlightenment-influenced expectations. It is flattened out and simplified, used as a weapon against other people and a prop for pet political and theological positions. And so I see a lot of people leaving their Bibles behind on the bookshelf when they leave fundamentalism. This is understandable, but heartbreaking and unnecessary.

Leaving fundamentalism means learning to accept the Bible on its own terms, loving it for what it is, not what we want it to be. It has been such a joy to rediscover the Bible in a way that respects the cultures and contexts in which it was written and assembled. For example, the creation account of Genesis 1 is arguably more meaningful and more profound when we understand it, not as a modern science text, but as an ancient Near Eastern temple text that honors Elohim as ruler over creation. Similarly, it will not do to simply shrug off as irrelevant those sections of the epistles that seem to relegate women to certain roles. Instead, we have to get a better sense of their context and purpose, which in my experience has revealed them to be radically progressive and Christ-centered, meaning quite the opposite of what they are often said to mean. Of course, there are still those texts that trouble me profoundly—the genocidal conquests of Canaan, for example—but I've come to believe that wrestling with the Bible is better than ignoring it. To those willing to keep digging, the Bible will not disappoint.

2. CHURCH

This one has been a real struggle for me, and I know it's a struggle for others as well. One of the hardest things for a recovering fundamentalist to find is a community of faith where they feel safe yet challenged, included yet taught. I don't know about you, but sometimes it seems like cynicism follows me through every church door, nipping at my heels like a pesky dog as I find my place in the pews. If you're like me, you're a little bit scared, a little bit picky, a little bit tired. You're rolling your eyes about the American flag in the corner, or the special music, or the building fund, or the lack of diversity. Sometimes it's just easier to stay in bed. (Okay, often it's just easier to stay in bed.) But we have to be careful of applying the same fundamentalist attitude we're trying to leave behind to our thoughts and reactions to church. It's not about finding the perfect community; it's about helping to build the right community. . . . Now if someone could tell me exactly how to do that, I'd love to know.

3. DISCIPLINE

There's legalism, and then there's discipline. One is practiced out of guilt and fear; the other out of love. One sucks all the grace out of faith; the other nurtures grace and helps it grow. I know a lot of people who, after leaving a more legalistic church environment, go through a period of detox in which they avoid any sort of spiritual discipline—prayer, fasting, tithing, etc.—altogether, as these things had always been used as measures by which Christians judged one another. This detox period is understandable and perhaps even necessary. But it can be helpful to reintroduce these disciplines into your life when you're ready, when they can be practiced out of love and commitment to Christ rather than guilt.

4. FRIENDSHIPS

It can be tricky navigating relationships with old friends after you've left fundamentalism. Some will inevitably be changed; others will be lost. Often, in an effort to get a new start, folks will cut off all their connections to a certain faith community. In some extreme cases, this may actually be the only healthy thing to do. But most of the time, it's worth putting in the extra effort to maintain relationships with friends and family with whom you disagree. This may mean some uncomfortable moments over coffee or at the dinner table, but as much as it depends on you, look to Christ as your example and try to live peaceably with the people around you, even when they start yelling about Barack Obama being the anti-Christ.

5. HOLINESS

This is a scary word because it can be easily manipulated and lorded over people to require submission and conformity. But I've known many people to leave fundamentalism only to make a string of bad choices that alienate them from God, themselves, and other people. Folks who had once been forbidden from drinking any alcohol at all find themselves getting drunk every weekend. Those who had once been forced to find their identity in their virginity end up swinging the opposite direction by growing reckless with their sexuality. Those who had once been made to feel guilty for each purchase end up succumbing to materialism. Perhaps the hardest part of being released from prison is knowing what to do with your freedom. But leaving fundamentalism doesn't mean leaving behind your self-respect or your commitment to imitating Christ. It means pursuing holiness out of love, not fear or guilt.

Originally posted on November 28, 2012.

Dear Pastors—Tell Us the Truth

Dear Pastors,

Tell us the truth.

Tell us the truth when you don't know the answers to our questions, and your humility will set the example as we seek them out together.

Tell us the truth about your doubts, and we will feel safe sharing our own.

Tell us the truth when you get tired, when the yoke grows too heavy and the hill too steep to climb, and we will learn to carry one another's burdens because we started with yours.

Tell us the truth when you are sad, and we too will stop pretending.

Tell us the truth when your studies lead you to new ideas that might stretch our faith and make us uncomfortable, and those of us who stick around will never forget that you trusted us with a challenge.

Tell us the truth when your position is controversial, and we will grow braver along with you.

Tell us the truth when you need to spend time on your marriage, and we will remember to prioritize ours.

Tell us the truth when you fail, and we will stop expecting perfection.

Tell us the truth when you think that our old ways of doing things need to change, and though we may push back, the conversation will force us to examine why we do what we do and perhaps inspire something even greater.

Tell us the truth when you fall short, and we will drop our measuring sticks.

Tell us the truth when all that's left is hope, and we start digging for it.

Tell us the truth when the world requires radical grace, and we will generate it.

Tell us the truth even if it's surprising, disappointing, painful, joyous, unexpected, unplanned, and unresolved, and we will learn that this is what it means to be people of faith.

Tell us the truth and you won't be the only one set free.

Love,
The Congregation

Originally posted on February 16, 2011.

Bringing Healing, Not a Cure
A REFLECTION BY TANYA MARLOW

If you've grown up as a Christian with clear, safe lines of good and bad, doubt is a terrifying thing. It's not simply that one aspect of your life is wobbling, like waning enthusiasm for cello practice or a bad time with your boss; it is black lava winding its way through your brain, it's a shaking of your soul like an ongoing earthquake, it's a dark smoke-plume of loneliness cutting you off from friends, community, yourself, and God. If you're a Christian leader with doubt, it is a double whammy: You have lost the lenses through which you saw the world, so everything is a blurry mess, yet people keep asking you for directions and you are supposed to help them.

I had been a nonordained Christian leader for a decade, teaching people how to interpret and preach the Bible, when the doubt came for me. An underlying autoimmune disease flared up after I gave birth, and I became bed-bound, as helpless as the baby I was trying to care for. All the theological training and clean intellectual answers I had were utterly inadequate, and from my heart came a roar of pain: "If you are a good God, why are you treating me like this?" Once that big question emerged, thousands followed—about the fairness of hell, methods of interpreting the Bible, and why so many church leaders seemed such a bad advert for Christ. In my bed, cut off from church and society, I found Rachel's Twitter and blog. Her blog post "Holy Week for Doubters" described the loneliness of doubting while being surrounded by believers who were so cheerful—so sure of everything. I wept because I was seen, and because it held out hope.

What I loved about her was that her priority for others wasn't necessarily a return to faith but finding healing, however that came (which she defined differently from "curing," where everything was magically fixed). She was a second John the Baptist, who had little patience for hypocritical Christian leaders but whose faith wobbled as he questioned whether Jesus was the Messiah, and who introduced others to Christ. She didn't merely protest the church; she examined her own soul with humility and created safe havens for those who had been crushed by the church.

Her blog post "Dear Pastors—Tell Us the Truth" is a plea to seemingly Teflon-coated, unshakable pastors. "Tell us the truth when you are sad, and we too will stop pretending," she wrote. "Tell us the truth when you fail, and we will stop expecting perfection." Everything Rachel listed in her request for other leaders was what she modeled herself. She was a truth-telling leader, a prophet, pastor, and healer: questioning and listening, bold yet vulnerable, intellectual but humble. A decade on, still chronically ill, I owe her a debt of thanks for inviting me into a deeper faith with space for mystery, showing me a better way to lead, and for bringing healing, not a cure.

Let's Build Bigger Banquet Tables

To the church in North America,*

I write to you as one of your own at a time when many in my generation have abandoned you. As the church in the developing world continues to grow, the church in North America is in decline. Some are predicting our imminent demise, while others foresee a glorious rebirth. Most seem to think that we're in the midst of an identity crisis, one that will determine the shape and direction of the North American church for many years to come.

According to the statistics, we are a people of (relative) wealth and (relative) generosity. We control most of the world's wealth and we give much of it away. Though we struggle with materialism, we value charity.

But are we people of the Kingdom?

That is the question at the heart of this crisis, and as we struggle together to answer it, I am convinced that what we don't need is bigger buildings or fancier sound equipment, better pastors or more parishioners, newer ministries or deeper pockets.

---

* This post was Rachel's contribution to the online Eighth Letter Project, which invited participants to compose letters to the North American Church, in the same spirit as John's seven letters to various churches in the Book of Revelation. The project is no longer available online.

What we need is bigger banquet tables.

Jesus loved banquets. He performed his first miracle at a wedding reception in Canaan and spent so much time feasting with tax collectors and prostitutes that the religious called him a glutton. Jesus was never too busy to stop and eat—sharing fish and bread with five thousand fans, a traditional Jewish supper with his closest disciples, and breakfast with the friend who denied him three times. When Jesus returns, he plans to throw a great banquet in honor of his bride, the Church. How fitting that in his absence, we remember him by eating together.

Jesus often compared his Kingdom to a great banquet that includes people from every tribe, tongue, and nation reclining at a single table. He made it clear that this banquet table is open to all, but that the rich and powerful will likely decline his invitation because they are just too busy to stop, slow down, and feast with their neighbors. So instead, Jesus invites "all who look like they need a square meal, all the misfits and homeless and down-and-out you can lay your hands on" so that his house will be full [Luke 14:21, MSG].

I guess this is why Jesus tells us to do the same: "The next time you put on a dinner, don't just invite your friends and family and rich neighbors, the kind of people who will return the favor. Invite some people who never get invited out, the misfits from the wrong side of the tracks. You'll be—and experience—a blessing. They won't be able to return the favor, but the favor will be returned—oh, how it will be returned!—at the resurrection of God's people" [Luke 14:12–13, MSG].

I suspect that Jesus used all of this delicious imagery because he knew that there is a difference between feeding people and dining with people.

Feeding people means keeping the hungry at arm's length.

It means sending checks now and then, making Thanksgiving baskets once a year, preaching about justice, and launching new ministries . . . all while sitting comfortably at the head of a tiny table, dropping scraps from our abundance to the floor. Americans are good at feeding people.

But dining with people is an entirely different matter. Dining together means sitting next to one another and brushing arms, passing the bread basket and sharing the artichoke dip. It means double-dipping and spilling drinks, laughing together and crying together, exchanging stories, ideas, recipes, and dreams. According to Jesus, it means leaving the seat at the head of the table ceremoniously empty so that all are guests of honor and all are hosts. Dining together isn't charity; it's friendship.

For the church in North America to grow in a good way, we need to break down this distinction between those who serve and those who are served. The abundance must truly be shared. At the local level, this may mean hosting literal banquets, complete with Jesus-style invitation lists. At the global level, it may mean sacrificing some of our own comforts so that when we care for our far-away neighbors we can still feel their presence beside us at the table. In every case, it means slowing down long enough to savor both the food and the company.

So let's build bigger banquet tables.

Let's eat fruit that is in season and drink coffee that is fairly traded so that Latin farmers can join us at the table with their heads held high. Let's share the reputation of Jesus and dine with those who the religious love to hate—gays and lesbians, divorcees, single moms, junkies, dreamers, and doubters. Let's squeeze in a little tighter to make enough room for people of all political persuasions, all religious backgrounds, all ethnicities, and all denominations. Let's eat a little less so that everyone has enough and let's linger a little longer so that everyone gets a chance to share what's on their mind. Let's invite "all who look like they need a square meal, all the misfits and homeless and down-and-out you can lay your hands on, and bring them here."

Originally posted on August 30, 2010.

PART FOUR

ALL RIGHT, THEN, I'LL GO TO HELL

Essays on Gender and Sexuality

"All Right, Then, I'll Go to Hell"

If I had to pick a favorite American writer, it would be Mark Twain, and if I had to pick a favorite scene from an American novel, it would be the one where his unlikely hero, Huckleberry Finn, accepts his fate in hell.

It's the moral climax of *Adventures of Huckleberry Finn*. The duke and dauphin have betrayed Jim and sold him to the Phelpses "for forty dirty dollars," and the Phelpses have locked Jim in their shed, where he awaits his return to his rightful owner for a two-hundred-dollar reward. Huck goes back to the raft to figure out what to do next, and there he gets to thinking about the lessons he learned in Sunday school about what happens to people like him who assist runaway slaves.

"*People that acts as I'd been acting about [Jim],*" he'd been told, "*goes to everlasting fire.*"

(After all, the Bible is clear: "Slaves obey your earthly masters with respect and fear"—Ephesians 6:5.)

Huck feels genuine conviction regarding his sin and, fearful of his certain fate in hell unless he changes course, he decides to write a letter to Jim's owner, Miss Watson, to tell her where Jim can be found, and at first, he feels this is the right choice. But then, Huck sits for a moment with the letter. His thoughts turn toward Jim "before me, all the time; in the day, and in the night-time."

He considers all of Jim's kindnesses and his care along with their shared adventures.

"It was a close place," according to Huck. He takes up the letter he had written, turning Jim in as a runaway slave, "and held it in my hand. I was a trembling, because I'd got to decide, forever, betwixt two things, and I knowed it. I studied a minute, sort of holding my breath, and then says to myself: 'All right, then, I'll go to hell'—and tore it up."

It is a moment of true moral courage, complicated though it is by troubling ingrained cultural assumptions. (Later, Huck can only make sense of Jim's kindness to him and Tom Sawyer by concluding he must be "white on the inside," a comment that reveals Twain's gift for creating characters that both critique yet fully inhabit their cultural contexts.)

I often think about Huck's resolution when I am told by religious leaders that "the Bible is clear" on this or that, and that I've got to stop listening to those gut feelings that tell me maybe we've gotten a few things wrong, that maybe there's more to the story than we're ready to see.

"Your feelings don't matter," they say.

"Your feelings cannot be trusted," they say.

"Once you start listening to your feelings, over and beyond the plain meaning of Scripture, it's a slippery slope to hell," they say.

A part of me agrees. I want to be faithful to the inspired words of the Bible, not bend them to fit my own desires and whims. Being a person of faith means trusting God's revelation, even when the path it reveals is not comfortable.

But another part of me worries that a religious culture that asks its followers to silence their conscience is just the kind of religious culture that produces two-hundred-dollar rewards for runaway slaves. The Bible has been "clear" before, after all—in support of a flat and stationary earth, in support of wiping out entire people groups, in support of manifest destiny, in support of Indian removal, in support of anti-Semitism, in support of slavery, in support of "separate but equal," in support of constitutional amendments banning interracial marriage.*

In hindsight, it all seems so foolish, such an obvious abuse of Scripture.

. . . But at the time?

Sometimes true faithfulness requires something of a betrayal.

A few months ago, I was invited to serve communion at a church in San Diego that included quite a few LGBTQ+ Christians in its membership. A lot of things happened in that service that would make some of the leaders in my evangelical religious community very angry: a woman serving the bread and the wine, a lesbian couple partaking of the elements with their baby daughter in tow, a gay man embracing me in a big bear hug and telling me that it was the first time in twenty years he felt worthy to come to the Table.

In that moment—the one with the big bear hug—I knew what my Sunday school teachers would say. They would say that this man was most certainly *not* worthy to come to the Table, that I was most certainly *not* worthy to serve, and that daring to participate in this endeavor would surely take me one step closer to "everlasting fire."

"The body of Christ, broken for you," I said anyway.

"The blood of Christ, shed for you," I said anyway.

"The body of Christ, broken for you," he said anyway.

"The blood of Christ, shed for you," he said anyway.

As we embraced, I knew in a way that I cannot put into words that sharing communion with this man was the right thing to do,

---

* "in support of slavery," see Rachel Held Evans, "Is Abolition 'Biblical'?," Rachel Held Evans Blog, February 28, 2013, https://rachelheldevans.com/blog/is-abolition-biblical.

that it was an act of bravery and grace for both of us—together unworthy, together worthy, brother and sister, in the mystery of the Eucharist.

So when the thought of my Sunday school teachers' disapproval crossed my mind, the only words to surface to my lips were, "*All right, then, I'll go to hell.*"

Perhaps grace, like the Bible, was never meant to be "sivilized" anyway.

Originally posted on May 23, 2012.

Rachel Goes to Hell

A REFLECTION BY BRIAN D. McLAREN

In 2013, I was finishing up my book *We Make the Road by Walking*, and I had a problem. I grew up evangelical, and my early books had been written for "my people," an evangelical audience. But with each book, I lost more of that audience. On their way out the door, quite a few of them consigned me to "the outer darkness where there is weeping and gnashing of teeth."

Meanwhile, I was gaining new readers, the de-churched and unchurched: post- and ex-evangelicals, mainline Protestants and progressive Catholics, and spiritual but not religious folks. As I listened deeply to their questions and tried to respond, I realized that I was becoming like a refugee who was immersed in a new culture: I was losing my native fluency in speaking, writing, and thinking evangelical.

That would have been fine, except for one thing: I still cared about evangelicals. I hoped to keep lines of communication open for at least a little longer.

I needed someone who could offer me suggestions for keeping my manuscript as evangelical-friendly as possible. This "beta reader" would need to (a) retain that fluency in "speaking evangelical" and (b) understand what I was trying to do in my book to offer constructive feedback.

Of course I thought of Rachel. I asked her for feedback on my manuscript, and she generously responded.

About a year earlier, Rachel had written one of her most daring blog posts: "All Right, Then, I'll Go to Hell."

By telling the story of Huck's moral dilemma next to a personal story of her own moral dilemma, Rachel transcended normal religious discourse that was based on exegeting verses, pitting verses against each other, debating definitions, resorting to the Greek and Hebrew, applying rules of hermeneutical logic, and ultimately, trying to corner people into conclusions they could not escape (i.e., "evidence that demands a verdict").

By transcending conventional religious discourse, Rachel was following the example of Jesus himself, who frequently told fictional stories—in rapid succession—to lift people to a higher and deeper level of discourse. By abducting them into the imaginative realm of storytelling, he gave them permission to picture themselves in a real-life situation: a parent being asked by a hungry child for bread; a father with two beloved sons, each wayward in his own way; a person robbed and beaten and lying at the roadside; a farmer whose ox has fallen into a ditch on the Sabbath day.

Jesus invited his hearers to take their deepest moral intuitions seriously, even if doing so meant they would challenge conventional notions and longstanding biblical interpretations. Rachel followed his example.

Rachel's blog post was especially subversive and creative for this reason: If hellfire is the "trump card" used by religious conservatives (in Mark Twain's time and our own) to keep people in bondage to cruel biblical interpretations and religious practices, Rachel dared to trump the trump card. She cast out the fear of hell with love for neighbor. That took courage. And it took a good bit of cleverness too.

Rachel had both. So may we.

Responding to Homophobia in the Christian Community

Recently, Thabiti Anyabwile wrote a post entitled "The Importance of Your Gag Reflex When Discussing Homosexuality and 'Gay Marriage,'" which was posted on his Gospel Coalition–hosted blog.*

I debated whether to engage a post that is just as disturbing as the title suggests, but after speaking with an editor and several writers at the Gospel Coalition, as well as some of my gay and lesbian friends, I've decided it's important to offer an alternative to the attitude presented in this post and, perhaps more importantly, to explore/discuss how Christians ought to respond when we encounter homophobia in our own faith communities.

Now let me be clear: I believe the post exhibits homophobia, not because of the author's conservative position on same-sex marriage, and not because the author intended to be hateful, but because the post employs degrading, fear-based language to dehumanize gay and lesbian people.

---

* Thabiti Anyabwile, "The Importance of Your Gag Reflex When Discussing Homosexuality and 'Gay Marriage,'" TGC: The Gospel Coalition, August 19, 2013, https://www.thegospelcoalition.org/blogs/thabiti-anyabwile/the-importance-of-your-gag-reflex-when-discussing-homosexuality-and-gay-marriage/.

Responding to New Zealand's recent legalization of gay marriage, Anyabwile laments the fact that pro-gay-marriage advocates have effectively argued their case by appealing to civil rights and by emphasizing loving, committed relationships between gay and lesbian people. Confessing with some agitation that he too found one gay advocate to be "kind, winsome, insightful and reasonable," Anyabwile concludes that the best way to turn the tide back against gay marriage is to "return the discussion to sexual behavior in all its yuckiest gag-inducing truth."

Christians should indulge their "gag reflexes," he says, and "return to the yuck factor" when they think and talk about gay and lesbian people, particularly in the context of gay marriage.

He then proceeds to graphically describe gay sex before telling the reader: "That sense of moral outrage you're now likely feeling . . . that gut-wrenching, jaw-clenching, hand-over-your-mouth, 'I feel dirty' moral outrage is the gag reflex. Your moral sensibilities have been provoked—and rightly so."

He concludes: "That reflex triggered by an accurate description of homosexual behavior will be the beginning of the recovery of moral sense and sensibility when it comes to the so-called 'gay marriage' debate."

Obviously, the post fails miserably in the logic department by arguing that because some people have a "gag reflex" when they think about gay sex, then gay sex must therefore be immoral. Let's think about this. A person might get a bit squirmy at the thought of his parents having sex, but it does not then follow that his parents' sex is inherently immoral. Furthermore, there are heterosexual acts that can be considered immoral—adultery, for example—but that might not induce Anyabwile's handy "gag reflex." (Not to mention the fact that much of what he describes as "gay sex" happens in heterosexual sex as well and that any sort of sex, when described purely biologically, can sound kinda gross;

let's face it.) So positioning "icky" as the barometer for morality is just poor argumentation. If, as Anyabwile suggests, this is really the best argument those opposed to gay marriage have, then the movement is in serious trouble.

But far more serious than Anyabwile's logical failings is the failure of this post to extend any sort of grace or dignity to the LGBTQ+ people in question. Instead, he invites those who may already have hostile feelings toward gay and lesbian people to indulge their revulsion and anger.

Concerned that the civility and decorum exhibited by many LGBTQ+ rights advocates might make their arguments more persuasive, Anyabwile suggests that the key to "winning" the same-sex marriage debate is to speak more graphically about gay sex in order to induce the "gag reflex." When discussing homosexuality, Christians should seek to create "gut-wrenching, jaw-clenching, hand-over-your-mouth, 'I feel dirty,' moral outrage" regarding gay and lesbian people seeking to get married.

This is why the post is so damaging and potentially dangerous. Sensing that the consideration of full personhood might sway the gay marriage debate toward legalization, he suggests we should deliberately move away from speaking of gay and lesbian people as multidimensional human beings and instead reduce them to sex acts in order to make others more repulsed by them. It is an unabashed attempt to single out, stigmatize, and ostracize an entire group of people, which is the exact opposite of what the gospel calls us to do. Anyabwile frequently uses terms like "dirty," "yucky," "repulsive," "disgusting," and "icky" to describe fellow human beings, created in the image of God, and this is unacceptable.

Can you imagine Jesus reducing those with leprosy to their disease? Or the bleeding woman to her "impurity"? Can you imagine Philip reducing the Ethiopian eunuch to his anatomy or Peter the gentile Christians to the food they ate? Can you imagine God reducing us to our sin?

And what's with this idea that our impulses necessarily lead us to truth? Are we justified in indulging our gag reflex when we encounter people who are sick, or homeless, or different from us? What about our violent reflexes? Or our indulgent reflexes? Or our racist reflexes? Our greedy reflexes?

Reflex doesn't make right. And anyone who believes in the pervasiveness of sin within our hearts should agree.*

RESPONDING TO HOMOPHOBIA . . .

Not everyone who opposes same-sex marriage is homophobic, of course. But I do come across what can only be described as homophobia and I suspect I am not alone. I suspect you too may have been in the presence of Christians cracking crude jokes about gay and lesbian people or muttering under their breath about a "disgusting" gay co-worker. Or perhaps you've been in a Bible study where it is suggested that all gay people are pedophiles or watched as kids who bully effeminate classmates are given a free pass.

(How easy it is to forget that there are gay people sitting in the pews of our churches. This is not an "us-vs.-them" thing; this is an "us" thing, a humanity thing. Many gay people are Christians, and many Christians have children, parents, friends, and loved ones who are gay.)

So how should we respond when fellow Christians engage in name-calling, bullying, lying, or hateful attitudes like these?

---

* In the original post, Rachel included this aside: "For those eager to defend Anyabwile, I recommend reading this post from Richard Beck (https://experimentaltheology.blogspot.com/2013/08/on-love-and-yuck-factor.html) in which he anticipates such defenses and responds well to them. Please also consider reading Beck's book, *Unclean*, which discusses how disgust is a dehumanizing emotion."

Four things come to mind:

1. Call it out.

Ignorance and hateful attitudes thrive when they are normalized and accepted without pushback. Your friends may just assume you agree with them when you don't speak up about their homophobia. On more than one occasion, I've heard Dan calmly respond to a crude homophobic joke with something simple like, "Hey, man. That's not funny. You're talking about real people here. Please don't say that kind of stuff around me." It's awkward for about ten seconds. But it's better than replaying that conversation over and over and wishing you had said something. And it sends the signal that not everyone is okay with crude jokes or ugly language at the expense of gay and lesbian people. More often than not, there will be someone else in the group who is relieved you said something and may even offer support. And sometimes, there will be someone in the group who is relieved to know he or she is not also hated or despised by you. Try thinking ahead of time about a line or two you can use in situations like these so you're ready.

In the case of this article, it would be appropriate to leave a comment saying you do not accept gay and lesbian people being spoken of in these terms, especially by those waving the banner of the "gospel," or by urging editors at the Gospel Coalition to remove the post entirely. Or, if the article is shared by your friends, speak up. It would be especially helpful if more conservative folks would push back a bit. Remember that silence in this regard can often communicate approval.

2. Be informed.

Hate grows in the soil of ignorance, and when it comes to sexuality, there's a lot of ignorance to go around. I can't tell you how many times I've heard a well-intentioned Christian say something about how children in gay families suffer (this is not true) or how all gay people are pedophiles (also not true).* We can debate the merits of same-sex marriage, certainly, but let's do it based on facts, not myths. And we can discuss how the Bible and Christian tradition factor into things as well, but let's be informed about our convictions.

3. Get to know some LGBTQ+ people and read their perspectives on things.

One of my gay friends said that Anyabwile's article was the most overtly hateful thing he has read about homosexuality from a Christian blog. My guess is Anyabwile probably didn't intend his post to be hateful, but had he taken a minute to imagine how it would read to a gay or lesbian teen, for example, he might have chosen his words more carefully.

Deliberately listening to and considering the perspectives of LGBTQ+ people can make a huge difference in how we engage conversations around marriage, the Bible, and church. You will learn how phrases like "the gay lifestyle" and "love the sinner, hate the sin" sound to those most impacted by them, and your stereotypes will be shattered. (You will also learn why Anyabwile's statement that "'gay' and 'homosexual' are polite terms for an ugly practice" is wrong. Those terms generally refer to sexual orientation.)

If you haven't already, be sure to check out *Torn: Rescuing Christians from the Gays-vs.-Christians Debate* by Justin Lee, my favorite book on the topic from a gay Christian's perspective. For a more

---

* Evelyn Schlatter and Robert Steinback, "10 Anti-Gay Myths Debunked," SPLC: Southern Poverty Law Center, February 27, 2011, https://www.splcenter.org/fighting-hate/intelligence-report/2011/10-anti-gay-myths-debunked.

conservative viewpoint, you might like Wesley Hill's *Washed and Waiting*. I'd also recommend *Does Jesus Really Love Me?* by Jeff Chu.

4. Preach and live the gospel.

Of course, the very best thing we can do in response to any sort of fear or hate or stigmatization is to preach the gospel like crazy, to spread the good news that, through Christ, God is making all things new and the Kingdom of Heaven is open to all who long for it.

For those who are weary and burdened by religious rules and expectations, Jesus promises rest. For those who hunger for righteousness, Jesus promises satisfaction. For those who are thirsty for refreshing, life-giving truth, Jesus promises streams of living water. For those who have been marginalized and cast aside, Jesus promises a banquet and a place of high honor. For those who long for reconciliation and forgiveness of sins, Jesus promises mercy and grace. For those deemed "unclean," Jesus promises embrace. For those who long for communion, there is bread and wine. And for those who long to be baptized, there is water.

The good news is that we aren't welcomed into God's family based on our merits or our skills. We aren't welcomed based on which theological beliefs we can check off a list or how well we fit the religious mold. You don't have to be straight to be part of this family. You don't have to be a Republican or a Democrat or an American. You don't have to be rich. You don't have to pray just the right words or know all the right answers. You don't have to be sinless. You don't have to have it all figured out. You just have to come. It's an adoption, not an interview.

The good news is that God doesn't reduce us the way we reduce one another. God does not see dirty people and clean people, good people and bad people. God sees beloved people. And nothing can separate us from that. Nothing.

Now be warned: Some people find this gospel offensive. They don't like the idea of sharing a table with all these undeserving, messed-up, "icky" people. They don't like the idea of this grace thing getting out of hand. But for the suffering, for the hurting, and for the ones who have nothing left to lose, this is very good news.

So preach it, and if you dare, live it.

Originally posted on August 23, 2013.

She Held Up a Lantern Ahead of Me
A REFLECTION BY JEN HATMAKER

Back then, I had twenty blogs bookmarked, alerts set so as not to miss a single new post from the thought leaders I was privately listening to. For me, it was a season of reading, watching, secretly examining all the comment sections, listening to forbidden podcasts with AirPods, clicking links, and following hashtags.

But if I had to pick one voice, the primary influence on my then-evangelical life that led me into a fully affirming position for my LGBTQ+ neighbors, it was Rachel Held Evans.

My community knows me *now*—an outspoken ally practically draped in glitter at this point. But I want to take you back to 2013 or so, when my head and heart were misaligned, and my evangelical edges were fraying into a spiritual crisis. I was desperate to find a faithful, thoughtful hermeneutic that made sense of the Spirit I knew, one that didn't leave the LGBTQ+ community exiled or begging for crumbs. I couldn't bear the cognitive dissonance anymore.

Rachel was this brilliant thinker with a backbone of steel and a heart of gold. I'd never encountered anyone like her and haven't since. She patiently and thoroughly examined every verse, every context, every biblical argument, every interpretation. She led her community with care and courage, but she would *go to the mat* to defend the marginalized communities she loved. The theology bros absolutely hated her, primarily because they couldn't best her.

Meanwhile, evangelical darling Jen Hatmaker was listening, listening, privately listening. Finally, I sent the barest DM: "Hello. I am Jen. How is . . . the weather?" or some nonsense. She took the obvious bait and let me into her orbit. As long as I live, I'll never get over the patience she showed me as I fumbled my way through womanist interpretations, sexual and biological science, original biblical language, historical context, all information she diligently curated.

Rachel held open a door for my questions and ignorance, making room for my evolution. She held generous assumptions for those of us mangling our way through the early stages of forbidden curiosity while never once allowing her space to become unsafe for LGBTQ+ folks, the hardest needle to thread. Her brilliant mind and pastor's heart paved a way not around the Bible but straight through it to an affirming position with a clear conscience.

I was stumbling through the dark, and she held up a lantern ahead of me, lighting the way. And when I finally got there, and my evangelical world crumbled, it was Rachel who mentored me through the storm. She told me to stand in the raging wind, plant my feet, and hold steady. She reminded me that no one suffers more than our LGBTQ+ beloveds at the hands of unaffirming theology. In one of her many emails, she wrote: "This work is hard. Stay faithful." Those words now stand as artwork in my home.

For every person who has responded to my leadership in their life toward spiritual evolution, know there was a Rachel in mine first.

Her singular gift and relentless commitment to justice meant so much to me, I hardly know how to describe it. Her mentorship in my life included dismantling religious patriarchy, Christian nationalism, gender limitations, selective biblical obedience. She modeled fearlessness while never taking herself too seriously. She seemed immune to bullying. Her intelligence was ferocious.

But she was somehow also funny; I once took her tiny newborn daughter straight out of her arms at Evolving Faith and just . . . left. She tweeted: "Jen Hatmaker has taken my baby and I may never see them again." (This felt justified since this baby was practically born on my podcast. I interviewed Rach while she was *having contractions one minute apart*.)

Rachel was younger than me, but I looked up to her like a wise mentor. She led me into better theology, better leadership. Throughout it all, she was a true friend. Loyal and good, supportive and patient. When I think about how much we need her voice today, I could weep.

I sit here in utter gratitude that I shared planet space with Rachel Held Evans. She quite literally changed my life. Her lantern was so bright, and it continues to burn. Her legacy is great. Well done, good and faithful servant. The work was hard, and you were faithful. You made the church and the world safer for my own daughter and all the sons and daughters.

Thank you. I miss you.

The False Gospel of Gender Binaries

Not long ago I had the pleasure of working with Adrian, a visual artist with a quick wit, easygoing spirit, and creative eye.* After an afternoon of laughter and collaboration, Adrian opened up about what it's been like working with other religious people, particularly evangelicals.

"I'm intersex," Adrian said, with a shrug of the shoulders. "Evangelicals don't have a category for me, so there's no real place for me in their church."†

Adrian's words hurt my heart, but I knew they were true. Over the past two years, I've heard similar sentiments expressed by transgender Christians (people whose gender identities differ from what is associated with the sex they were assigned at birth), and of course by gay, lesbian, and bisexual Christians. Often I hear of childhoods plagued by bullying, exclusion, depression, and fear, all made worse when the churches that were supposed to love and care for them rejected them because they did not fit into rigid gender binaries.

---

* Rachel changed the name to protect this individual's privacy.
† Rachel included this note: "Intersex is a term used for a variety of conditions in which a person is born with a reproductive or sexual anatomy that doesn't seem to fit the typical definitions of female or male. Learn more here: https://isna.org/faq/what_is_intersex/."

"God made male and female," culture warriors like to thunder. "Any deviation from traditional gender and sexuality norms represents a serious sin and threat to the gospel."*

This claim is often punctuated by advocacy for rigid, hierarchal gender roles based on stereotypes in which all men are described as being "wired" one way (as providers, leaders, and fighters), and all women are described as being "wired" another way (as followers, nurturers, and homemakers).

Even the Vatican reinforced this message this week in an international forum on marriage where "complementarity between man and woman in marriage" was described by Pope Francis as "the root of marriage and family."†

While most people indeed have a heterosexual orientation and identify with a single gender that was assigned to them at birth, it has become increasingly clear that this is not the case for everyone, that gender and sexuality might better be understood as manifesting themselves along continuums, with male/female, masculine/feminine, heterosexual/homosexual existing at the poles but with a variety of identities, orientations, and expressions in between.‡ Science and psychology continue to confirm this as a reality, with the American Psychological Association no longer characterizing variations in sexual orientation and gender identity as disorders, only warning that stigmatization based on them can negatively affect mental health.

---

* Rachel included this note: "And because someone is bound to bring it up, please read Matthew 19 in context. As you will see, Jesus is responding to a question about divorce, not about gender binaries."

† Adam Withnall, "Pope Francis Declares Union Between Man and Woman 'At Root of Marriage' in a Blow to Gay Rights," *Independent*, November 18, 2014, https://www.independent.co.uk/news/world/europe/pope-francis-declares-union-between-man-and-woman-at-root-of-marriage-in-blow-to-gay-rights-9867561.html.

‡ Sam Killermann, "Breaking Through the Binary: Gender Explained Using Continuums," IPM: It's Pronounced Metrosexual, accessed April 19, 2025, https://www.itspronouncedmetrosexual.com/2011/11/breaking-through-the-binary-gender-explained-using-continuums/.

People do not typically choose their sexual orientations or gender identities the way one might choose to wear a watch or to take cream in their coffee. Most of my gay and lesbian friends recall feeling different from a young age, frightened at the prospect of being disowned from their families and cast out of their churches because of something they simply could not change. Efforts intended to reverse sexual orientation through prayer and counseling, once popular within evangelicalism, have proven not only ineffective, but destructive, leading to multiple apologies from former leaders of those movements.* Sadly, for many LGBTQ+ Christians, those apologies came too late, and the messages they received through "conversion therapy" led them into marriages based on secrets, or, tragically, to suicide.†

Nearly all of us would fail to conform to the generalizations made by the most strident complementarians, but intersex people like Adrian, and LGBTQ+ people like those you might meet at the Gay Christian Network, are truly in the minority. And unfortunately, they are consistently subjected to stigmatization and marginalization by religious people who refuse to share bathrooms with them,‡ who disassociate with churches that welcome them,§ who mock and ridicule them and compare them to

---

* Maya Rhodan, "9 Ex-Leaders of the Gay Conversion Therapy Movement Apologize," *TIME*, July 31, 2014, https://time.com/3065495/9-ex-leaders-of-the-gay-conversion-therapy-movement-apologize/.
† Tim Rymel, "I'm a Gay Man Who Married a Straight Woman," The Good Men Project, November 9, 2014, https://goodmenproject.com/featured-content/im-gay-man-married-a-straight-women-try/.
‡ Denny Burk, "The Transgender Revolution Marches Forward," Denny Burk Blog, January 2, 2014, https://www.dennyburk.com/the-transgender-revolution-marches-forward/.
§ Michael Gryboski, "Southern Baptist Convention Cuts Ties with California Church over Pro-Gay Marriage Stance," *Christian Post*, September 25, 2014, https://www.christianpost.com/news/southern-baptist-convention-cuts-ties-with-california-church-over-pro-gay-marriage-stance-127029/.

pedophiles and idolaters,* and who withhold money from charities that employ them.† Christians are told that sharing civil liberties with LGBTQ+ people constitutes religious persecution, that sexual minorities should induce a "gag reflex,"‡ and that defending gender binaries is as essential as defending the gospel itself.

But what sort of gospel is only good news for the majority? What sort of gospel leaves people behind just because they are different?

The gospel of Jesus Christ is not so fragile as to be unpinned by the reality that variations in gender and sexuality exist, nor is it so narrow as to only be good news for people who look and live like Ward and June Cleaver. This glorification of gender binaries has become a dangerous idol in the Christian community, for it conflates cultural norms with Christian morality and elevates an ideal over actual people.

No doubt some will argue that we cannot build our theologies around "exceptions" like Adrian. When I bring up intersex people in conversations about gender and sexuality, I am typically met with blank stares, shrugged shoulders, and dismissive platitudes about how most people fit neatly into male and female categories and generalities, so we shouldn't worry about the outliers.

But if Jesus started with the outliers, why shouldn't we?

If Jesus started with the poor, the sick, the marginalized, and the minorities, then why would we dismiss them as irrelevant to our theology of gender and sexuality?

I can't help but think of the Ethiopian eunuch from Acts 8. He

---

* Andrew Wilson, "The Case for Idolatry: Why Evangelical Christians Can Worship Idols," *Think*, November 12, 2014, https://thinktheology.co.uk/blog/article/the_case_for_idolatry_why_evangelical_christians_can_worship_idols.

† Here, Rachel linked to her own posts about the World Vision controversy, previously covered in this book.

‡ See "Responding to Homophobia in the Christian Community" in this book.

was a sexual and ethnic minority, and it was considered "unbiblical" for him to even enter the assembly of God, much less be baptized (Leviticus 21:20; Deuteronomy 23:1). But when the eunuch learned about the gospel through his reading of Isaiah and the witness of Philip, his response is profound: *"Look! There is water! What is to prevent me from being baptized?"*

Philip could easily have responded by quoting Bible verses and appealing to tradition. He could have dismissed the eunuch as an anomaly, not worth the time and effort to fight for his inclusion in this new family of God. But instead, Philip baptized the eunuch in the first body of water the two could find. He remembered that what makes the gospel offensive isn't who it keeps out, but who it lets in . . . *starting with you and me.*

Now, I'm not suggesting we abandon conversations about the Bible and sexual ethics, nor am I interested in promoting a "genderless society" (as some have bizarrely claimed, somehow supposing that acknowledging the existence of gray requires dismissing the existence of black and white). I am suggesting, however, that Jesus didn't die on the cross to preserve gender complementarity. Jesus didn't die on the cross to ensure that little girls wear pink and little boys wear blue. Jesus lived, taught, died, and rose again to start a new family in which Jew and gentile, slave and free, male and female are all part of one holy Body. Certainly there will be those who reject the gospel because of the cost of discipleship, but let it be because of the cost of discipleship, not the cost of false fundamentals, not because they've been required to change something they cannot change.

There is this tendency within certain sectors of Christianity to assume that if our theology "works" for the relatively privileged (often for straight, upper-middle-class, Western men), then it should work well enough for everyone else, and the rest of the world should conform to it. But if our theology doesn't "work" for the least of these to whom Jesus first brought the gospel and through whom Jesus still presents himself today, then it doesn't work at all.

If the gospel's not good news for Adrian, then it's not good news.*

Originally posted on November 19, 2014.

---

* Rachel included this note for her readers: "Finally, be sure to check out Dr. David Gushee's recent lecture at the Reformation Project entitled, 'Ending the Teaching of Contempt Against Sexual Minorities' https://youtu.be/G2o3ZGwzZvk."

A Scandalously Inclusive Gospel
A REFLECTION BY AUSTEN HARTKE

"What makes the gospel offensive isn't who it keeps out, but who it lets in."

This often-repeated phrase first appeared in Rachel's writing in 2013 as she shared honestly about moving away from the rejection of LGBTQ+ people that she'd been taught and toward a fuller understanding of queer folks as beloved siblings in Christ. While the concept of radical inclusion continues to be a North Star for many of us as we navigate the waters of faith, when I remember Rachel I think less about the conclusions she came to and more about how she got there.

Rachel was a relationship person. Once she knew you it almost felt like she'd pinned some kind of special GPS locator on your shirt when you weren't looking, because you'd get these messages out of the blue encouraging you about a project, or checking in on you when you were having a difficult time. She was genuinely curious about other people, and she spent a lot of time listening. I remember reading *A Year of Biblical Womanhood* when it came out in 2012 and then Googling Rachel afterward, a little nervously, to see if she'd ever written anything negative about transgender people. As it turned out, the first time the word *transgender* showed up on her blog was just a year earlier, and it wasn't because she wanted to state her own thoughts or feelings—it was because she was passing the mic to Lisa

Salazar, a trans Christian woman, as part of a question-and-answer series. Rachel allowed the relationships she forged with other people to challenge her, to change her, and to strengthen her.

When Rachel and Nadia Bolz-Weber created the Why Christian? conference in 2014 they chose Allyson Dylan Robinson, the first openly trans pastor ever ordained by a Baptist church, as one of their keynote speakers. I was a volunteer during that conference, and I remember sitting in a pew on the side of the staging area while Rachel shared her conviction that her job in the progressive Christian world from now on was to take the spotlight shone on her work and point it toward the up-and-coming leaders with marginalized identities who often went unnoticed. I'd never heard anyone say anything like that before, and it radically reshaped my vision of what leadership could look like. When I got to chat with her afterward, I asked if I could give her a hug, and I got not only one of the best hugs I've ever received, but the beginning of a friendship that would change my life. From that time on, Rachel was in my corner and unlocking doors to rooms I never thought I'd see.

She was a guide for so many of us, showing us how to stand bravely in the not-knowing, how to let ourselves be changed by love, and how to give away the power we were given. She was a master at connecting the dots to explain how oppression of one group is often built on top of the subjugation of another, so that you can't fight for women's equity in the church without also fighting for the end of homophobia and transphobia as well. Rachel taught me how to be a leader, but beyond that, she taught me how to be a person of integrity living in community with others, so that every time I open a door I make sure to hold it wide for those who come after me. May we all follow her example as we seek to embody a scandalously inclusive gospel.

The Absurd Legalism of Gender Roles, Exhibit D: "Biblical" Manipulation

It's been a while since I've written here about Christianity, gender roles, and the whole egalitarian/complementarian divide, but a couple things prompted today's post.

First, our recent dive into parenthood has made me exceedingly glad we ditched the strict gender roles promoted by conservative evangelical culture in favor of a relationship characterized by mutuality and flexibility. Dan has risen to the occasion of fatherhood with more sweetness and energy than seems possible, changing diapers, doing seemingly infinite loads of laundry, rocking and burping the baby, making pot after pot of coffee (which we now refer to as "liquid hope"), researching baby poo on the internet, and so on. Owen Strachan of the Council on Biblical Manhood and Womanhood may characterize this shift in his priorities as a "man fail," but for us, it's working beautifully.* I've never loved and respected my husband more.

Second, John Piper recently posted an article at Desiring God entitled "Six Things Submission Is Not," intended to explain to

---

* Owen Strachan, "The 'Dad Mom' and the 'Man Fail'," Patheos, "Thought Life," last updated November 2, 2011, https://www.patheos.com/blogs/thoughtlife/2011/11/the-dad-mom-and-the-man-fail/.

women how they should and shouldn't submit to their husbands under a complementarian (patriarchal) understanding of a "biblical" familial structure.* While I appreciate Piper's rightful condemnation of a husband who demands his wife seek his permission before using the bathroom, I believe Piper's entire premise—that wives must be subordinate to their husbands—is faulty, and that this article's application of that premise can actually damage marital relationships by, among other things, impeding honest communication.

To review: In their letters to the early church, the apostles Peter and Paul include what you might call a Christian remix of the traditional Greco-Roman household codes, which detailed the responsibilities of a male head-of-house, his wives, slaves, and adult children (see Ephesians 5, Colossians 3, and 1 Peter 3).

Complementarians like Piper believe these instructions are universally binding and argue that what makes the New Testament household codes countercultural is their rejection of feminism in favor of male headship. However, Peter and Paul didn't live in a feminist culture; they lived in a patriarchal one. Noting that wives are to submit to their husbands and slaves to their masters was nothing radical. The authors were essentially stating the obvious about the nature of their time and place in the world and expected social norms. What makes the New Testament household codes radical is that they take a step toward mutuality by directing all members of the household—those with power and those who are powerless—to emulate the humility of Jesus Christ in their relationships. Piper's post about "what submission is not" contains a glaring omission, then—the fact that "biblical" submission is not meant to be one-way. In his letter to the Ephesians, Paul calls both

---

* John Piper, "Six Things Submission Is Not," Desiring God, February 26, 2016, https://www.desiringgod.org/articles/six-things-submission-is-not.

wives and husbands, men and women to "submit to one another out of reverence for Christ" (Ephesians 5:21). Directing a "how to submit" list to women alone perpetuates the mistaken notion that the deference and humility celebrated in the New Testament household codes are exclusively feminine virtues.

(Perhaps the strongest argument against Piper's hermeneutical approach to the New Testament household codes is the fact that the very same hermeneutic has been applied to these passages to justify slavery. All three of the biblical passages that instruct wives to submit to their husbands are either directly preceded or followed by instructions for slaves to obey their masters, with phrases like "likewise" and "in the same way" connecting them. If the New Testament household codes mean that patriarchy is a good, God-ordained system for all places and times, then to be consistent, one must also argue that slavery is a good, God-ordained system for all places and times. There's really no getting around that.)

I (and many biblical scholars and fellow Christians) would argue the point of these passages is not that patriarchy is the best foundation for marriage, but rather that the humility and service of Jesus Christ is the best example for marriage . . . and any relationship. That's a posture one can carry in a patriarchal culture or an egalitarian one, so faithfulness to Scripture does not require an embrace of patriarchy. If it seems as though I'm repeating myself, it's because I've written on this topic dozens of times, including an entire series on the New Testament household codes, which you can still read.*

Not surprisingly, trying to force first-century societal norms onto modern-day marriages has proven . . . complicated . . . even among those who subscribe to this approach. I remember countless

---

* Rachel Held Evans, "Additional Resources for Mutual Submission," Rachel Held Evans Blog, August 31, 2013, https://rachelheldevans.com/blog/mutual-submission-resources-marriage-books-egalitarian.

conversations in the dorm rooms of my conservative Christian college about how to defer to a guy as the "spiritual leader" in a relationship, an ideal that far too often resulted in women deliberately diminishing their own gifts, ideas, and dreams in an effort to better play second fiddle.

Forced gender roles impact relationships in countless negative ways, but the one I want to unpack here is the way this form of legalism can hamper honest communication between spouses by requiring women to "influence" their husbands without ever actually leading them.

In his post, Piper says, "submission does not mean you do not try to influence your husband" and suggests that a good test of proper male headship in a relationship is to examine who says "*let's*" most often—as in, "*let's* go out to eat, *let's* try to get our finances in order, *let's* get to church on time next Sunday." He seems to be saying that a woman can guide her husband, but not directly, not overtly.

Piper expands on this idea in his book *Recovering Biblical Manhood & Womanhood*, in which he advocates for what he calls "non-directive leadership."

"To the degree that a woman's influence over a man is personal and directive will generally offend a man's good, God-given sense of responsibility and leadership," he writes, "and thus contradict God's created order . . . A wife who 'comes on strong' with her advice will probably drive a husband into passive silence, or into active anger." Instead, "a woman who believes she should guide a man into a new behavior should do it in a way that signals her support of his leadership."

Ironically, his choice for an example of "beautiful non-directive leadership" is the biblical Abigail, who in talking David out of killing Nabal, "exerted great influence over David . . . but did so with amazing restraint and submissiveness." Missing from Piper's analysis is the fact that Abigail was far from submissive to her actual husband at the time (Nabal), rejecting his leadership by going behind his back to gather the provisions requested by the king and appearing quite pleased when he keeled over from a heart attack. (Also missing is any mention of the fact that the supposedly model marriage between David and Abigail included multiple wives and concubines.)

Here's the problem, as I see it: When women are instructed to "influence" men without leading them, to "guide" them without offending their fragile masculinity by using scary words like *let's*, we end up with women who must resort to nondirect communication in order to try and achieve their ends. The result is a relationship characterized by repression and manipulation.

Indeed, I've endured plenty church-sponsored bridal showers in which the older women instruct the younger ones on how to get their way by *"making him think it was his idea."* Even sadder, I've listened with a broken heart to women recount decades of frustration and pain that went unaddressed because they believed a good Christian wife avoids saying things like, *"I want"* or *"I need"* or *"let's."*

Few things make me ache more than watching decent, Jesus-loving people struggle under the weight of legalism, and I've received countless messages from couples who did just that before casting off the ill-fitting roles imposed onto their marriage by complementarianism. Anyone who knows anything about healthy relationships knows direct communication is key. You can't expect your spouse to read your mind, and you can't build an effective partnership by beating around the bush in an effort to stick to unnecessary hierarchal roles.

Dan and I discovered early into our relationship that being honest and direct with one another saved a ton of time and spared us all sorts of needless frustration. Dan's masculinity is not threatened when I'm up-front about what I think or when I tell him exactly what I want us to do. In fact, he prefers not having to guess at those things. And contrary to everything you've heard from the complementarian camp, in nearly thirteen years of egalitarian marriage we've never reached that big, bad hypothetical impasse in which we simply cannot agree and need someone to play a gender-based trump card to prevent paralysis. It just hasn't happened.

When both parties look to the example of Jesus, decisions can be made together, with *mutual* humility, gentleness, and deference.

While I'm sure it's not Piper's intention to encourage repression or manipulation in marital relationships, I'm convinced that's often the result when women are instructed to protect the fragile male ego by practicing "non-directive leadership."

You know what's way easier, and more natural?

Honest, direct communication of wants, needs, and ideas.

In my experience, most men—indeed, most people—respond much better to that anyway.

So let's give it a shot.

Originally posted on March 11, 2016.

If My Son or Daughter Were Gay . . .

So someone shared this short film with me last week and I haven't been able to get it out of my mind.*

The creative premise is a world in which homosexuality is the norm and heterosexual people are bullied and marginalized. What really moved me was its depiction of bullying, which is based on real reports from LGBTQ+ kids.

With or without the gay-straight "flip," I think the film helps viewers understand better what it's like to be in the minority, to be different. I hadn't spent much time thinking about what it's like for gay kids to overhear their parents talking about gay neighbors with derision and fear, for example, or how narratives about judgment and hell can be processed by kids in some pretty destructive ways. I hadn't thought much about what it would be like to have a gay son or daughter either.

The film is meant to be provocative, of course, so not everyone will like it. But it reminded me of one important, reality-based fact: Most people begin to recognize their sexual orientation when they are just kids, when they are young and vulnerable like this little girl. So when we, in the church, discuss homosexuality as though it were an issue faced by "other people" who are "out there," when we

---

* The video to which Rachel refers here is no longer available online.

resort to stereotypes and language about hell and judgment and damnation, we may be doing serious damage to the most precious and vulnerable among us. Even our casual conversations with one another can be picked up by little ears and internalized in destructive ways. We must never forget that there are kids struggling with the implications of their sexuality in our pews, in our classrooms, and at our own kitchen tables.

I am reminded of Jesus's strong words about having to give an account for our careless words and about the consequences of making any of these little ones stumble.

This is one reason why the Southern Baptist Convention's recent condemnation of the Boy Scouts was so upsetting to me: It targeted kids. It sent the message to young gay boys that they are a problem, unwelcomed in the church and a "threat" to their friends. As if they needed one more voice telling them that! As if they needed the bullies to have one more excuse to pick on them!

Still, I am hopeful that things will change for the better, and that the next generation will lead the way. I've spoken at several events for Christian teens in my travels, and let me tell you, to a person, they find antigay bullying abhorrent and are very concerned with how the church has treated their gay friends. I've already heard from a mom whose son came home from a Scout meeting in which he and his friends were informed that the church that sponsored them was pulling their funding because the Scouts no longer discriminate against gay boys. The mom said her son was angrier than she'd seen him in a while. But he wasn't angry at his gay friends; he was angry at the church.

So if I harp on this topic more than you would like, it's because I'm rooting for this generation and I long for them to find a place in the church. There have been too many secrets, too many bruises, too many suicides, and too many broken families already. Let's be careful with our words, our assumptions, and our attitudes. What makes the gospel offensive isn't who it casts out, but who it lets in, and the true mark of our holiness as a church is in how well we love the least of these.

If God blesses Dan and me with a child who is gay, I would want that child to know without a doubt that he or she is loved unconditionally. I would want her to know nothing could separate her from the love of God in Christ. I would want her to know that she isn't broken, she isn't an embarrassment, she isn't a disappointment.

May I be part of creating a world in which I will not have to protect her from the bullies.

And may I be part of creating a world in which I will not have to protect her from the church.

Originally posted on July 1, 2013.

"Mom, I Want to Tell You Something."
A REFLECTION BY OSHETA MOORE

"Mom, I want to tell you something."

We were parked in our driveway after I'd picked him up from a hangout. The house was alive with bedtime routines—baths, books, brushing teeth—but my teenage son was on his own schedule. He sat in the passenger seat, staring at his hands, the overhead light casting a warm glow between us.

"Yeah?" I asked, turning to face him.

He cleared his throat, fiddled with the leather bracelet on his wrist, and finally said, "I'm bi, Mom."

Bi. Bisexual. My son, fifteen and full of life, love, and curiosity, had just shared something deeply personal. And while my heart was racing a mile a minute—God, don't let the Apple Watch give me away—I knew three things for certain.

First: The Kingdom of God is made up of beloved children of God, fearfully and wonderfully made. This Beloved Bi young man, my son, was created with the capacity to love expansively, beautifully, and indiscriminately. That's the sacredness of being bi—the ability to see the "fearfully and wonderfully made-ness" of all people, regardless of gender.

Second: As my friend Rachel Held Evans once wrote, "My son or daughter would belong in my church, my family, my home, my embrace." If my body was his first home, then my arms would always be his forever. In any and every way he chooses to return, this will always be true. Isn't this what we learned in the story of the Prodigal Son? Home waits. Home watches. Home *welcomes.*

And third: This was a defining moment—for him and for me. How I responded would forever shape how he remembered sharing this part of himself with me. Rachel's words echoed in my mind: "Most people begin to recognize their sexual orientation when they are just kids, when they are young and vulnerable." I would not ruin this for him.

So, I cleared my throat, adjusted my watch to buy a few seconds, and said, "Alright, Bubbs. Thanks for telling me. I have some questions for clarification."

He sighed, that classic teenage exasperation, and said, "Fine. Shoot."

I flipped into Mom Mode, asking questions about the difference between appreciation and attraction, what he imagined a potential relationship with a guy would look like compared to a girl, and—of course—safety concerns. Because hormones and identity often make for stormy seas, and I'm no fool.

He answered each question with maturity and grace, and I felt something shift in me. My son's courage gave me hope, and his clarity gave me direction. It wasn't just about parenting a queer child. It was about embracing the call to create a world where my son—and other queer Beloveds—would not have to be shielded from the church but *welcomed* by it.

In the months following his coming out, my husband and I had many late-night talks about our role in this movement. We agreed it wasn't enough to stand on the sidelines, nodding politely. We needed to root ourselves in a faith community that was committed to radical inclusion, to "creating a world in which [queer Beloveds] do not have to be protected from the church."

But something else was happening in those months—something deeper, more personal. As I worked to parent my son through his coming out, I found myself reparenting little Osheta.

Little Osheta, who watched *Labyrinth* and fell desperately in love with Jareth and desperately in lust with Sarah (but didn't know it at the time—she just thought she wanted to *be* Sarah).*

Teenage Osheta, who felt jealous when her best friend got a boyfriend even though she had a perfectly adorable boy to kiss backstage during musical rehearsals.

Young adult Osheta, who felt strangely at home with her queer friends but told herself she was just showing them the love of Jesus. Spoiler alert: Baby Queer Osheta was just searching for her people.

And grown-up Osheta, who is wildly in love with her husband but still gets butterflies whenever she sees a certain woman soccer player with swagger, charisma, and the most perfect free kick.

My son's brave confession challenged me to be brave too. One evening, during a walk with my husband, I stopped and said, "Babe, I need to tell you something."

He puffed on his cigar, looked at me with curiosity, and said, "Shoot."

"I'm bi. Like . . . bisexual. Like."

He stopped walking, placed his hands gently on my waist, and said, "Baby, I know."

I blinked, startled. "Wait, what? You *knew*?"

"I've always known," he said simply. "Since we started dating. We just didn't have the words back then. But you're good, baby. We're good."

In that moment, I thanked God for Rachel's post, for the way it

---

* *Labyrinth* was a 1986 film starring David Bowie (as Jareth) and Jennifer Connolly (as Sarah).

mothered me, little queer Osheta, so that I could mother my son. Rachel's words gave me the framework to love him well, to embrace him fully, and—eventually—to embrace myself.

I miss Rachel every day. But I carry her legacy forward by creating safe, joyful, and loving spaces for my queer siblings. And if I've learned anything from her, it's that love is always worth the risk. Always.

Unstoppable Grace: Thoughts on the Gay Christian Network Conference

We have a saying in Christianity that "you will know them by their fruit." Drawn from Jesus's teachings in Matthew 7, the expression means that the true test of faithfulness to Christ is not in simply believing or saying the right things, but in displaying the fruit of the spirit—love, joy, peace, patience, kindness, goodness, gentleness, and self-control.

"A good tree cannot bear bad fruit," said Jesus, "and a bad tree cannot bear good fruit."

I spent this past weekend with Christians bearing very good fruit.

I went to the Gay Christian Network's "Live It Out" conference in Chicago a little unsure of what to expect, a little perplexed that someone like me would be invited, and a little freaked out about what to say as a straight woman to a group of gay, lesbian, bisexual, and transgender Christians—many of whom have been severely wounded by the church.*

But within a few hours of arriving, it became apparent to me

---

* The Gay Christian Network has since changed its name to Q Christian Fellowship and is no longer led by Justin Lee.

that I had little to teach these brothers and sisters and everything to learn from them.

I speak at dozens of Christian conferences in a given year, and I can say without hesitation that I've never attended a Christian conference so energized by the Spirit, so devoid of empty showmanship or preoccupation with image, so grounded in love and abounding in grace.

As one attendee put it, "This is an unapologetically Christian conference."

Indeed. There was communion, confession, powerful worship, and fellowship. There was deep concern for the Word. (The breakout sessions about the Bible and same-sex relationships were by far the most popular, with Matthew Vines's session so packed there wasn't even standing room!) There was lots of hugging and praying and tears . . . and argyle.

I spoke with attendees from a multitude of denominational backgrounds—Catholic, Southern Baptist, Nazarene, Churches of Christ, Pentecostal, Mennonite, you name it. I met gay Christians who felt compelled by Scripture and tradition to commit their lives to celibacy (Side B) and gay Christians who felt free in Christ to pursue same-sex relationships (Side A). And I heard story after story of getting kicked out of church, of being disowned by parents, of losing friends, of moving from despair to hope.

"I think we connect with your work because you write so much about Jesus," a man who came all the way from Australia said. "For a lot of us, everything about religion has been taken away. All we have left is Jesus. So we love to talk about Jesus."

The event wasn't perfect, of course. As with any conference, there were tensions and disagreements, a few awkward moments and misunderstandings. But these were handled with such profound patience and grace I couldn't believe what I was witnessing. Many of these folks have every right to walk around with permanent chips on their shoulders, but over and over again I encountered nothing but grace . . . big, wide, unstoppable, unexplainable grace.

I suppose this is what happens when a bunch of Christians get together and actually tell one another the truth.

About our pain.

About our sin.

About our fear.

About our questions.

About our sexuality.

About ourselves.

Telling the truth has a liberating effect on everyone else in the room, and this was evident in the final night of the conference when we listened to one another's stories:

From the young woman who had been called vicious names since grade school and who told us that this was the first time in her life she felt safe among other Christians.

From the brave mom who, choking down tears, told us that before this weekend she had been ashamed of her son, afraid to tell her Christian friends and family that he was gay. Now she had the courage to tell the truth and love him better.

From the man who, after twenty years of trying desperately to force himself to speak differently, dress differently, move his hands differently, and love differently decided to finally tell himself the truth.

From the conservative pastor who used to be an apologist against homosexuality, but whose friendship with a lesbian woman slowly, over many years, changed his mind. "*Her life was her greatest apologetic,*" he said, before openly weeping. "*I was wrong. And when I hear about the pain many of you have experienced, I know that I was the cause of some of that pain. I am so sorry. I am so, so sorry. Please forgive me.*"

From the man in the wheelchair who declared, "I'm Black. I'm disabled. I'm gay. And I live in Mississippi. What was God thinking?!"

From the lesbian couple whose conservative church chose to break with its denomination rather than deny them membership.

From the young man who said that when he finally worked up the courage to come out to his parents *"it didn't go as well as I hoped,"* and in the painful silence that followed, far too many understood.

From the denominational leader whose peers wanted him to "see what these people are so angry about" and who choked up as he said, *"I'm going to go back and tell them you're not angry. You weren't anything like I expected you to be. I'm going to go back and tell them you've been hurt and it's our denomination that needs to change, not you."*

From the parents who said they learned, too late, to love their gay son "just because he breathes."*

It was church if I've ever experienced it. And as I wiped tears from my eyes, I became as convinced as ever that if the church continues to marginalize and stigmatize LGBTQ+ Christians, then the church as a whole will suffer. It will miss out on all this energy, all this wisdom, all this truth, all this fruit. It will miss out on these beautiful people, these beautiful families, these beautiful relationships.

I was in a conversation with someone the other day who said he wondered if perhaps LGBTQ+ Christians have a special role to play in teaching the church how to engage thoughtfully around issues about sexuality.

I think he's wrong. After this conference, I'm convinced

---

* "'Just Because He Breathes'—Rob & Linda Robertson at Gay Christian Network 2014 Conference," YouTube, Q Christian Fellowship, April 24, 2015, https://www.youtube.com/watch?reload=9&v=Jk_-9Jlx1Bs.

LGBTQ+ Christians have a special role to play in teaching the church what it means to be *Christian*.

After all, movements of the spirit have never started with the "right" people. The gospel has never made as much sense among the powerful and religious as it makes among the marginalized. As I said in my keynote, what makes the gospel offensive isn't who it keeps out but who it lets in.

. . . And who it calls to lead.

I realize that standing with and affirming LGBTQ+ Christians—both those who identify as Side A and those who identify as Side B (though, for reasons I can explain later, I'm personally inclined toward A)—puts some of my work in jeopardy. I realize that this post will be used to discredit me and that I may lose readers and opportunities as a result. But here I stand—not to lead, but to follow; not as a mere "ally," but as a sister; not because I have it all figured out or have all my questions answered, but because I know in my heart it's the right thing to do.

I'm so grateful to GCN for welcoming me into your family last weekend. You told the truth. You extended grace. You let me ask dumb questions. You loved me well.

And as long as you are part of the church, I think her future is bright.

Originally posted on January 15, 2014.

Her Questions, Her Invitations, and Her Critiques Flowed from Her Deep Love

A REFLECTION BY MATTHEW VINES

January 2014 was the first time I met Rachel in person. It was at the Gay Christian Network conference in Chicago, where she was—no surprise—the most anticipated keynote speaker among a great lineup. Despite her celebrity status, she was as down-to-earth as anyone else, staying up late into the night to meet attendees and hear their stories in the hotel lobby.

In this blog post after the conference, Rachel wrote that she had "little to teach these brothers and sisters and everything to learn from them." This posture of openness and humility was classic Rachel—and it made her leadership all the more profound, as it embodied the servant leadership of Jesus himself.

The timing of this post was significant, too. While mainline Protestant denominations had been debating same-sex relationships for decades, evangelical communities had remained closed to any theological perspective affirming same-sex unions. That began to change around 2014, due in no small part to Rachel's courageous engagement with the topic.

My own connection with Rachel had begun a few months earlier, in September 2013, when she shared my viral video about the Bible and same-sex relationships with her substantial readership. (I was thrilled.) Then, a month or so after the conference, I was over the moon when Rachel sent my publisher a passionate endorsement of *God and the Gay Christian*. They immediately decided to put it on the front cover because they knew that Rachel's endorsement mattered. In her years of public blogging and writing, Rachel had cultivated a dedicated, ideologically diverse audience who recognized that her ideas and arguments had to be taken seriously.

Rachel was not a provocateur, challenging for the sake of challenging. What made her special was how clearly her questions, her invitations, and her critiques flowed from her deep love for her faith, the Bible, and her fellow family of God. She insisted on asking difficult questions because she insisted on conforming her life to the life of Jesus—even when doing so sometimes elicited condemnation from religious leaders.

"Unstoppable Grace" was one of several memorable milestones in Rachel's journey toward more public advocacy for gay, bisexual, and transgender Christians. While many progressive evangelicals were asking these questions privately at this time, Rachel was unusual in her willingness to wrestle with them publicly—no matter the blowback she might (and did) receive. Her observation here that LGBT Christians had "a special role to play in teaching the church what it means to be Christian" reflected her longstanding recognition that those who had been wrongly marginalized by the church often understand Jesus's message with a visceral clarity—and are therefore very much worth listening to.

A decade later, the evangelical conversation around gay, bisexual, and transgender people remains challenging, and in many ways, we are still in its early phases. But Rachel's writing helped create crucial early room for this dialogue to unfold. Through posts like this one, Rachel showed fellow Christians that engaging these questions with humility and empathy wasn't a threat to orthodox faith. Instead, it was an expression of it. Rachel was a woman of valor, nailing her proverbial theses to the digital church door and helping fuel much-needed reform. I am deeply grateful to have known her, and I am privileged to be one of many today who are continuing to walk on the path that she helped forge.

How to Win a Culture War and Lose a Generation

When asked by the Barna Group what words or phrases best describe Christianity, the top response among Americans ages sixteen to twenty-nine was "anti-homosexual." For a staggering *91 percent* of non-Christians, this was the first word that came to their mind when asked about the Christian faith. The same was true for 80 percent of young churchgoers. (The next most common negative images?: "judgmental," "hypocritical," and "too involved in politics.")

In the book that documents these findings, titled *unChristian*, David Kinnaman writes: "The gay issue has become the 'big one,' the negative image most likely to be intertwined with Christianity's reputation. It is also the dimension that most clearly demonstrates the unchristian faith to young people today, surfacing in a spate of negative perceptions: judgmental, bigoted, sheltered, right-wingers, hypocritical, insincere, and uncaring. Outsiders say [Christian] hostility toward gays . . . has become virtually synonymous with the Christian faith."*

---

* David Kinnaman and Gabe Lyons, *unChristian: What a New Generation Really Thinks About Christianity—and Why It Matters* (Baker Books, 2012), 92.

Later research, documented in Kinnaman's *You Lost Me*, reveals that one of the top reasons 59 percent of young adults with a Christian background have left the church is because they perceive the church to be too exclusive, particularly regarding their LGBTQ+ friends. Eight million twenty-somethings have left the church, and this is one reason why.

In my experience, all the anecdotal evidence backs up the research.

When I speak at Christian colleges, I often take time to chat with students in the cafeteria. When I ask them what issues are most important to them, they consistently report that they are frustrated by how the church has treated their gay and lesbian friends. Some of these students would say they most identify with what groups like the Gay Christian Network term "Side A" (they believe homosexual relationships have the same value as heterosexual relations in the sight of God). Others better identify with "Side B" (they believe only male/female relationship in marriage is God's intent for sexuality). *But every single student I have spoken with believes that the church has mishandled its response to homosexuality.*

Most have close gay and lesbian friends.

Most feel that the church's response to homosexuality is partly responsible for high rates of depression and suicide among their gay and lesbian friends, particularly those who are gay and Christian.

Most are highly suspicious of "ex-gay" ministries that encourage men and women with same-sex attractions to marry members of the opposite sex in spite of their feelings.

Most feel that the church is complicit, at least at some level, in antigay bullying.

And most . . . *I daresay all* . . . have expressed to me passionate opposition to legislative action against gays and lesbians.

"*When evangelicals turn their antigay sentiments into a political campaign,*" one college senior on her way to graduate school told me, "*all it does is confirm to my gay friends that they will never be welcome in the church. It makes them bitter, and it makes me mad too. This is why I never refer to myself as an evangelical. Ugh. I'm embarrassed to be part of that group.*"

I can relate.

When Tennessee added an amendment to the state constitution banning same-sex marriage (even though it was already illegal in the state), members of my church at the time put signs in the yard declaring support for the initiative. From my perspective, the message this sent to the entire community was simple: EVERYONE BUT GAYS WELCOME.

Dan and I left the church soon afterward.

Which brings me to North Carolina and Amendment One.

Despite the fact that the North Carolina law already holds that marriage in the eyes of the state is only between a man and a woman, an amendment was put on the ballot to permanently ban same-sex marriage in the state constitution. The initiative doesn't appear to change anything on a practical level (though some are saying it may have unintended negative consequences on heterosexual relationships) but seems to serve primarily as an ideological statement

. . . an expensive, destructive, and impractical ideological statement.

Conservatives in the state—who you would think would be more opposed to tampering with constitutions—supported the amendment, and last night it passed. Religious leaders led the charge in support of the amendment, with ninety-three-year-old Billy Graham taking out multiple ads in publications across the state supporting the measure.

As I watched my Facebook and Twitter feeds last night, the

reaction among my friends fell into an imperfect but highly predictable pattern. Christians over forty were celebrating. Christians under forty were mourning. Reading through the comments, the same thought kept returning to my mind as occurred to me when I first saw that Billy Graham ad: *You're losing us.*

I've said it a million times, and I'll say it again . . . (though I'm starting to think that no one is listening):

My generation is tired of the culture wars.

We are tired of fighting, tired of vain efforts to advance the Kingdom through politics and power, tired of drawing lines in the sand, tired of being known for what we are against, not what we are for.

And when it comes to homosexuality, we no longer think in the black-and-white categories of the generations before ours. We know too many wonderful people from the LGBT community to consider homosexuality a mere "issue." These are people, and they are our friends. When they tell us that something hurts them, we listen. And Amendment One hurts like hell.

Regardless of whether you identify most with Side A or Side B (or with one of the many variations within those two broad categories), it should be clear that amendments like these needlessly offend gays and lesbians, damage the reputation of Christians, and further alienate young adults—both Christians and non-Christians—from the church.

So my question for those evangelicals leading the charge in the culture wars is this: *Is it worth it?*

Is a political "victory" really worth losing millions more young people to cynicism regarding the church?

Is a political "victory" worth further alienating people who identify as LGBT?

Is a political "victory" worth perpetuating the idea that evangelical Christians are at war with gays and lesbians?

And is a political "victory" worth drowning out that quiet but persistent internal voice that asks—*What if we get this wrong?*

Too many Christian leaders seem to think the answer to those questions is "yes," and it's costing them.

Because young Christians are ready for peace.

We are ready to lay down our arms.

We are ready to stop waging war and start washing feet.

And if we cannot find that sort of peace within the church, I fear we will look for it elsewhere.

Originally posted on May 9, 2012.

I Was Listening

A REFLECTION BY MICHA BOYETT

I've said it a million times, and I'll say it again . . .
(though I'm starting to think that no one is listening):
My generation is tired of the culture wars.
—RHE

Rachel wrote of her concern that no one was listening, but people *were* listening in 2012. I was one of them, reading her posts as quickly as they hit my blog reader. Rachel said the things I wanted to say, but louder and clearer. With the sort of courage I hadn't yet discovered in myself. I copied and pasted, reposted.

We were young women then—girls who had the brains, passion, and spiritual calling for the pulpit, but rarely the opportunity. We had been groomed to accept our fates: lady thinkers, writers, readers with ideas from a religious tradition that patted us on the head. Rachel wasn't having that.

She was thirty when she penned this post in 2012. I was thirty-three, recklessly writing my way through the unstitching and mending of my faith. We didn't yet have the language for faith deconstruction. I called it questioning; she called it evolving.

Months before Rachel died, Stephen Patterson released *The Forgotten Creed*, a scholarly work on Paul's letter to the Galatians, chapter 3. He made the case that Paul recites what is most likely the earliest creed in the church, a creed that would have been recited at baptism by the very first believers: ". . . you are all children of God through faith . . . There is neither Jew nor Gentile, neither slave nor free, nor is there male and female, for you are all one in Christ Jesus" (Galatians 3:26, 28, niv). This was the center of the Jesus movement that became the early church. *In the Spirit, all that divides us is undone.*

I doubt Rachel read this book in those months before she left us. Her kids were little. She was writing a new project, working on the final Why Christian? conference, the next Evolving Faith conference. But sometimes I like to imagine what she would have written in response. She would have known the creed to be true, in the part of her that knew love was the force of all creation, that God was broader, more pliable, and less defined than the rules of the belief system we'd been handed. Christianity at its core is a religion of radical equity and muscular inclusion. The Jesus movement in its earliest iteration opened up the doors that much of Christianity's religious structures have since worked to seal, lock, and dismiss.

In "How to Win a Culture War and Lose a Generation," Rachel was speaking to the ones who protect the sealed doors. *Open them back up!* she shouted. At the time, eight million twenty-somethings had left the church over its exclusion of the LGBTQ+ community. Now, as the numbers swell, I think she would point us to that earliest of Christian creeds, the backbone of our spiritual ancestors: *There is no longer race or class, no longer gender or sexuality, no longer disabled or non-disabled! All are one in Christ Jesus.*

As she later wrote in *Searching for Sunday*, "Imagine if every church became a place where everyone is safe, but no one is comfortable. Imagine if every church became a place where we told one another the truth. We might just create sanctuary."

I spent an evening with Rachel a few days before she went into the hospital. She didn't feel great, thought she was "catching something" after a long weekend conference. I brought over the best blanket, made her toast and tea. What would I have said that night if I'd known we'd lose her?

I would have asked her about that early baptismal creed. Her eyes would have sparkled like they did when she had a fresh idea. I would have said, *Rachel, your courage to say the truth has led us to be our bravest selves*. I would have promised that we would keep moving toward that earliest vision of Christianity.

I would have reminded her that she had been remaking and re-imagining the church all along. That her words would keep moving us even when she was gone.

I would have said, *Rachel, we have been listening*.

PART FIVE

STILL A BIBLE NERD

Essays on Scripture

I Would Fail Abraham's Test (and I Bet You Would Too)

It's right for God to slaughter women and children anytime he pleases ... God is God!

—JOHN PIPER*

It's a test I'm certain I would have failed:

Get your son. Get a knife. Slit his throat and set him on fire.

I'd like to think that even if those demands thundered from the heavens in a voice that sounded like God's, I'd have sooner been struck dead than obeyed them.

Regardless of one's interpretation of this much-debated and re-imagined text (which makes a bit more sense in its ancient Near Eastern context), the story of Abraham's binding of Isaac should unsettle every parent and every person with a conscience. Yes, God provided a lamb, but only after Abraham gathered the wood,

---

* John Piper, "What Made It Okay for God to Kill Women and Children in the Old Testament?," Desiring God, February 27, 2010, https://www.desiringgod.org/interviews/what-made-it-okay-for-god-to-kill-women-and-children-in-the-old-testament.

loaded up the donkey, made the journey, arranged the altar, tied his son to the stake, and raised the knife in the air.

Be honest. *Would you have even gathered the wood?*

I think I would have failed Abraham's test. And I think you would have too.

And I'm beginning to think that maybe that's okay.

Peter Enns's interpretation of the genocide of the Canaanites got me thinking once again about how Scripture informs our conscience and how our conscience informs our interpretation of Scripture.*

In the story in question, God leads the Israelites on a years-long conquest of Canaan, with instructions to kill every man, woman, and child of Canaanite ethnicity.

Those who defend these stories as historical realities representative of God's true desires and actions in the world typically respond to challenges to that interpretation by declaring: "God is God, and if God orders ethnic cleansing, we have no business questioning it."

According to this view, God is glorified in seeing swords driven through the chests of curly-haired toddlers, in pregnant women being stabbed in the belly before being murdered themselves, and in old men and women begging for mercy but being denied it—just as God was glorified in the death of all the firstborn Egyptian males (Exodus) and in the taking of twelve- and thirteen-year-old girls as spoils of war (Numbers).

An endorsement of such actions raises about a million questions, the most pressing of which is: If God ordained ethnic cleansing in the past, might God ordain it in the present or future?

The Puritans certainly believed so, and pointed to the conquest

---

* Rachel Held Evans, "Canaanites, Reality Checks, and Letting the Bible Out of the Box," Rachel Held Evans Blog, September 16, 2014, https://rachelheldevans.com/blog/peter-enns-bible-tells-me-so.

of Canaan in Scripture as justification for their decimation of the Pequot tribe, whom they designated "accursed seeds of Canaan."[*]

"Sometimes the Scripture declareth women and children must perish with their parents," wrote Captain John Underhill of the 1637 massacre. "We have sufficient light from the Word of God for our proceedings."[†]

Belief in a cruel God, they say, makes a cruel man.

I have often been told by pastors and apologists that my misgivings about these biblical passages represent a weakness of faith, and that my persistent questions about suffering, evil, and violence in God's name betray a deep distrust in a God who owes me no explanations.

"You have to take your emotions out of it," a Reformed pastor once told me. "You're letting the humanism so pervasive in our culture affect your sense of justice."

"But why would the very God I believe imprinted us all with a conscience—with a deep sense of right and wrong—ask me to deny that conscience by accepting genocide as just?" I asked. "And how could I ever bring myself to worship a God who, if these accounts are true, ordained and derived glory from actions I believe are evil?"

"Stop right there," the pastor said. "I want you to hear the pride in that statement: 'How could I ever worship a God who . . . ?' That is not for you to decide, Rachel. God is God. You worship God because He's God."

God is God.

When people say this, what they seem to be saying is that God

---

[*] Lee Sultzman, "History of the Pequot Indians," Society of Colonial Wars in the State of Connecticut, accessed April 9, 2025, https://www.colonialwarsct.org/1637_pequot_history.htm.

[†] Quoted in John Mason, *A Brief History of the Pequot War* (Applewood Books, 2009), 81.

is power. And if God is power, God gets to define love however God pleases.

While I agree we can't go making demands and bending God into our own image, it doesn't make sense to me that a God whose defining characteristic is supposed to be love would present himself to his creation in a way that looks nothing like our understanding of love. If love can look like abuse, if it can look like genocide, if it can look like rape, if it can look like eternal conscious torture—well, everything is relativized! Our moral compass is rendered totally unreliable. We have no moral justification for opposing Joseph Kony's army of children, for example, because Joseph Kony claims God is giving him direction. If this is the sort of thing God does, who are we to question it?

This is a hard God to root for. It's a hard God to defend against all my doubts and all the challenges posed by science, reason, experience, and intuition. I once heard someone say he became an atheist for theological reasons, and that makes sense to me. Once you are convinced that the deity you were taught to worship does evil things, it's easier to question the deity's very existence than it is to set aside your moral objections and worship anyway.

I tried for many years to follow the pastor's advice and disengage my emotions and intellect and keep them a safe distance from my faith. I tried to click into robot-mode when I walked into church. But disengaged is no way to live. Disengaged is no way to believe. A disengaged faith is not really faith.

So I kept asking questions . . .

When Rob Bell released *Love Wins*, a book that made a compelling biblical case against the exclusivist theology that all non-Christians will be condemned to eternal conscious torment in hell, the Southern Baptist Convention released a resolution that stated: "Being troubled, even deeply troubled, by the implications of the biblical text does not give us a reason to abandon the text or force it into a mold that rests comfortably with us. It should be our goal to let the Bible be the source and shaper of our doctrine."

In other words, Christians cannot allow their instincts or conscience to inform their theology, only Scripture.

But as I argued, this rationale represents a major inconsistency in Baptist teaching:

> If the members of the Southern Baptist Convention truly believe that only those who place personal faith in Jesus Christ will be saved and that no concessions to this belief should be made on the basis of its troubling moral implications, then for consistency's sake, they must also vote to condemn the teaching of the age of accountability.
>
> The age of accountability refers to a belief that children under a certain age (usually twelve or so) will be granted salvation regardless of the religious affiliation of their parents. Most Baptists I know believe in the age of accountability, and even the SBC's Baptist Faith and Message makes it implicit in its statement that people are not morally accountable until "they are capable of moral action."
>
> And yet this concept is never explicitly stated in Scripture, nor does it appear in any of the historic Christian creeds. The age of accountability is a concept born from the compassion of the human heart, from a deep and intrinsic sense that a loving, good, and just God would not condemn little children or the mentally disabled to such suffering when they could certainly bear no responsibility for their faith. It is a theology created by discomfort...
>
> ...The very formation of the Southern Baptist denomination—rooted in support of slavery—reflects the disastrous consequences of confining morality to that which is explicitly stated in Scripture

to the neglect of the conscience. Conscience should be tested with Scripture, certainly, but it should never be silenced by it.*

My point is this: It is intellectually dishonest to say Christians make moral judgment calls based on Scripture alone. Conscience, instinct, experience, culture, relationships—all of these things (and more) play important roles in how we assess right and wrong.

Most of us condemn slavery in spite of Colossians 3:22, genocide in spite of Deuteronomy 20:17, and women-as-property in spite of Exodus 20–21.

I suspect this has something to do with being conformed to the image of Jesus Christ, not the Bible, something to do with God's presence both inhabiting and transcending the pages of Scripture, something to do with having a God-given conscience, interpreting with wisdom, and going with your gut. And I suspect it has something to do with love.

When I visited Amish Country during my "year of biblical womanhood," I had dessert with a sweet, grandmotherly lady in her enormous, bustling kitchen. As we feasted on Shoofly pie, my guide pointed out that there was an extra leaf in the woman's table. It was for family that had left the Amish way of life, my guide explained, to the nodding head of our bonneted host. According to the religious rules, such family should be shunned and forbidden from sharing a table with their parents, brothers, and sisters. And so this woman added an extra leaf to her table, so that technically she wouldn't be eating with her shunned family members . . . even though she was.

I've long been fascinated by the stories of people who defied— or "worked around"—their religion in the name of love, and these

---

* Rachel Held Evans, "Rob Bell, the SBC, and the Age of Accountability," Rachel Held Evans Blog, June 22, 2011, https://rachelheldevans.com/blog/rob-bell-sb-age-of-accountability.

stories are plentiful among parents. I once heard from a mother who defied her pastor by ensuring that her daughter received the depression medication she so desperately needed. I know of a father who, though he had once been convinced parents of LGBTQ+ children should "hand them over to Satan" as recommended by John MacArthur, just marched in his first pride parade right alongside his gay son. And then there is the conservative Southern Baptist mom who bravely defended the experiences of her transgender child.

These are people of conviction, people whose faith is important to them and who long for the approval of their religious leaders and the favor of God. *And yet they risked all of that for love.*

I guess I'm just not convinced that such actions reveal a lack of faith, nor am I convinced that these people would be better off if they disengaged their emotions in the name of obedience.

I am not yet a mother, and still I know, deep in my gut, that I would sooner turn my back on everything I know to be true than sacrifice my child on the altar of religion.

Maybe the real test isn't in whether you drive the knife through the heart.

Maybe the real test is in whether you refuse.

Originally posted on October 14, 2014.[*]

---

[*] Rachel published a follow-up piece to this highly engaged post about a week later with additional resources: "Responses & Resources for the Abraham/Isaac Question," October 22, 2014, https://rachelheldevans.com/blog/abraham-isaac-resources.

The Bible Was "Clear"...

In 1982:

The Bible clearly teaches, starting in the tenth chapter of Genesis and going all the way through, that God has put differences among people on the earth to keep the earth divided.
—Bob Jones III, defending Bob Jones University's policy banning interracial dating/marriage.* The policy was changed in 2000.

In 1823:

The right of holding slaves is clearly established by the Holy Scriptures, both by precept and example.
—Rev. Richard Furman, first president of the South Carolina State Baptist Convention†

---

* "Bob Jones University," Wikipedia, accessed April 19, 2025, https://en.wikipedia.org/wiki/Bob_Jones_University#cite_note-10.
† "Excerpts from Rev. Dr. Richard Furman's EXPOSITION of The Views of the Baptists, RELATIVE TO THE COLOURED POPULATION of the United States IN A COMMUNICATION To the Governor of South-Carolina," 1838, SUNY Ulster, accessed April 19, 2025, https://people.sunyulster.edu/voughth/Furman_Slavery.htm.

In the sixteenth century:

People gave ear to an upstart astrologer who strove to show that the earth revolves, not the heavens or the firmament, the sun and the moon. This fool . . . wishes to reverse the entire science of astronomy; but sacred Scripture tells us that Joshua commanded the sun to stand still, and not the earth.

—Martin Luther in "Table Talk" on a heliocentric solar system[*]

In 1637:

Sometimes the Scripture declareth women and children must perish with their parents . . . We have sufficient light from the Word of God for our proceedings.

—Captain John Underhill, defending the Puritan decimation of the Pequot tribe[†]

In 1846:

The evidence that there were both slaves and masters of slaves in churches founded and directed by the apostles, cannot be got rid of without resorting to methods of interpretation that will get rid of everything.

—Rev. Leonard Bacon, in defense of American slavery[‡] (Christian ministers wrote nearly

---

[*] Martin Luther, *Table Talk* (H. G. Bohn, 1566), 1539.
[†] "The History," Mystic Voices: The Story of the Pequot War, accessed April 19, 2025, http://www.pequotwar.com/history.html.
[‡] Mark Noll, *The Civil War as Theological Crisis*, rpt. ed. (University of North Carolina Press, 2015), 45.

half of all defenses of slavery, often citing Scripture to make their case.)

In 1869:

The Bible is the revealed will of God, and it declares the God-given sphere of woman. The Bible is, then, our authority for saying woman must content herself with this sphere . . . Who demand the ballot for woman? They are not the lovers of God, nor are they believers in Christ, as a class. There may be exceptions, but the majority prefer an infidel's cheer to the favor of God and the love of the Christian community.

—Rev. Justin Dewey Fulton in his treatise against women's suffrage[*]

In 1960:

Wherever we have the races mixed up in large numbers, we have trouble. . . . These religious liberals are the worst infidels in many ways in the country; and some of them are filling pulpits down South. They do not believe the Bible any longer; so it does not do any good to quote it to them. They have gone over to modernism, and they are leading the white people astray at the same time; and they are leading colored Christians astray. But every good, substantial, Bible-believing, intelligent, orthodox Christian can read the Word of God and know that what is happening in the South now is not of God.

—Bob Jones Sr., in his treatise against integration entitled "Is Segregation Scriptural?"[†]

---

[*] Justin Dewey Fulton, *The True Woman: A Series of Discourses* (Lee & Shepherd, 1869), 36.

[†] Justin Taylor, "Is Segregation Scriptural? A Radio Address from Bob Jones on Eas-

Of course, for every Christian who appealed to Scripture to oppose abolition, integration, women's suffrage, and the acceptance of a heliocentric solar system, there were Christians who appealed to Scripture to support those things too.

But these quotes should serve as a humbling reminder that rhetorical claims to the Bible's clarity on a subject do not automatically make it so. One need not discount the inspiration and authority of Scripture to hold one's interpretations of Scripture with an open hand.

It's easy to look down our noses at the Christians who have come before us and discount them as unenlightened and uninformed. But to accept Galileo's thesis, our seventeenth-century forbearers would have had to reject sixteen hundred years of traditional Christian interpretations of passages like Psalm 93:1, Ecclesiastes 1:5, and Joshua 10:12–14. And to accept the arguments of the abolitionist, our great-great-grandparents had to see beyond the "plain meaning" of proof texts like Ephesians 6:1–5; Colossians 3:18–25, 4:1; and 1 Timothy 6:1–2 and instead be compelled by the general sweep of Scripture toward justice and freedom.

We like to characterize the people in the quotes above as having *used* Scripture to their own advantage. But I find it both frightening and humbling to note that, often, the way we make the distinction between those who *loved* Scripture and those who *used* Scripture is hindsight.

So before you share that MLK quote on Facebook today, ask yourself: If your pastor told you that integration was "unbiblical" and MLK was a dangerous, anti-Christian communist (which is what plenty of white pastors in the South did), which side would

---

ter of 1960," TGC: The Gospel Coalition, July 26, 2016, https://www.thegospelcoalition.org/blogs/evangelical-history/is-segregation-scriptural-a-radio-address-from-bob-jones-on-easter-of-1960/.

you have chosen? Would you have defied your own religious community to stand with MLK?

I wish I knew for sure what I would have done . . . but I don't. I'm humbled, and a little frightened, by how often true justice is only recognized as such in hindsight.

Originally posted on January 20, 2014.

How to Love Jesus Without Needing to Be Right About Everything

A REFLECTION BY ZACK HUNT

God may know everything, but not even God knew as much as I did when I was an evangelical teenager on fire for Jesus. I was an expert on everything from evolutionary science and women's health to human sexuality and, most important, the Bible. Though it was easy to be an expert on the Bible since all I had to do was quote it. Nothing could stop me. Certainly not a sense of humility.

It took a long time and a lot of humbling revelations for me to finally accept the possibility that maybe, just maybe I might be wrong about some things, possibly even some of the things I thought the Bible was very clear about. It took me even longer to publicly own my delusions of omniscience.

Rachel helped folks like me find the courage to admit we were wrong—which is no small thing when you grow up thinking being wrong could send you to hell. She was an exvangelical showing us it was possible to deconstruct your faith and still love Jesus long before "exvangelical" and "deconstruction" were parts of our collective lexicon. Not that she would care. Branding and needing credit were never her thing. She was too focused on learning how to better love her neighbor to care whether strangers thought she was cool.

It was that authenticity that resonated so much with me and helped folks like me feel comfortable trusting her. She wore her humility on her sleeve the way so many of us once wore our WWJD bracelets so proudly. It was a breath of fresh air for all of us who, like Rachel, grew up in a culture of dogmatism that made being right, never doubting we were right, and making sure everyone else knew *they* were wrong, our divine calling. Being able to love Jesus free from the shackles of fundamentalism and evangelicalism was something most of us who grew up fundamentalist or evangelical never thought possible.

Rachel showed us how to do the impossible. She showed us how to love Jesus without needing to be right about everything. Instead of proselytizing strangers, she asked questions. Instead of damning others to hell, she built a bigger table. And she invited us to join her on her journey. But she would be the first to tell you she wasn't a saint. She made mistakes just like the rest of us. Unlike a lot of us, she owned those mistakes publicly. Her fearlessness gave folks like me the courage to openly admit when we were wrong too, even when it was painful and embarrassing to do so.

I was wrong about evolution. I was wrong about abortion. I was wrong about my LGBTQ+ neighbors. I was wrong about the Bible. I was wrong and Rachel helped to show me that not only is that okay, but admitting when we're wrong can actually lead to a healthier, more honest, and more loving faith.

Everyone's a Biblical Literalist Until You Bring Up Gluttony

... Or divorce, or gossip, or slavery, or head coverings, or Jesus's teachings on nonviolence, or the "abomination" of eating shellfish and the hell-worthy sin of calling other people idiots.

Then we need a little context.
Then we need a little grace.
Then we need a little room to disagree.

I got to thinking about this after I was criticized for my essay about loving gay kids unconditionally.* Some folks were very upset that I had the audacity to write an entire blog post about putting a stop to LGBTQ+ bullying without including a Bible-based condemnation of LGBTQ+ people, or at least a theological discussion around the issue of homosexuality and Scripture.

Bible verses were quoted. Open letters were written. End Times predictions were made.† Pillows in my home were thrown record distances.

---

* See "If My Son or Daughter Were Gay . . ." in this book.
† Elizabeth Prata, "Rachel Held Evans Asks 'What If My Son or Daughter Were Gay,' and Gets a Response from Dr. Joel McDurmon," *The End Time*, accessed April 19, 2025, https://the-end-time.blogspot.com/2013/07/rachel-held-evans-asks-what-if-my-son.html?showComment=1373054805631.

It's funny. Yesterday, I posted a quote from Mark Twain in which he referred to a snake oil salesman as an "idiot," but no one left an angry comment warning me of hell based on Jesus's teaching in Matthew 5:22 that "if you call someone an idiot, you are in danger of being brought before the court; and if you curse someone, you are in danger of the fires of hell."

Nor did anyone raise any biblical objections regarding gluttony a few weeks ago when I casually mentioned overdosing on Sweet Frog frozen yogurt (strawberry, with a pile of chocolate chips, Oreo crumbs, and chocolate animal crackers on top, if you must know), or about materialism when I shared pictures of our new car. (Hey, for some people, a brand new Honda Civic is pretty flashy.)

And in spite of the flood of emails I get each week condemning my support of women in ministry, I've never received so much as an open letter criticizing my refusal to wear a head covering, even though my website is full of photographic evidence of what the apostle Paul calls a "disgrace" in 1 Corinthians 11:6.

We may laugh at these examples or dismiss them as silly, but the biblical language employed in these contexts is actually pretty strong: Eating shellfish is an abomination, a bare head is a disgrace, gossips will not inherit the Kingdom of God, careless words are punishable by hell, guys who leer at women should gouge out their eyes.

Heck, you could make a pretty good biblical case for gluttony being a "lifestyle sin" that has been normalized by our culture of "Supersized" portions and overflowing buffet lines, starting with passages like Philippians 3:19 ("their god is their belly"), Psalm 78:18 ("they tested God in their heart by demanding the food they craved"), Proverbs 23:20 ("be not among drunkards or among gluttonous eaters of meat"), Proverbs 23:2 ("put a knife to your throat if you are given to appetite"), or better yet, Ezekiel 16:49 ("Now this was the sin of your sister Sodom: She and her daughters were arrogant, overfed and unconcerned; they did not help the poor and needy").

Yet you don't see weigh-ins preceding baptisms or people holding "God Hates Gluttons" signs outside the den of iniquity that is Ryan's Steakhouse.

And we haven't even touched on materialism, or the fact that on the day I stuffed my face with froyo, thirty thousand kids died from preventable diseases and many more went hungry.

It seems the more ubiquitous the biblical violation, the more invisible it becomes.

So why do so many Christians focus on the so-called clobber verses related to homosexuality while ignoring clobber verses related to gluttony or greed, head coverings or divorce? Why is homosexuality the great biblical debate of this decade and not slavery (as it once was) or the increasing problem of materialism and inequity?* Why do so many advocate making gay marriage illegal but not divorce, when Jesus never referenced the former but spoke quite negatively about the latter?

While there are certainly important hermeneutical and cultural issues at play, I can't help but wonder if something more nefarious is also at work. *I can't help but wonder if biblical condemnation is often a numbers game.*

Though it affects more of us than we tend to realize, statistically, homosexuality affects far fewer of us than gluttony, materialism, or divorce. And as Jesus pointed out so often in his ministry, we like to focus on the biblical violations (real or perceived) of the minority rather than our own.

In short, we like to gang up. We like to fashion weapons out of the verses that affect us the least and then "clobber" the minority

---

* About slavery, see Rachel Held Evans, "Is Abolition 'Biblical'?," Rachel Held Evans Blog, February 28, 2013, https://rachelheldevans.com/blog/is-abolition-biblical.

with them. Or better yet, conjure up some saccharine language about speaking the truth in love before breaking out our spec-removing tweezers to help get our minds off of these uncomfortable logs in our own eyes.

We see this in the story of the religious leaders who ganged up on the woman caught in adultery. She was such an easy target: a woman, probably poor, disempowered, and charged with the go-to favorite of the self-righteous—sexual sin. When they brought her to Jesus, they were using her as an example to test him, to see how "biblical" his response to her would be. (See Deuteronomy 22:23–14.) Jesus knelt down and scribbled in the sand before saying, "He who is without sin can cast the first stone." They dropped their stones.

While self-righteousness avoidance certainly affects our selective literalism, we also have good reasons for not condemning one another for the more ubiquitous biblical violations (again, real or perceived) in our culture.

It's hard for me to flatly condemn divorce, for example, when I know of several women whose lives, and the lives of their children, may have been saved by it, or when I hear from people who tell me they would have rather *come* from a broken home than *grown up* in one. We have a natural revulsion to the idea of checking people's BMI before accepting them into the church, especially when obesity is not necessarily reflective of gluttony (often, in this country, it is a result of poverty), and when we know from our own experiences or the experiences of those we love that an unhealthy weight can result from a variety of factors—from genetics to psychological components—and when some of our favorite people in the world (or when we ourselves) wrestle with a complicated relationship with food, whether it's through overeating or undereating.

Again, it's a numbers game. It's hard to "other" the people

we know and love the most. It's become a cliché, but everything changes when it's your brother or sister who gets divorced, when it's your son or daughter who is gay, when it's your best friend who struggles with addiction, when it's your husband or wife asking some good questions about Christianity you never thought about before. Our relationships have a tendency to destroy our categories, to melt black and white into gray, and I don't think God is disappointed or threatened by this. I think God expects it. It happened to Peter when he encountered Cornelius and Philip when he encountered the Ethiopian eunuch. Suddenly it became a lot harder to label your friends "unclean" or "unworthy."

After all, when God became flesh and lived among us, the religious accused him of hanging out with "sinners" (even gluttons!) never realizing that this was the whole point, that there were only "sinners" to hang out with.

Of course, all of this raises questions about when it's right or wrong to "call out" sin, and I confess I'm no good at sorting that out. I'm as hypocritical as the next person, judgmental of those I deem judgmental, self-righteous, indulgent, a gossip, too careless with my words, too quick to get angry at certain people with certain theological views, too easily seduced by money and notoriety and . . . my favorite things in the whole entire world . . . AWARDS! LISTS! ACCOLADES!

I too need reminding that, for all my big talk about a "Christocentric hermeneutic," more often than not, I'm following a "Rachelcentric hermeneutic" when I read the Bible, complete with my own biases, preferences, insecurities, and opinions guiding how I "pick and choose." (Oh I can wield every Bible verse that challenges Calvinism like a knife, but I'd rather not talk about how I'm actually applying the Sermon on the Mount to my life or what I really think about enemy-love.)

Should we stop discussing which biblical instructions apply

today and how we ought to apply them? Certainly not. Should we remain silent when the vulnerable are oppressed and exploited or when injustice and immorality pervade our culture? No. Do we abandon our convictions about what the Bible says is sin? No, not even when we disagree on that. Are rhetorical questions overused in blog posts? Yes.

But it's good to remind ourselves now and then that just as Southern slaveholders had a vested interest in interpreting Colossians 3:22 literally, so we tend to "pick and choose" to our own advantage.

And when we make separate categories for the "real sinners," when we reduce our fellow human beings to theological issues up for constant debate who cannot even be told they are loved without qualifiers, when our hermeneutic conveniently renders others the problem and us the heroes, maybe it's time to sit across a table and get to know one another a little better, to break up some categories and make some new friends. Maybe it's time to drop our stones for a while and pass the bread.

. . . healthy, whole grain, organic bread, of course.

Originally posted on July 8, 2013.

When Rachel Asked, She Gave Me Permission to Ask, Too

A REFLECTION BY MATTHIAS ROBERTS

"I can't help but wonder if biblical condemnation is often a numbers game."

There's a moment with Rachel I will always remember. We were recording a podcast conversation together, and I had paused in an attempt to force my thoughts to coalesce into words. They wouldn't. Because I am not a particularly skilled interviewer (I lean upon the magic of editing to boost my perceived intelligence), I laughed nervously and admitted I'd lost my train of thought.

This isn't rare. I warn people to expect it from the start, and most generously wait. But that wasn't Rachel. She joined my tentative chuckle with her own kinder laugh and jumped in, proposing we switch places. Maybe she could take the reins of the interviewer for a moment. Would I be okay with that?

"Are rhetorical questions overused . . . ?"

I don't think so. Here's the thing about Rachel's questions: Whether or not she meant them as rhetorical, they were part of her. She carried them with her, from her blog posts, to the way she named her events, to her daily conversations. A more straightforward way of saying this is that Rachel was curious. That's what I remember.

Years before, when a twenty-two-year-old me sat at my desk reading her blog, yearning to come out but not yet feeling brave enough, wondering if I would seal my fate as an apostate by publicly muttering the words "I'm gay," her questions were far from rhetorical. They were questions I didn't have the words for. When Rachel asked, she gave me permission to ask, too.

"Why do so many Christians focus on the so-called clobber verses related to homosexuality while ignoring clobber verses related to gluttony or greed, head coverings or divorce?"

I had secretly wondered about a less coherent version of this question, but I didn't know I was allowed to ask it. The times I had tried, the levels of anger it prompted in those around me surprised me. I didn't know. But something wasn't adding up.

It's a lachrymose thing, returning to Rachel's earlier writings now that she's gone and my own questions feel clearer. I don't know if I'm a Christian anymore, and I haven't thought about the phrase "biblical literalism" in years. Yet her words still resonate. Something that Rachel seems to circle around here, a point that she developed more cogently in her later works, is the idea of context. Not just biblical context, but each of our own contexts. Rachel wonders, if I may take the liberty of paraphrase: Might our own contexts matter as much, if not more, when we approach the text? When we approach people who are different from us?

At this point in my life, the answer is obvious. Of course. But, when she first helped usher me into these questions, it was like she was opening that closet door, letting more and more light in. In case it sounds romanticized, think about the last time your eyes were used to the dark and you met a flash of light. It's not comfortable. It wasn't easy to sit with the idea that maybe the people who had taught me how to read the Bible were biased, in the same way they told me I was biased for asking questions about their bias. But, if they were biased, and I was biased too, maybe being biased wasn't a sign of straying, but just of being human.

"After all, when God became flesh and lived among us, the reli-

gious accused him of hanging out with 'sinners' (even gluttons!) never realizing that this was the whole point, that there were only 'sinners' to hang out with."

I cherish that moment when I didn't have words, when Rachel, once again, asked a question. Her curiosity, and the quiet permission she extended through her work, has become part of my context. I can't separate who I am from who she helped me become, and I imagine you might feel this, too. She left a mark on us, giving us language, and so much more. Perhaps on our good days, we are a bit more open, a bit more willing to ask, to listen. She is part of all our contexts now, her questions carried with us as we continue on.

Oh Beloved, Just You Wait

A REFLECTION BY RACHEL KURTZ

I am a fat, queer, divorced, single mother of three. If my teenage self would have known my future self, she would have prayed for me, hard! I was raised in the Pentecostal Church and spent the first nineteen years of my life with very strong beliefs that I learned from the men in my church growing up as the Word of God and lucky for me I was a much thinner non-sinner. I wasn't struggling with my sexuality. I wasn't making out, drinking, or doing drugs. I was very good. I went to church at least three times a week. I was part of the worship team and sang solos to cassette tracks of Sandi Patty, Russ Taff, and Amy Grant. I prayed, oh did I pray, that I would live into the life I was created for. According to the Scriptures, I did practice some gluttony, and boy did I love to hear a juicy bit of gossip (still do, I am a sucker for a good story), but none of the truly "bad sins." I lived according to the gospel of the white, patriarchal, narrow-scoped ideas of many earnest God-fearing and people-condemning people. I truly didn't know any better, and I trusted the leaders with my whole heart. Then I grew up, I met people, I loved my friends, and I realized over time perhaps the people whom I had pleased so much with my Bible quoting and worship leading didn't actually hold the keys to the truth of Scripture like I was taught.

This is something I adore about the life and writing of Rachel Held Evans. She was always quick to say, I was wrong, or I understand things differently, now that I know better, I will do better. Rachel was a voice for the marginalized. She was also a "Christian's Christian." She might not have been a Missionette like me, but she knew Scripture and knew which ones have been fashioned into weapons against God's beloved. She denounced white supremacy and patriarchy without hesitation. She spoke truth to power. And in her post "Everyone's a Biblical Literalist Until You Bring Up Gluttony" she speaks directly to the Christians and says, Beloved, can't you see the blatant truth? We are categorizing sin. We are hollering about things that don't pertain to us. We are weaponizing Scripture to condemn others and never put the same spotlight on things we commit all the time! Rachel is not unkind in her honesty, but she is calling us to wake up.

I am so grateful to have learned that the beginning of our story doesn't have to tell the end of it. I am grateful I learned about grace, I learned about love, I learned about myself, and I talk so sweetly to the earnest young Christian I was and say, Oh beloved, just you wait. You will live a life beyond your wildest dreams, you will love and be loved. You will live a life that is saturated in the Spirit and it will look nothing like the terrifyingly angry or deeply disappointed and grieved God of your youth. She will use your loud mouth, and even your love of your fat body will be a blessing against self-hatred. You have a future and a hope, just not like you had planned.

Sunday Superlatives: Rachel Was Both

A REFLECTION BY ALISE CHAFFINS

Editor's note: Sunday Superlatives was a popular series of round-up links featuring the work of fellow writers or anything that Rachel found that might interest her readers. She introduced her selections as "Best Analysis" or "Most Challenging" or "Most Likely to Say It Perfectly" or even "Lightest Packer" (she jokingly awarded that one to herself for managing to get a week's worth of luggage into a carry-on bag).

There were few thrills of affirmation like being included in Rachel's Sunday Superlatives and the uptick of clicks, comments, and even book sales that followed. Often playful, always interesting, Sunday Superlatives were one small way Rachel fostered community online and remained committed to her larger goal of amplifying other voices.

Charlotte's Web has been one of my favorite books since Miss Fett read it to our third-grade class. Stories about unlikely friendships always resonate with me, and I think that book is part of the reason why. Charlotte, the spider, uses her ability to write to save her pig friend, Wilber. It's also the book that comes to mind when I think about Rachel.

One of my best friends pointed me to Rachel's blog before her book *Evolving in Monkey Town* was published. Her posts resonated with my questions about my faith journey, and I quickly joined the conversation in the comments of her posts, eventually forming an online friendship with Rachel that spilled over into the real world.

Many bloggers at the time would use certain days to share items they stumbled across during the week. A piece of music that caught your ear. A video that made you laugh. A book that made you think. And always the words of other writers on the internet you connected with.

No one had a more thorough list than Rachel with her Sunday Superlatives.

Each Sunday, she would highlight dozens of posts she had read throughout the week. They would include essays of all sorts: politics, religion, humor, science. Nothing was off the table in the Superlatives. And no one was off the table in the Superlatives.

And this is why Charlotte and Rachel are linked for me. Charlotte had a short life but used it to help her friend. Through her Sunday Superlatives and overall generosity, Rachel gave a place for writers to have their words seen more broadly. She allowed women and queer people and people of color access to a platform that was traditionally controlled by men. She amplified voices that might not have otherwise had an opportunity to be heard.

She allowed me that access.

I don't write the kinds of essays I wrote back then. These days, I'm a film critic, which feels far removed from a woman who wrote about her faith. But I'm still a writer because Rachel gave me that courage by sharing some of my earliest work. I'm still a writer because Rachel introduced me to some of my best writing friends. I'm still a writer because Rachel's words inspired me to want to write better.

I think a lot of people who found themselves on Rachel's Sunday Superlatives might say the same.

The last line of *Charlotte's Web* is, "It is not often that someone comes along who's a true friend and a good writer. Charlotte was both."

Rachel's generosity made it possible for some authors to find publishers. Rachel's generosity made it possible for some to find an audience. Rachel's generosity almost certainly saved some lives by allowing people a seat at a table they had been asked to leave.

Rachel was a good writer. She was a good friend. Charlotte only ever wrote "Terrific," but I'd use the word "Superlative."

I Love the Bible

It is said that after Jacob wrestled with God, he walked with a limp.

So it has been with the Bible and me.

I have wrestled with the Bible, and it has left me with a limp.

But I am glad. I am glad because this limp has slowed me down a bit. It has humbled me. It has forced me to stop running so fast and sure down the path of certainty that I forget to listen, to pay attention, to ask questions, to build altars, to wait.

I have wrestled, and I love the Bible more now than I have ever loved it before. I love it more than when I demanded that it answer all of my questions, more than when I forced it to fit my cultural categories, more than when I tried so desperately to make it all resolve, more than when I pretended like it never bothered me.

I have wrestled with the Bible. I have spoken my fears out loud—about the genocidal conquests in Canaan, about the slaves, about the "untouchables," about the seven days, about the concubines and sister wives, about the instructions on silence and submission and head coverings. I have lived in the tension, and I live in it still.

I have wrestled with the Bible, and, try as I may, I cannot make it in my own image. I cannot cram it into an adjective, or force it into a blueprint, or fashion it into a weapon to be used against my political and theological enemies. It simply will not be tamed.

But oh, how I have tried to tame it!

Because a blueprint would be easier.

Because a to-do list would be easier.

Because an inspirational desk calendar would be easier.

Because an affirmation of everything I already believe would be easier.

But the Bible is not a blueprint. It isn't a list of bullet points to be followed or a to-do list to be obeyed. It can't be crammed into an adjective or forced into a theology.

No, the Bible is a sacred collection of letters and laws, stories and songs, prophecies and proverbs, philosophy and poems, spanning thousands of years and multiple cultures, written by dozens of authors and inspired by God. It is teeming with metaphor and imagery, tension and contrast. It defies our every effort at systemization. It defies our every attempt at mastery. Indeed, it forces us into community—with God and with one another—*precisely* because it is difficult to understand, *precisely* because it was never meant to be read alone.

Differences in interpretation should not lead us to question one another's passion or commitment to Scripture, but rather invite us into conversation with the shared assumption that we are all struggling toward truth, all trying to figure it out.

Those of us who have wrestled know that no one's interpretation is inerrant. Those of us who have wrestled know we can be wrong.

I love the Bible more now than ever before because I have finally surrendered to God's stories.

God's long, strange, beautiful stories.

We asked questions.

God told stories.

We demanded answers.
God told stories.
We argued theology.
God told stories.

And when those stories weren't enough, when the words themselves would not suffice, the Word became flesh and dwelt among us, laughed among us, wept among us, ate among us, told more stories among us, suffered among us, died among us, and rose among us. The Word entered our story and invited us into his.

The Word became flesh and said, "Watch me. Follow me. See how I do it. This is what I desire."

And the Word loved—
Loved the poor,
Loved the rich,
Loved the sick,
Loved the hungry,
Loved the zealots,
Loved the tax-collectors,
Loved the lepers,
Loved the soldiers,
Loved the foreigners,
Loved the insiders,
Loved the slaves,
Loved the women,
Loved the untouchables,
Loved the religious,
Loved the favored,
Loved the forgotten.
Loved even the enemy.

When words were not enough, the Word took on flesh and *became* the story.

I love the Bible, but I love it best when I love it for what it is, not what I want it to be . . . when I live in the tension and walk with the limp—

The limp that slows me down,

The limp that delights my critics,

The limp I wouldn't change for the world,

The limp that led me to God.

Originally posted on October 10, 2012.

Her Nerdy Love of the Bible
A Reflection by Mihee Kim-Kort

When I was growing up in a Korean immigrant church, it was made clear to me early in my life that the Bible was central to our faith community. We were given multiple versions of Bibles at different ages, but also to commemorate special occasions (I was given one when I graduated high school). We read diligently and followed various Bible-reading plans, we memorized verses and sometimes whole passages, and it seemed so many gatherings were organized around the Bible—services, revivals, regular studies. Not only the stories and narratives but the languages of the Bible became our language: how we encouraged each other, prayed for each other, admonished one another, inspired each other.

And so it was that I found a kindred spirit in Rachel and her nerdy love of the Bible. Although our church didn't participate in programs like Awana, the way she told stories about faith felt familiar—I could tell that she also grew up in a community that lived and breathed the stories in the same ways. When I first came across her work on her blog in 2010 and then later in her book *A Year of Biblical Womanhood*, I heard a resonant way of engaging the biblical texts for faith. Several years after I graduated from seminary with a new kind of relationship with the Bible I saw in her an example of how the stories of the Bible can challenge us and help us grow as individuals and communities in new, beautiful ways.

One of the ways Rachel showed me the beauty of the sacred texts of our faith as more than proof texts or static or calcified cultural documents was simply through her message of love. I often tell people who may not know of her or have heard of her—that's okay. All you need to know really is that she loved us, loved the church through her witness, her stories, her words. Even if you never met her or talked to her in person, you can know who she was through her books—that's her.

I can still say without an ounce of hyperbole that Rachel was someone whose work changed the trajectory of American Christianity, but she was also totally grounded in her family and friendships—she was authentic and generous, always with her time and help. She was an advocate for the work of people on the margins, for the voices of women, people of color, LGBTQ+ people; and she was relentless in that, courageous and fierce but always erring on the side of compassion, always lifting up our humanity. And all of this, I think, came from her deep love and understanding of the Bible as a story about God's love of humanity throughout history, in the present, and in the future.

Someone once asked me whether I knew her well, and I paused before saying yes, but what I really wanted to say was, actually, she knew *me* well, she knew my heart, and she loved me. That was who she was with countless people. She encouraged me to share my own stories and message of love, but more than that she encouraged me to know and trust and love myself.

As she wrote in *Inspired*, "Jesus invites us into a story that is bigger than ourselves, bigger than our culture, bigger even than our imaginations, and yet we get to tell that story with the scandalous particularity of our particular moment and place in time. We are storytelling creatures because we are fashioned in the image of a storytelling God. May we never neglect the gift of that. May we never lose our love for telling the tale."*

---

* Rachel Held Evans, *Inspired: Slaying Giants, Walking on Water, and Loving the Bible* (Thomas Nelson, 2018), 164.

PART SIX

TELLING THE TRUTH

Essays on Life in the Midst of It All

You Don't Hate Me. You Hate My Brand.

Last week, after a hurried, seven-hundred-word article of mine generated exactly 2.5 gazillion responses on the internet, I found myself lying facedown on top of the covers on our bed in the middle of the day.*

Like, for an hour.

Dan finally walked in to make sure I wasn't dead . . . or worse, watching a Netflix series without him.

"What's up?" he asked.

"I'm just so sick of RHE," I said, my voice muffled by our comforter. "I really need a break from her."

It's funny how, as bizarre as that sounded, Dan knew exactly what I meant. There's the Rachel whose strengths, weaknesses, dreams, quirks, passions, failings, and pet peeves he knows so intimately; the one still in her pajamas at 4 in the afternoon and pouting on his side of the bed; and then there's the Rachel Held Evans who smiles from the corner of a website, cheerfully drumming up blog posts, page views, books, lectures, and the occasional controversy to be digested by the public each day.

---

* Rachel Held Evans, "Why Millennials Are Leaving the Church," CNN Belief Blog, no longer available online.

They aren't complete opposites of one another, of course, but they aren't exactly the same either.

One uses a lot more profanity.

In the publishing industry, we talk a lot about a writer's "brand"—the general impression an author leaves with readers based on her personality, writing style, favorite topics, marketing, packaging, and audience. But these days, you don't have to have a book deal or a literary agent to cultivate a "brand." You just need a little online real estate.

Over time, as your life gets distilled into these little pixels, it's easy for the people who see them—be they friends, acquaintances, or perfect strangers—to assume they represent you in your totality. Even more frightening, as you gather feedback and gain friends/followers/subscribers, you can start to believe it too.

But we are not our messages, no matter how much we believe in them. We are not our filtered photos, or our tweets, or our political and religious ideologies. We are not even the stories we tell, no matter how carefully and truthfully we tell them.

We are not our brands.

We are human beings—little bundles of cells and relationships and hopes and fears that can never be crammed into images or words.

I have to remind myself of this now and then, when I see people discussing me on the internet in terms that dehumanize and reduce. They are caricatures, really, the sort of portraits you can pay a street artist in New Orleans to draw for you. The features are exaggerated, but they are based on just enough reality to look familiar, to make me a little more mindful of those warts and moles and wrinkles. Other artists accentuate the positives, of course, but those are glamor shots and no matter how many I hang in my locker, we all know they're not entirely true; it's all about the lighting.

It would be easier to ask for grace if I'd done a better job of extending it. But I too objectify other people. I've assumed that Mark Driscoll *is* his bullying, macho-man brand, and John Piper the sum of his views on women. While these brands certainly don't spontaneously generate, and while these ideas should be discussed, debated, and sometimes denounced, I find myself reluctant to retweet the fake Twitter accounts or join in any online jeering. Because it's a heck of a lot easier to dish it out than it is to eat it up, let me tell you, and I think sometimes we inadvertently perpetuate celebrity culture by railing so loudly against it, by feeding into the caricatures with our derision.

As much as I find Mark Driscoll's "brand" highly distasteful and seriously problematic, I don't know the man, so I have no business hating him. And as much as you may love or hate the RHE brand, most of you don't really know the girl behind it, no matter how candid I am with you, no matter how hard I try to be real.

The truth is, that dude whose blog posts totally rub you the wrong way may be the best person in the world with which to watch a football game or talk theology over beer. That acquaintance on Facebook whose pictures make her life seem perfect may struggle with self-doubt, depression, and fear. That stuffy Calvinist you love to hate may melt into a goofy, delightful playmate when he's tickling his kids on the living room floor. The feminist you always imagine shouting other people down may have an unbelievably tender heart. The pastor you think is always wrong probably gets a few things right. And the pastor you think is always right definitely gets some stuff wrong.

Perhaps the most radical thing we followers of Jesus can do in the information age is treat each other like humans—not heroes, not villains, not avatars, not statuses, not Republicans, not Democrats, not Calvinists, not Emergents—just humans. *This wouldn't mean we would stop disagreeing*, but I think it would mean we would disagree well.

It's hard acknowledging the limits of a medium through which my own writing career has flourished, but I want you to know: The conversations we have here—as encouraging, informative, and life-changing as they can often be—are meant to be brought to dinner tables, coffee shops, AA meetings, parks, church fellowship halls, long car rides, dorm rooms, and diners, among people who (whether they agree or disagree) can look you in the eye and take you in, not as a brand but as a human being. It's riskier, I know, but it's truer. It's better. And I think it's what good writing is intended to accomplish—to connect us to the truth in one another, our world, and the divine . . . in real life, not just our heads.

As if this post wasn't self-indulgent enough, I should confess I've been experiencing some growing pains. I love that the blog is growing and that more people are reading my articles and books, but I'm in that awkward teenage stage when your arms and legs are suddenly longer so you're knocking stuff over and running into doors. I'm upsetting apple carts I didn't even mean to upset, apparently making theological statements about views I didn't even know existed. I feel a little in over my head, to be honest.

(Let's get real. When all you've got is an English literature degree and they're asking you to comment on substitutionary atonement at Christian colleges and church trends on CNN, something's gone amiss.)

So I'm recalibrating a bit, figuring out what it means to steward whatever influence I have in ways that are both creative and sustainable, and that perhaps give some other folks the chance to step up to the mic. I'm also pouring the best of myself into a new book, which means posts may be a bit spottier . . . and weirder, as they will likely have been written after 1 a.m.

Thanks for your patience, wisdom, support, and willingness to call me on my crap. You've helped me grow my brand, yes, but you've also made me a better person. I hope we get the chance to really know one another someday.

Originally posted on August 15, 2013.

Stay and Complicate
A REFLECTION BY GLENNON DOYLE

During a conversation about the cage of masculinity, I asked the poet Ocean Vuong if he still identified as a man. He said, "I go by he/him pronouns, even when I don't always feel at home in it or amongst its ranks . . . I don't think the work is finished in maleness. Just because it's been poorly demonstrated does not mean that it's finished . . . My decision is to stay and complicate."*

There are groups who find their identity and power in whom they let in and whom they keep out. Some of us are born into and raised in that water. Then one day, we rub our eyes and suddenly see for the first time the murkiness of the water we've been swimming in. Others of us are born on the shore but we become so afraid by the uncertainty and chaos of life that we jump in the water ourselves—lured in by the false certainty and safety offered by strongmen.

Either way, we do wake up. Doubts and questions stir in our innermost beings. Privately, at first, we wonder what we'll do. Will we choose to keep the safety of the community and abandon our individuality, moral conscience, and intellectual integrity? Or will we abandon our community—all those we love—so that we don't have to abandon ourselves? What will we choose?

---

* We Can Do Hard Things Episode 84, https://podcasts.apple.com/ca/podcast/we-can-do-hard-things/id1564530722?i=1000556261871.

There are some of us, like Jesus, like Ocean, like Rachel Held Evans, who choose neither. They care too much about the people in the group to leave them—and they care too much about the people outside the group to leave them out. They find themselves unable to abandon their own faith or to cede their power to participate in the ongoing struggle of defining that faith for themselves and for the world. So they find a third way. They stay and complicate. They stand in the doorway of the castle and they use their entire body, mind, heart, and voice to hold the door open. They refuse to budge.

I don't know how Rachel did it. Day after day, year after year, I watched her deepen and widen the definition of Christian. She stood strong, right in the belly of the beast, refusing to abandon herself, her people, or her God. She brought truth to the gatekeepers—pushing, correcting, and growing them. When they fired back, she absorbed their arrows so that those outside the gates—those already so exhausted from defending their humanity—would not have to. She sneaked people in and out of the gates. And, because she was so full of the God she loved, she kept loving them all: the gatekeepers, the gated, and those outside the gates. Somehow, she just kept loving them all.

God bless those who refuse to believe that that work is finished. And God bless those who love them all, for theirs is the Kingdom of God.

Scattered Thoughts on My Life in the Christian "Industry"

A lot of churches have green rooms these days.

And I'm not sure how I feel about that.

I sit in the green room, fidgeting with my water bottle and trying not to make eye contact with the famous preacher whose pictures line the walls. I wonder if they're expecting someone like him today, and I wonder if I'll ever be able to speak in front of a room full of people without getting pee-in-my-pants nervous about it, without feeling out-of-place.

Afterward, people will have questions.

Questions I don't have the answers to.

And I'll watch the disappointment spread across their faces when they realize that I'm just as frightened and confused as they are about this thing we call faith, that I'm not the authority figure they think that they need.

There are microphones and there are lights, and sometimes it feels like a big performance. I wish Lady Gaga would show up and do it instead.

I fit in best with those who don't fit in.

A group of two hundred people, half of whom identify as

LGBTQ+, laughs at all the right spots, waits patiently through the hiccups, embraces me like a sister.

There is bread and there is wine, and sometimes it feels like heaven come to earth. And I am grateful in a way I've never known before.

A man comes up to me afterward and says it was the first time in fifteen years he felt brave enough to take communion. We were brave together, I think.

But I soon forget the conversation because I'm too busy arguing with my publisher. They won't let me use the word "vagina" in my book because we have to sell it to Christian bookstores, which apparently have a thing against vaginas.* I make a big scene about it and say that if Christian bookstores stuck to their own ridiculous standards, they wouldn't be able to carry the freaking Bible.

I tell everyone that I'm going to fight it out of principle, but I cave within a few days because I want Christian bookstores to carry the sanitized version of my book because I want to make a lot of money, because we've needed a new roof on our house for four years now, and because I really want a Mac so I can fit in at the megachurches.

I feel like such a fraud.

And then a reader bakes me cookies. And then I get an email of encouragement from Australia. And then I share a meal with fellow searchers. And then I sit next to the cutest little girl on the flight home, and she reminds me of the true marvel that is soaring above the clouds.

---

* Rachel's readers snagged onto this comment, which resulted in several follow-up posts that she jokingly referred to as "Vagina-Gate." You can read more at "On Keeping Vaginas Out of Christian Bookstores," Rachel Held Evans Blog, March 23, 2012, https://rachelheldevans.com/blog/vagina-christian-bookstore-a-year-of-biblical-womanhood.

And I want to do well by these good people.

And then my inbox gets a bit too full. And then a commenter calls me a whore. And then Mark Driscoll gets interviewed by Piers Morgan. And then I am warned not to tell anyone about the "gay church." And then I start to worry about my "brand." And then I've gone weeks without seeing my real-life friends and neighbors because I'm too busy traveling the country telling other people to love their friends and neighbors.

And I get overwhelmed and angry and tired in a way I've never been tired before.

Can this . . . industry . . . be good for the soul?

I PULL INTO THE DRIVEWAY AFTER A LONG TRIP, AND witness a miracle.

Pip, the gray wren who shows up every spring, is rebuilding her nest in the corner of our carport again. I thought for sure that she had kicked the can last year, when she suddenly disappeared, leaving a baby bird behind. Yet here she is again! She has pushed the baby bird's bones out of the nest and lined her house with fresh twigs. (We have witnessed a lot of life and death in our carport through the years.)

At the sight of her silhouette in my headlights, I put my head on the steering wheel and cry.

Maybe it's because I'm overtired.

Maybe it's because I'm just glad to be home.

Or maybe it's because the first story I ever wrote was about a bird and a nest.

It was third grade, and I wrote the story to read out loud at the annual third grade talent show. It was called "A Helping Wing," and it told of a little robin who broke her wing and needed help building her nest. A troupe of local mockingbirds and cardinals, sparrows and owls brought pieces of their own nests to add to hers, and they all lived happily ever after.

After the talent show, the mother of another student came up to me and said that my story made her cry . . . in a good way.

And that was when I knew I wanted to be a writer.

Now I'm crying into the steering wheel because it's been harder than I thought to stay the course, harder than I thought to remember why I'm doing all of this in the first place.

But Pip has just reminded me: I'm here to write about how a little gray wren builds her nest in our carport every year and to wonder what this might say about God.

It's that simple.

It's that hard.

It's that wonderful.

But a lot of churches have green rooms these days.

And I'm not sure how I feel about that.

Originally posted on March 14, 2012.

Everything Will Pass

A REFLECTION BY CINDY WANG BRANDT

I followed Rachel before she became RHE. I cheered along with her when she got to guest blog for larger platforms, when her posts would go viral, when she herself became the larger platform that she generously lent to others. I was an OG fangirl. Perhaps because I knew of her way back when, I was able to observe the demeanor in which she handled her fast growing fame. I remember one time she said, "I am well aware that one day, this may all go away." She was speaking of how fleeting and fickle online fame can be, how the tides could turn with a switch of algorithms, or any number of unknown factors. None of us could have predicted we would lose her to illness at her young age.

Her humility and how loosely she held her notoriety allowed her to do her work with integrity. As someone who was a part of the blogging ecosystem in the late 00s, she was one of very few who modeled that authenticity. She didn't write to pad her ego; didn't suffer the indignities of online criticism for her own gain; she wrote for the love of her craft, her ideas, and her faith. She worked hard and smart and she did it knowing it could all go away.

RHE was and is a powerful force. She helped me find my voice as a woman of color embedded in a faith tradition that didn't honor my worth the way I deserve. She empowered me to be loud, to be fierce, to stake my claim with audacity among men and other authority leaders. She inspired me to work hard, project my voice, and demand that what I had to say was important and mattered.

But Rachel reminds me that none of it does; that everything will pass. Rachel helps me breathe, she coaxes me to rest, and she ingrained in me that I matter not just because of what I do and say, but because I am.

I need both, the ferocity to assert myself and the humility to step back. I carry RHE and Rachel in me, hard and soft at the same time.

My Parents

It's far and away the most common question I get asked.

You pose it in the comment section, at book signings, during the Q&A session after a talk, in emails and tweets and handwritten letters.

What about your parents? you ask. *Do they approve of all these changes in your faith? How have they reacted to your questions and doubts? What is your relationship like?*

And I know that for many, there is a question behind the question . . . and often a world of hurt too.

I remember the young woman in Nashville who pulled me aside, tears brimming in her blue eyes, to tell me about how her mother worried about her, argued with her, and was deeply disappointed in her . . . for going to seminary and becoming a pastor (when "the Bible clearly teaches" women cannot serve in such a way). I remember too the college student in Seattle who straight-up begged, *Can you PLEASE write a letter to my parents and tell them that just because I vote for Democrats doesn't mean I'm going to hell!* I've listened as a whole group of twenty-somethings exchanged stories of awkward interventions and emotional meltdowns and dramatic lines-in-the-sand, all over differences of opinion regarding theology or politics or ecclesiology.

There are parents who refused to attend their grandkids'

baptism (because they didn't approve of the method), parents who scheduled pastoral counseling sessions on behalf of their kids (because they were afraid Biology 101 had convinced them to accept evolution), parents who—somewhat endearingly—gift the black sheep of the family a different apologetics book every Christmas (because Lee Strobel is better than socks!). And of course there is the gut-wrenching story of the young man who worked up the courage to come out to his parents only to be told by his father, *"This is worse than if you had died."*

Lord, have mercy.

When I hear these stories, I empathize, but I can't relate.

Because my parents have been wonderful.

We don't always agree on theology or politics (the 2016 election promises to raise the pitch of our dinner conversations a few decibels), but my parents have always prioritized maintaining our relationship over maintaining ideological uniformity.

They never expected their kids to turn out just like them. They never expected my sister and me to parrot their opinions. Rather, they raised us to think for ourselves, to disagree gracefully, and to tell them the truth without fear of judgment. Even when the local gossip flared up around my supposed apostasy, my parents weren't ashamed. On the contrary, they bragged. They hung articles about me on the refrigerator and shared pictures on Facebook of me preaching from a pulpit (an act forbidden in the church in which I grew up). They were, and are, proud of me. They are glad that I am following Jesus—even if it's in my own way, even if it's with *The Book of Common Prayer* tucked under my arm.

It has taken me a long time to appreciate the gravity of that, the gift of it.

I cannot imagine what would have happened if, in those first scary years of doubting and deconstructing my faith, my parents had responded like so many of my friends and tried to fix me. Even when I blustered and fulminated and foolishly rocked the boat for the sake of rocking it, they refused to treat me like a problem or an embarrassment or something to fear. They loved me unconditionally.

And I'm pretty sure their response helped preserve my faith.

I'm certain it preserved our relationship.

Which is why there are times when I want to track these other parents down, grab them by the shoulders and shout: *Don't you get it?! The easiest way to alienate your child for good is to make your love and acceptance of them conditional upon what they believe! Are your political and theological convictions really more important than that relationship?*

One of the most destructive mistakes we Christians make is to prioritize shared beliefs over shared relationship, which is deeply ironic considering we worship a God who would rather die than lose relationship with us.

I'm often asked about how to preserve important relationships in the midst of doubt and change. (In fact I'm thinking of making this a theme in the next book.) There is much that could be said about this, of course, and I've learned much of what I've learned from making mistakes, but I think the most important thing is this: Invest in love. *Risk* in love. Because as the apostle Paul put it, "Three things will last forever—faith, hope, and love—and the greatest of these is love." Beliefs will change, political and theological convictions will alter, even faith and hope will falter. But "*love never fails.*"

God does not demand that we all agree. God only asks that we love one another well.

No parent who loves their child unconditionally is a failure.

And sometimes love means biting your tongue and holding back, even when you don't understand or agree or approve. Unity does not require uniformity.

I'm so grateful for my parents, and for my sister and for Dan, who have loved me through a whole lot of religious change—which has often been public and often been clumsy. And as I finally find myself settling into something of a steady rhythm of faith (dappled, as always, with doubt), it is made all the sweeter by the steadfast love of my mom and dad, which is one of the few things in the world I have never had to question.*

Originally posted on March 27, 2015.

---

* Rachel linked to a guest post written by her father, Peter Held, "For Parents of Doubting Children," at Rachel Held Evans Blog, April 6, 2011, https://rachelheld evans.com/blog/doubting-children-peter-held.

She Never Had to Doubt Their Love

A REFLECTION BY REV. CAROL HOWARD

Rachel and I sat down at one of those unassuming places in rural Tennessee that may have had the world's best vegetables. The restaurant was situated close to where Rachel lived, and where I served as a pastor. After ordering, our conversation quickly turned to theology.

"Do you think I'm a fundamentalist?" Rachel asked.

Startled, I answered, "No!" When I looked up, I realized that Rachel wasn't accusing me or defending herself. In a strange way, the question wasn't even about her. She wanted to explore what I thought.

We had been embedded in a Twitter war over the resurrection for weeks. We were not on opposing sides, exactly. We both believed in the resurrection, but we had differing nuances.

I argued that a person didn't have to believe in the resurrection to be a Christian.

Rachel felt like the resurrection was an essential belief.

Then, I said something on Twitter. I don't really remember the words exactly, but it amounted to, "We need to allow room for smart people in our faith." Which, when you think about the flip side of that statement (and I did not), was incredibly condescending.

Twitter leaped to the occasion. In the swirl of aggressive algorithms, fury became a contagion. I was branded as an insufferable arrogant heretic, while Rachel was branded as not smart.

I'm hoping the former was wrong. We all know that the latter could not have been farther from the truth.

As we ate our greens and mac and cheese, we talked about the "five fundamentals of the faith" and the fundamentalist modernist controversy. Rachel had done a deep dive on the fundamentalist side. I had been taught the modernist side. We compared notes. And then we dreamed about upcoming books.

I loved Rachel's brain. Not only was she brilliant, but she was endlessly curious and open.

I guess she got it honestly, because she also had an open and honest relationship with her parents. Her father was a highly regarded academic where I served. Before the world knew Rachel Held Evans, middle Tennessee knew Dr. Peter Held. So, people often asked Rachel what her parents thought. She answered that her parents sometimes disagreed with her, and they always loved her. She never had to doubt their love.

Here we are, living in this black and white world, endlessly splitting and polarizing. We cut off our families in the frustration of deconstruction. Our youth group buddies unfriend us on Facebook because of our vote in the last election. But Rachel reminds us of a different way. What if we all held beliefs, questioned rigorously, and prioritized relationships above all? What if we never had to doubt love? What a different world this would be.

What I Learned Turning My Hate Mail into Origami

For Lent this year, I wanted to learn a new creative skill that would enable me to turn something ugly into something beautiful, so I resolved on Ash Wednesday to turn some of my hate mail into origami.*

As I wrote back in February, "It felt a little awkward at first, but as I moved my fingers across those painful words, folding them into one another to make wings, then a neck, then a crooked little beak, healing tears fell, and I let my fingers pray."

I've been making origami off and on for forty days now, letting my fingers pray out little swans and sailboats and flowers and foxes, and I've learned some things: about reverse folds and crimp folds, about trial and error, about patience, about retracing steps and following directions, about forgiveness, about letting go, about redirecting some of my anxious and self-focused energy into purposeful acts of creativity and healing, about building bridges, about asking for help.

---

* Rachel Held Evans, "Swords into Plowshares and Hate Mail into Origami," Rachel Held Evans Blog, February 22, 2013, https://rachelheldevans.com/blog/origami-hate-mail.

That last one—asking for help—turned out to be the most instructive part of them all.

The consummate contemplative, I had originally imagined this Lenten practice to be a solitary one. It would be all quiet and meditative and poetic and introspective.

But it was my friend Melissa who mailed me the origami books.

It was my brother-in-law Tim who helped me make my first sailboat.

It was my friend Monika who sat at my kitchen table and made blackout poems out of the most hateful letters, spending Holy Saturday—our special day—forming crooked little pelicans, ducks, and penguins out of scraps of paper.

It was a reader's idea to work some beautiful, affirming words into the process too, inspiring me to scribble the prayer of Teresa of Avila and the fruit of the spirit onto the colored origami paper.

It was my sister who made the jumping frog while we waited for Easter dinner.

It was Dan who managed to make the perfect origami crane in a matter of fifteen minutes . . .

. . . while I only managed to make something that most resembled crumpled paper.

It was the author of one of those letters who emailed an apology, upon learning about my Lenten practice.

It was that email that inspired me to issue a few apologies of my own, to be just a little quicker to listen, slower to speak, and slower to get angry.

What I learned turning my hate mail into origami is that we're meant to remake this world together. We're meant to hurt together, heal together, forgive together, and create together. Far from being all quiet and meditative and poetic and introspective, this practice turned out to be full of laughter, cluttered tables, shared grumbles of frustration, and shared exclamations of delight—*"That totally looks like a flamingo!"*

And in a sense, even the people who continue to hate me and call me names are a part of this beautiful process. Their words, carelessly spoken, spent the last forty days in my home—getting creased and folded, worked over, brushed aside to make room for dinner, stepped on by a toddler, read by my sister, stained with coffee, shoved into a closet when guests arrive, blacked out, thrown away, turned into poems, and folded into sailboats and cranes and pigeons that now sit smiling at me from my office window.

Because I am a real human being, living a very real life, with a very real capacity to be hurt, to be loved, to heal, and to forgive.

And so are my enemies.

And something tells me we would all be a little more careful, a little more gentle, if we knew how long our words linger in one another's lives, if we imagined those words sitting on one another's kitchen tables, shaped like foxes.

Something tells me we would all be a bit slower to speak if we knew just how long it takes to work those ugly, heavy words into something beautiful, something that can float or fly away.

Originally posted on April 1, 2013.

The Afterglow Is Brilliant
A REFLECTION BY DR. PETER ENNS

As I write this, Rachel has been gone for more than five years. I still feel sadness, disbelief, and anger that her light went out at midday.

Rachel was destined to be her generation's Barbara Brown Taylor or Anne Lamott. That is what I feel we have lost. And this still grieves me personally, thinking of the impact Rachel had on me and my family.

I have to confess, I am still working to internalize what Rachel saw clearly at half my age. Turn hate mail into origami. Indeed. Don't answer back in kind, but own it and make something beautiful out of it. Well done, Rachel. I'll keep trying. I promise. But it's hard sometimes . . . I know you know that.

What I miss most is the impact she had on some people I care for. One of them was my daughter. While at a Christian college, she struggled mightily with her faith (as most Christian college students usually will). Believing had become more complicated than youth group and teen study Bibles had led her to believe. The faith of her youth wasn't cutting it. Her faith was evolving, though she did not yet have the language to express it.

Rachel gave her that language. My daughter had so many questions—and deep doubts—which was unsettling enough. But it was compounded by the nagging feeling that the very act of questioning at all was a sign of a faith that was weak and unraveling, and deeply disappointing to God.

I gave her a copy of *Faith Unraveled*—back when it had the way cooler title: *Evolving in Monkey Town*. She devoured it, and when I saw her soon thereafter . . . well . . . her face was peaceful, her tone joyful. She was transformed.

She had found in Rachel—finally—someone who understood her, someone who articulated her experience and who was asking her questions. Someone who was brave enough to be vulnerable and honest enough to write it all down, humor and kindness thrown in. "What a relief. Maybe I'm not alone. Maybe I'm not broken or dirty. Maybe God doesn't hate me." How many people have been able to say this, too, because of Rachel's loving words?!

Rachel helped my daughter (and so many others) catch a vision for a bigger God who loved her as she was, who was not annoyed at her questions, and in fact welcomed them.

I miss Rachel and wish she could still be that living voice of power and peace for young people, especially women. I feel her loss acutely for the sake of my college students, many of whom are trying to figure some things out and who might also need to hear what my daughter heard years ago.

They still can, of course. Though it's not the same, we still have her books and blogs. The light has gone out, but the afterglow is brilliant—a guide for others following Rachel's path of embracing belief and doubt.

Ashamed

I am ashamed.

I am ashamed that we feast while our neighbors go hungry.

I am ashamed of our selective memory.

I am ashamed of the bumper stickers, the T-shirts, the logos, the fog machines, the light shows, the celebrities, and that paralyzing fear of Silence we're so bound and determined to avoid that we keep shouting and shouting and shouting at one another till our words are just clanging cymbals echoing off church walls.

I am ashamed of the walls. They are built high, with circles of barbed wire around the top, to keep pests away from our bread and wine, to keep the Silence from getting in.

I am ashamed of the abuse, the shaming, the cover-ups, the secrets, the millstones being forged in Sunday school classrooms and pastors' offices where people are supposed to be safe, and the way I want to watch those millstones drag a few more bodies down to the bottom of the sea.

I am ashamed of the violence—in our theology, in our words, in myself.

I am ashamed of how we have confused two kingdoms—demanding God's name on Caesar's coins, invoking God's will in our wars, reducing God's Word to *against* or *for*. We've turned the Bible into a position paper.

I am ashamed of our mindless routines: segregated Sunday mornings, men up front and women in the back, the Romans Road and the Sinner's Prayer, "*what were you wearing to make him say/think/do that?*," the relentless chase after the American dream.

I am ashamed of mission trips that hurt more than help, of hijacked stories and imagined heroics, of our industrial savior complex, and most of all, my own stubborn complicity in the very injustices I decry. There is "slavery stitched into the fabric of my clothes" but I've learned to ignore the itch.*

I am ashamed that the church has become the scariest place to come out instead of the safest, that it routinely shuts out the most vulnerable, the most hurting, the most despised, when those were the people Jesus started with, the people he loved most.

I am ashamed that we are so quick to speak and so slow to listen.

I am ashamed by our lack of imagination, ashamed by our hypocrisy, ashamed by the heavy loads we bind up to place on people's backs, ashamed by the logs in our eyes and the stones in our hands.

I am ashamed by our failure to love.

I am ashamed of the way I judge those I deem judgmental, the way I stumble through my day without prayer, the way I issue praises to heaven in one breath and curse my brothers in the next, the way I talk a big game about loving others and then brush past the woman crying in the airport, the way cynicism seeps into my bones, the way I zone out in front of my wireless glowing mirror in a pathetic effort to avoid confronting it all. *Who's the fairest?*

I am ashamed, and I am sorry.

But I am not ashamed of the gospel.

I am not ashamed of this scandalous news, whispered first by

---

* The quotation is from a line in the song "Ain't No Reason," by Brett Dennen.

a pregnant Palestinian teenager whose dream for the world shattered the proud and lifted up the humble.

I am not ashamed of the carpenter anointed to restore sight to the blind and set prisoners free, or his ragamuffin band of fishermen and tax collectors and zealots, his friendship with prostitutes, his strange ways and long stories, his challenge to the religious, his radical notion that women are human.

I am not ashamed of the good news that we have it backwards: Privileged are the poor, the peacemakers, the merciful, and the suffering. Cursed are the rich, the full, the merciless, the hateful.

I am not ashamed that when God strapped on sandals and walked among us, God fed the hungry, wept with the mourning, touched the untouchable, turned water into wine, cracked jokes about religion, obeyed his mom, defended the defenseless, bantered with children, forgave his enemies, and reminded us that the whole point of it all is to love God and love our neighbors well. That's it.

I am not ashamed that when God strapped on sandals and walked among us, God rode a donkey instead of a war horse.

I am not ashamed of the good news that we don't have to wait around for the right leader or the right government because there's a new and better kingdom growing in us and around us, a kingdom that welcomes all to the table.

I am not ashamed of the good news that Jesus is Lord and Caesar is not.

And I am not ashamed of the very good news that when God strapped on sandals and walked among us and endured the very worst this world has to offer, the very ugliest inside of us, God looked upon it all and said, *"Father forgive them, for they know not what they do."*

And I am not ashamed of the very good news, first shouted by another unlikely woman in another garden, and then echoed through the centuries in every corner of the earth, that Jesus Christ has risen from the dead! *Risen indeed*, we say, even when we're not quite sure we believe it.

I am not ashamed of this great cloud of witnesses, kicking up dust ahead of me on the path. They are hermits and homemakers and sinners and saints and pilgrims and poets and mothers and activists and peacemakers and friends. They bind up wounds and stand up to bullies and offer rides and listen well and make meals and let things go and work hard and fail sometimes. But they keep telling the story—this story that sets both the oppressed and the oppressors free, this story that may even save me.

I am not ashamed of love. Love casts out fear; love knits us together; love conquers all.

I am not ashamed of the church. She is a survivor, after all, a work-in-progress, a stubborn bride-to-be. The gates of hell will not prevail against her, they say. So I guess I better quit hedging my bets.

I am not ashamed because there are all these little mustard seeds scattered across our broken, shameful world, some of them just now swelling and splitting underneath the dark soil; others breaking through the surface with a garish flash of green; others meandering toward the sun, desperate for light or rain or some sort of trellis; others growing slow and steady into tall shade tress with limbs like arms wide open to the world, welcoming the birds of the air to nest in their branches.

I am not ashamed because my roots are deep and the sky is tall, and there will always be some place to grow.

I am not ashamed because I am not alone.

Originally posted on March 7, 2013.

I Am Ashamed

A REFLECTION BY KATHY ESCOBAR

When people ask me if I'm a Christian, I always respond the same way, "Um, it depends on what you mean by Christian?"

For good reason, so many of us have become more ashamed to identify as Christian because of the misperception of what it has come to mean in our society. With the hazardous mash-up of Christian nationalism and unhinged political power in the USA hell-bent on dehumanizing women, immigrants, LGBTQ+, and pretty much everyone we love and care about, it's hard not to feel terribly ashamed—and afraid, too. It is painful to have ever aligned myself with a system so far removed from the ways of Jesus.

I think of Rachel so often in this current social climate that has become exponentially more toxic since her death. I miss her voice, her presence, her strength, her clarity, her vulnerability, her hope. Along with countless others, I long for her simple yet powerful words that so easily translated the dissonance we were experiencing into the language of our souls. What would she be posting today? Who would she make mad today? (a sure sign that she was on the right track). What would she be calling us to? What prophetic comfort would she offer to help us straighten our backs and still hold our heads high?

Her words are timeless, clarifying, empowering, strengthening, and needed now more than ever—reminders that disrupting power matters, that mustard seeds can move mountains, that we can't let toxic systems destroy our hope, that we can build a more equitable world, that a simple faith that doesn't have to be defended is enough, and most of all—that we do not ever have to be ashamed of love, equality, and hope.

Rachel, we're borrowing some hope from you right now. We really need it.

I Don't Always Tell You

I don't always tell you about the mornings I wake up and feel the absence of God as though it were a presence—thick and certain, remembered all over again the way you remember in the morning that someone you love has died.

Or about the days when the idea that a single religion can stop the CNN crawler from reporting one more missile strike, one more downed plane, one more bombed hospital, strikes me as freshly stupid, dangerously naïve.

I don't always tell you about how sometimes I'm not sure I want to bring kids into a world like this one, a world so full of suffering.

Because that sort of thing doesn't exactly sell off the shelves at Christian bookstores, does it?

What do you do when the religion that is supposed to give you comfort and direction is the cause of your pain and confusion?

What do you do when religious people respond to your questions by calling you names? By mocking you? By casting you out?

I don't always tell you about the depth of my doubt.

I don't always tell you about how the cynicism settles in, like a diaphanous fog.

Or about how sometimes, just the thought of reading one more Christian book I only half believe exhausts and bores me.

There is no need for a diagnosis. This isn't the sort of clinical depression with which so many good people struggle. Privileged as I am, I can cut off the flow of information—shut the laptop, turn off the news, and head outside—and my mood lifts. I can gaze into the dizzying blue of a clear sky and believe in God again, because at least for me, that sky isn't filled with missiles or bombs. I have the luxury of forgetting.

Sometimes it frightens me, how effortlessly I can move from belief to unbelief as one would move from room to room.

Kathleen Norris called it *acedia*, the noonday demon, a religious and relational apathy that "makes it seem that the sun barely moves, if at all."*

That sounds about right to me—stuck in the unforgiving glare of midday when every truth has a sharp edge.

I don't always tell you, because when a reader says, "I love it when you write something VULNERABLE!," I wonder if she really means it, if she really wants to know that the demon whose voice she thinks she's quieted in her own heart is screaming like hell in mine, and that the scariest thing about being VULNERABLE, about exposing myself to the world without a religion or a platform or a "brand" for protection is that I might lose them for good . . . or, perhaps, learn that I can breathe without them.

And that's not exactly the sort of born again experience the publishers pay for.

Originally posted on July 28, 2014.

---

* Evagrius Ponticus (345–399), *The Praktikos*, quoted in Kathleen Norris, *Acedia & Me: A Marriage, Monks, and a Writer's Life* (Riverhead, 2008).

Tending to the Spiritual Fire of Our Generation
A REFLECTION BY KAITLIN B. CURTICE

My favorite Rumi quote goes like this:

"Stay in the spiritual fire. Let it cook you."

As soon as I saw these words a few years ago, I knew it was both a comfort and a call, not just for me personally, but for all of us as human beings—we are called to stay in the spiritual fire, and to let it cook us.

I know that's an uncomfortable, if not violently culinary way to see our lives, but lean deeper in and ask what it might mean. We are called to show up in the world, but to do it in a steady, ready, tender, fierce way. I am a Potawatomi person, we are the firekeepers, and every day I think about the fire I carry and ask how I can help others carry their fires, too.

This is what Rachel Held Evans embodied for so many of us and continues to inspire in us today—a tending to the spiritual fire of our generation.

Rachel and I met in a Twitter debate with another author in 2017.

I still remember the day, in the car with my kids, about to take them to a park, and I had to pull off the road onto the curb of a small neighborhood road to check Twitter and continue the interaction. What I felt instantly with Rachel was a true sense of kinship, and the more we got to know one another, the more we deepened that care in our friendship, the more we tended to our own fires—together.

We especially bonded over the running joke that was announced in 2018 from the stage of the Why Christian? conference when Rachel shared photos of us from school, asking the audience who they thought was a better Christian: me, holding my Bible tight to my chest for a public school photo, or her, holding her Best Christian Attitude Award. The audience laughed and the two of us laughed because we knew the irony of it all, that we showed up to this liminal space of asking big questions of our faith when we grew up being trained to be so sure of it.

In her piece "I Don't Always Tell You" Rachel writes:

> I don't always tell you about the depth of my doubt.
> I don't always tell you about how the cynicism settles in, like a diaphanous fog.

Being a memoir writer and someone who explores spirituality, identity, and healing, I am part of the storytelling community, one in which we are all about vulnerability and honesty.

People love that, up to a certain extent.

They love it until they don't.

They love it until they realize how truly tired we are, or how we could never possibly tell *the whole truth*.

Sometimes Rachel and I would text or call each other up and talk about *that*, those liminal spaces, the complexities of being a writer, of asking questions of our faith and spiritual life when we live much of it so publicly.

But what I know is this: Keeping the spiritual fire burning, letting it *cook us*, is about what we don't always speak. It's about staying in the fire for the long haul, asking the questions we really won't want

BRAVING *the* TRUTH 349

to ask, acknowledging every doubt and shadow, and learning to love what they teach us about ourselves and the world.

Because of the way Rachel embodied solidarity and kinship with me and so many others, I am trying to find ways to do the same with other women, with a community of writers who need space to say the things we don't always know how to say, to name our fears, to whisper the things we don't want to tell others.

"You can show up to me as you are," I say.

"You can hold the complexity with me, and I'll listen," I text.

Because being a "spiritual writer" is hard as hell in a publishing world that often wants numbers and catchy titles, in a social-media-driven world that wants dualism, extremism, and hot takes to feed a transactional culture and toxic algorithm.

So we stop, breathe, pause, and remember that the same fire that has fed the prophets and teachers before us is the same fire that feeds us now, and on the hard days, we get to sit there with a book and a good cup of coffee and the steady presence and memory of a friend who will hold it all with us when we don't exactly know how to hold it ourselves.

Thank you for your spiritual fire, Rachel. It's still tending to our tired, weary, dreaming souls.

> My love,
> Let the fire
> cook you,
> but don't
> get fully
> cooked.
> We need
> you tender,
> soft and
> fleshy, bone

and skin still
reminding us
what it means
to hold the holy
in every second
so that future
generations can know
what it feels like
to be held
by that sacred
fire, too.

Hey Mommy Bloggers, Thanks

"So you're a mommy blogger?"

When I started blogging a decade ago, I got this question a lot, and at times I responded with a touch of antipathy. Childless and independent, with far more interest in the latest political and theological debates than trends in cloth diapering, I, like so many others, dismissed "mommy blogging" as trivial, jejune.

It didn't help that, back then, women writers of faith were such an underrepresented group online, several advertisers and publishers literally had no category for women like me, so they labeled me a "mommy blogger," whether the term fit my work or not.

"I do have a blog," I'd respond defensively, "but I'm definitely *not* a mommy blogger. I don't even have kids."

But my attitude toward "mommy blogs" changed once I actually started reading them. In between the photo dumps and product placements were some of the most honest, considered, and powerful essays I'd ever read, essays about things that really mattered: faith, doubt, feminism, race, mental health, addiction, community, friendship, mindfulness, grace, and the unique joys and challenges of raising children in our highly connected, yet increasingly isolating culture.

The women behind these blogs wrote with uncommon humor, courage, and insight, often posting multiple entries a week—a schedule that would make the most seasoned professional columnist sweat. As I subscribed to more and more of their feeds, I came to realize the term "mommy blog" was insufficient to describe the breadth and depth of what these women were writing about online.

Sarah Bessey's reflections on faith and feminism and Osheta Moore's practical guidance on justice and peace challenged me to live as a more faithful follower of Jesus in those quiet, unpublicized moments when faithfulness really matters.*

Denene Millner's posts about parenting Black boys as a Black mother did far more to wake me up to realities of racial injustice in this country than my subscription to *The New York Times*, and Kristen Howerton's "Rage Against the Minivan" blog introduced me to the concept of white privilege in a way that made sense and inspired change.†

Bunmi Laditan, Jenny Lawson, and Jen Hatmaker routinely had me in stitches at my laptop. Nish Weiseth basically made me a Democrat. Mihee Kim-Kort became one of my pastors.‡

Glennon Doyle, of course, used her disarming humor and candor to invite readers to get real about everything from addiction, to perfectionism, to bullying, to the futility of trying desperately to "seize the day" amidst the fog of parenting young children.§ (Glennon's gone on to write two bestselling books and raise millions of dollars for vulnerable women and children. The term "mommy blogger" doesn't exactly cut it.)

Though my life looked very different from the lives of these women, their work gave me permission to exhale, to relax into

---

* See https://sarahbessey.com; https://osheta.com/.
† See https://mybrownbaby.com/; https://rageagainsttheminivan.com/.
‡ See https://bunmiladitan.wordpress.com/; https://thebloggess.com/ (Jenny Lawson); https://jenhatmaker.com/; https://www.mkimkort.com/.
§ Originally posted at https://momastery.com/blog/. No longer available.

the spirit of "me too" that pervaded the comment sections. They taught me too that our biggest questions, our deepest desires and fears and joys, often meet us in the quotidian challenges of marriage, parenting, and home life—at the 3 a.m. feeding, in the tantrum at Costco, amidst piles of dirty laundry, at the community playground, in the bouquet of weeds left carefully on your pillow.

When I clicked through images of the largest protest in US history to see millions of women—old and young, married and single, parents and nonparents—marching peacefully through the streets of every major city in the US, I couldn't help but smile and think, *"Look: mommy bloggers."*

Never underestimate what women can do together.

Eighteen months ago, I became a mother myself. So far, parenting has been a lot like driving without a GPS. We bought the parenting books of course, and we can turn to friends and family for help and advice, but when things get especially hairy, I often find myself conjuring the wisdom of mommy bloggers, past and present, whose words guide me the way a local gives an out-of-towner directions: *"Turn left at the big red barn. Go down that road a few miles, maybe three. You'll see a tree that's been struck by lightning. Make a right there. Watch your speed because the sheriff's always out this time of day."*

This terrain is new, yet familiar.

The emotional ups and downs are intense, but not surprising. The hard days are hard, but not unexpected. The beautiful moments are everything they said they would be . . . and so much more.

Thanks to all those "mommy blogs," I knew ahead of time that feeling guilty, exhausted, and even angry didn't make me a bad mom, that it's okay to ask for help, to say you're not okay. Thanks to

---

* Here, Rachel is referencing the Women's March which took place on January 21, 2017, one day after the first inauguration of Donald Trump as president.

the courage of other moms, I knew ahead of time that pregnancy after a miscarriage would be scary, that just because breastfeeding is "natural" doesn't mean it's easy, that my marriage and body and worldview would inevitably change, that "sometimes you feel two feelings at the same time, and that's okay."

. . . Okay, so that last one is from Daniel Tiger . . . I can't help it; that cat's in my head.

I wanted to write about this because the other day, my son decided to turn another diaper change into a wrestling match, and in my exhaustion, I got so frazzled and frustrated, I started shaking. I felt out of control, and that scared me. Then, from somewhere in the past, I heard the voice of a mommy blogger: *Put him in his crib with some toys where he'll be safe, and give yourself three minutes in the bathroom to cry it out. It's better for you both if you take the time to regain your calm.*

I have no idea where I read that advice, but it saved my day.

So, to all the mommy bloggers—

Thanks.

Thanks for being brave with your words and with your lives. Thanks for telling the truth. Thanks for pushing through all the condescension and sexism and trivialization to share your point of view. Thanks for hitting "publish" even when it was hard.

I'm a better mom, a better Christian, and a better person because of you.

Originally posted on August 3, 2017.

The Risk of Birth

My son entered the world to the sound of laughter.

In February 2016.

When you've been married for thirteen years, you know exactly what kind of humor your partner will appreciate when she's actively pushing a baby out of her body, and Dan, sensing it would make me feel confident and safe, had the entire delivery room in stitches that night.

I don't remember much of what he said, but I remember my OB laughed so hard I worried she'd drop the scissors as she passed them to Dan to cut the cord, and I remember being the happiest I've ever been when that little boy's body was placed on my chest, all startled and slimy and mine.

A few days after my son's birth, Donald Trump won the New Hampshire primary. They said he'd never win the nomination, so I didn't worry too much. Our lives were utterly consumed with swaddling, nursing, burping, and maintaining the journal we meticulously updated with details of our baby's diaper contents to report to the pediatrician because we were completely, unabashedly *those parents*.

The days and nights that followed were, as everyone always says, a blur. One can never prepare for the physical and emotional demands of caring for a newborn for the first time, and I was lucky to have a relatively smooth delivery and postpartum experience. The great thing about motherhood is that it demands the best of you, and then some. It demands more from you than you ever knew you had, and it's empowering to rise to that occasion, to learn something new about yourself.

Eventually, days became days again, and nights, for the most part, nights. (We still get the occasional 3 a.m. wake-up call.) The more mobile our little guy gets, the more we see of his personality—athletic, intrepid, clever, and curious, with a sophisticated sense of humor and a penchant for bluegrass.

I knew I would love this little boy, of course, but I had no idea I would like him this much.

Somewhere between our baby's first laugh and his first clumsy crawl, Trump won the nomination. Just a few days before our baby's first steps, Trump won the presidency.

November, 2016.

What a world my boy toddled into. We like to refer to the "dumpster fire" of 2016. Memes abound (my favorite: "have you tried turning 2016 off and on again?"). From what seemed like a surge in celebrity deaths, to an especially divisive, racist, and misogynistic election, to what is beginning to look like a global shift toward authoritarianism and xenophobia, we have good reasons to be sad, good reasons to be deeply concerned.

And yet, rolling around on the floor with my baby yesterday, his nose pressed against mine as he squealed with laughter, I was reminded once again that 2016 was, by far, the best year of my life.

Oh, it was the hardest year on my marriage, for sure, and on my body, my faith, and my ongoing battle against cynicism, but there is no doubt in my mind that 2016 will always be remembered as his year, the one that brought the world his first yawn, his first giggle, his first fall, his first Christmas, his first word.

The year didn't belong to Donald Trump, after all. That's not something he can buy with his money or win with his pomposity.

We find ourselves in these strange juxtapositions from time to time, between the stories of our lives and the stories of the world around us. Sometimes they align with a sort of poetic symmetry—the gentle rain at the funeral on September 11, the divorce papers arriving the day you get the cancer diagnosis. Other times, the contrast is jolting—the baby cooing in your arms as news of another mass shooting scrolls across the TV, the wedding on Inauguration Day 2017.

For me, the dissonance of this strange year is compounded by the fact that motherhood turned my bleeding heart into a hemorrhage. It's as though I've become porous, my skin absorbing the pain of others, particularly other mamas and babies. (Speaking of which, why did all the good shows this year involve children in peril? I'm looking at you, *Stranger Things*!) Every night, as I nurse my boy in that cozy armchair in his nursery, I think of the Syrian mama nursing her baby in a raft adrift in the Mediterranean Sea. I think of the shell-shocked boy from Aleppo. I think of how every Latino kid taunted by classmates, every soldier sent to war, every autistic kid who will lose his therapy when ACA is repealed, every Black man shot by police is somebody else's baby boy, somebody else's most important person in the world. I still, almost every day, think of Sandy Hook.

"Compassion is the sometimes fatal capacity for feeling what it is like to live inside somebody else's skin," writes Frederick Buechner. "It's the knowledge that there can never really be any peace and joy for me until there is peace and joy finally for you too."*

Motherhood invited me into other people's skin in a way I've never experienced before. So my joy is big and real and consuming,

---

* Frederick Buechner, *Wishful Thinking: A Theological ABC* (HarperOne, 1993), 18.

but also incomplete. I am overwhelmed by the conviction that every mother should be able to feed her baby like this, in safety and contentedness, and I am haunted by the reality that this is still far from the case.

In 2016, I became more aware than ever of the darkness around us, and more invested than ever in lighting the path.

In 2016, the world bared its teeth and my baby giggled back.

Blessedly, in the aftermath of the election, I had the occasion to revisit Madeleine L'Engle's fantastic Genesis Trilogy, as I've been asked to write the foreword for a new edition. (If you want to know how I reacted to the honor of that request, watch Joe Biden win the Medal of Freedom for a visual approximation.)

"If I affirm that the universe was created by a power of love," wrote Madeleine L'Engle about her own fears of raising children during the Cold War, "and that all creation is good, I am not proclaiming safety. Safety was never part of the promise. Creativity, yes; safety, no. All creativity is dangerous . . . To write a story or paint a picture is to risk failure. To love someone is to risk that you may not be loved in return, or that the love will die. But love is worth that risk, and so is birth, its fulfillment."*

She refers, of course, to her famous Advent poem which begins:

> *This is no time for a child to be born,*
> *With the earth betrayed by war & hate*
> *And a comet slashing the sky to warn*
> *That time runs out & the sun burns late.*
>
> . . . .
>
> *When is the time for love to be born?*
> *The inn is full on the planet earth,*

---

* Madeleine L'Engle, *And It Was Good: Reflections on Beginnings* (Convergent, 1983), 15.

And by a comet the sky is torn—
Yet Love still takes the risk of birth.*

This was a strange year to have a baby.

Perhaps, for you, it was a strange year to lose your father, to be ordained, to become a citizen. But if the incarnation has anything to say about it, we don't get to wait around for ideal circumstances to begin creating, birthing, nurturing, planting, protesting, and working together to heal the world.

So my prayer for you today, and in the days, weeks, and months ahead, is this: No matter what it means to you, take the risk of birth. Don't be afraid.

Finish the book. Pursue the relationship. Begin the ministry. Push the boundaries. Join the march. Write the screenplay. Do the dishes. Plant the onions. Carry the child. Roll around on the floor with your giggling toddler as if the world was even fractionally worthy of his presence.

I'm so glad I did.

Originally posted on January 13, 2017.

---

* "The Risk of Birth," in L'Engle, *And It Was Good*, 15.

The Risks of Birth, and Life

A REFLECTION BY SARAH McCAMMON

I never met Rachel Held Evans, but in so many ways, I felt like she understood me completely.

We were born the same year, each went to Christian colleges, and married our college boyfriends—though my first marriage didn't last. We each wrestled with the God of evangelicalism—and found a spiritual home in the Episcopal Church.

We each had two children—although Rachel waited a bit longer than I did.

Which brings me to one of Rachel's writings that still moves me, both as a mother and as a journalist who has covered our nation's political debate around childbirth and women's bodies.

In "The Risk of Birth," Rachel reminisced the "dissonance" of coming to terms with a changing country as she also discovered the joys and exhaustion of new motherhood.

As someone who, by occupational hazard, thinks about the news far more than I'd sometimes like to, I find that Rachel's "strange juxtaposition" of the beauty of new life pressed up against the chronic ugliness of the world cuts deep.

I think of my own experience of Sandy Hook—coming home from a radio shift filled with what felt like wall-to-wall coverage, to my own son, almost the same age as those sweet souls, and sinking into bed in despair. I think of the January day I brought him home from the hospital, how I perceived the cold as if for the first time, in a way that made tears roll down my cheeks as I held him and watched the snowflakes out the window. I think of the physical risks of birth that too many women—particularly Black women—still face, before they even bring their babies home.

And I comfort myself with Rachel's words:

> But if the incarnation has anything to say about it, we don't get to wait around for ideal circumstances to begin creating, birthing, nurturing, planting, protesting, and working together to heal the world.
>
> So my prayer for you today, and in the days, weeks, and months ahead, is this: No matter what it means to you, take the risk of birth. Don't be afraid.

Office of the Night Watch: A Meditation on Nursing

Note: As you may know, Team Evans has officially expanded to become a family of three! Our sweet little guy met the big, wide world three weeks ago and we couldn't be happier . . . or sleepier. A textbook pregnancy ended with a textbook delivery, with all the right doctors and nurses in place. Dan has risen to the occasion of fatherhood with more energy, tenderness, and support than seems possible, and so far motherhood has proven exactly as my friends said—harder and better than I could ever imagine. This past year has taught me a lot about the limits and dangers of social media, so while I'll share some reflections on motherhood from time to time, I won't be posting pictures or details about the little guy himself on my public media channels. As a memoirist and blogger, I love sharing stories from my life with readers who care and relate, but not everything is for public consumption. Thanks ahead of time for respecting that boundary. Thank you, too, for all the heartfelt congratulations and encouragement. It has meant so much over these last nine months and will continue to buoy me in the challenging weeks and months (and years!) ahead. I am deeply, profoundly, inexpressibly grateful.

IF THIS IS NOT PRAYER—THIS WORDLESS, RHYTHMIC meeting of souls, this dance both utterly instinctual and pull-your-hair-out hard—then I don't know what prayer is. *Do you, little one?*

They say the church fathers gave us fixed-hour prayer, but now I know the church mothers marked sacred time long before these hours had names like lauds, sext, vespers, compline, matins, and the office of the night watch. Mamas have been keeping watch for as long as God has cooed and whimpered and shrieked through a baby's tiny lungs every hour . . . every two hours . . . or, if you're lucky, every three. If this is not prayer—this half-awake yet fully alive cycle of feeding and being fed, of fussing and fumbling through the dark—then I don't know what prayer is. *Do you, little one?*

Once, before you were born, I tried to keep the offices for forty days. Baby, I gave up after five! Only the joyless saints of bygone time, I reasoned, would wake at 3 a.m. to talk to God. But there is no giving up this time around. You are far more hungry for milk than I have ever been hungry to pray, little one. And so I rise again, and again, and again, never knowing if you will be sleepy or ravenous or recalcitrant, or if our next session will be like walking beside the still waters or wrestling with an angel.

Perhaps it's wrong to say it out loud, little one, but I suspect I will love you more than I will ever love God. Critics may call this a failure, but if three weeks of motherhood offer but a glint of the Ultimate Love coursing through the universe, then my heart could never bear its full force. I love God the way you love me—wholly, but not on purpose, the way you are learning to breathe without being told how to do it, the way you root and claw at my breast until you are filled. It worried me at first, how you only looked me square in the eyes for a few seconds before glancing away, but the doctors said this is normal, that those gazes just beyond my face are your way of taking me in without growing overwhelmed, of loving me without looking right at me. If this is not prayer, little one, then I don't know what prayer is.

The office of the night watch, between 1:30 and 4:30 a.m., is the hardest and the best. We are resting, yet working. We are two, yet one. We are saying everything there is to say to one another without uttering a single word. Sometimes it feels like we are the only two breathing bodies in the universe, the only two souls awake and alive. So I pray:

> Keep watch, dear Lord, with those who work, or watch, or weep this night, and give your angels charge over those who sleep. Tend the sick, Lord Christ; give rest to the weary, bless the dying, soothe the suffering, pity the afflicted, shield the joyous; and all for your love's sake. Amen.

The office of the night watch is the hardest and the best. We keep it together, little one, and I am so glad.

Originally posted on February 25, 2016.

The Gravity of Real Life
A REFLECTION BY WINNIE VARGHESE

You are but dust, and to dust you shall return.

Those are the words to be said as you make the cross with your thumb on foreheads with the ash from the burned palm leaves of the Palm Sunday of the previous year.

Rachel posted those words days before she went into the hospital.

It was Ash Wednesday.

This dust, the remnant of our hopes and ambitions and all of our hard work to be good and useful and loved and loving. At times I wish for the intensity of self-focus that fundamentalists have, even after they leave fundamentalism. The knowing that what you personally decide to do matters a lot to God. You matter a lot. Your project of understanding who God is beyond what the churches you grew up in told you. Your knowing that your life is playing out on a grand stage in this universe, populated with balls of dust like you, earnestly scrapping for something.

Rachel knew that God was to be known in us, despite everything she had been taught. Then she went out and found us and reintroduced us to a God who delighted in us, formed us out of dust, to love dust, as ephemeral as this life itself yet with the gravity of real life.

I am grateful for her wise sifting of the tradition she inherited for the truth she sought. I am grateful for her confidence that others would want to join her on this journey. I am grateful for her faith in a God who wants to be known by people like us.

Lent for the Lamenting

Editor's note: This is the final post Rachel wrote for her own blog on March 6, 2019. Just a few short weeks later, in mid-April, she entered the hospital and died on May 4, 2019.

> *There are recovery programs for people grieving the loss of a parent, sibling, or spouse. You can buy books on how to cope with the death of a beloved pet or work through the anguish of a miscarriage. We speak openly with one another about the bereavement that can accompany a layoff, a move, a diagnosis, or a dream deferred. But no one really teaches you how to grieve the loss of your faith, or the loss of your faith as it once was. You're on your own for that.*
> —SEARCHING FOR SUNDAY*

As the season of Lent commences, I am aware this year of all who find themselves in a season of frustration, grief, and lament over the church or their place in it. The evangelical embrace of Trumpism. The abuse scandals in the Roman Catholic Church and

---

* Rachel Held Evans, *Searching for Sunday: Loving, Leaving, and Finding the Church* (Thomas Nelson, 2015), 48–49.

Southern Baptist Convention. The United Methodist Church's divisions over LGBTQ+ inclusion. Not a day goes by that someone doesn't reach out to me, in person or online, to tell me they feel betrayed by their family of faith—by what has been done, and by what has been left undone.

This path of lament is a well-worn one for me, so for the next forty days, I'll be taking to social media to share quotes, music, books, podcast episodes, prayers, and other resources that have been especially helpful to me in acknowledging the wounding of the church (both personally and systemically) and working toward healing (both personally and systemically).*

If you want to read along, I'll be drawing most heavily from *Rilke's Book of Hours: Love Poems to God*, translated by Anita Barrows and Joanna Macy; *Forgive Us: Confessions of a Compromised Faith*, by Mae Elise Cannon, Lisa Sharon Harper, Troy Jackson, and Soong-Chan Rah; *Learning to Walk in the Dark*, by Barbara Brown Taylor; and *Searching for Sunday*, by Yours Truly. I hope the series will be helpful.

It strikes me today that the liturgy of Ash Wednesday teaches something that nearly everyone can agree on. Whether you are part of a church or not, whether you believe today or you doubt, whether you are a Christian or an atheist or an agnostic or a so-called none (whose faith experiences far transcend the limits of that label), you know this truth deep in your bones: "Remember that you are dust and to dust you will return."

Death is a part of life.

My prayer for you this season is that you make time to celebrate that reality, and to grieve that reality, and that you will know you are not alone.

Ashes to ashes, dust to dust.

---

* Rachel did share "A Lent for Lamenting" posts on social media off and on throughout that Lenten season, along with her usual social media presence.

Her Last Act as a Blogger
A REFLECTION BY AMANDA HELD OPELT

It wasn't uncommon for people to refer to Rachel as a prophet.

As her sister, I'd often hear her laugh when people assigned this title to her. She would roll her eyes, sip her coffee, and playfully grumble that her readers overstated her authority and profundity.

But insofar as a prophet speaks hard truths to power and reveals the hidden stories of the heart, I believe the moniker fit. Moreover, if a prophet has some special insight into the future, then—in at least one instance—Rachel's words did indeed act as a harbinger of things to come.

On March 6, 2019, Rachel wrote a blog in honor of Ash Wednesday and Lent—one that articulated the acute grief that comes with deaths of all sorts: the death of a loved one, the death of a dream, and the death of a faith as it once was. "Death is part of life," she wrote.

But could she have known that the death she was preparing us for was her own?

This Lenten reflection was the last blog she would ever write, for it was mere weeks later that Rachel became very sick, was hospitalized, and eventually died. Death is, indeed, part of life. And now *her* death will always be an unimaginable, unalterable, and undeniable part of *my* life.

In the Old Testament, grief had a huge role to play in the prophetic work. The prophet Jeremiah weeps and wails for a land desolated by Israel's suffering and unrepentance (Jeremiah 9:10). As Jeremiah prophecies, the Lord commands him to call for the wailing women. "Send for the most skillful of them" (9:17), God says, and tells them to train their daughters in the art of wailing. "Teach one another a lament" (9:20), God says.

There are times in life when lament must lead the prophetic work. For it is in wailing that we expose injustice and release the pain buried deep in our soul. It is through tears that we say what is true. Lament makes space for what the world too often tries to hide in shadowy corners, and a woman who howls is sometimes a holy messenger.

It is in this way, perhaps, that Rachel was *most* like a prophet. When I think of Rachel—of the deep love and compassion she had for her fellow weary travelers on the journey of faith—I think of her as a wailing woman, one as skilled as any Jeremiah may have summoned. Our ache was her ache. Our tears were her tears. Our healing was her great hope.

In a religious culture that too often derided questions and threatened dissenters with disownment, Rachel's cries made space for our pain. She gave an entire generation *permission*—permission to doubt, permission to ask, permission to wrestle with God, permission to be changed. She gave us permission to celebrate a newfound faith while also grieving the loss of faith as it once was.

And finally, in her last act as a blogger, she gave us prophetic permission to grieve for *her*.

AFTERWORD:
GO FORTH, WOMAN OF VALOR

BY SARAH BESSEY

On that particular autumn morning of 2018, I sat just behind Rachel as she stood at the podium onstage, welcoming everyone to the very first Evolving Faith conference. I was listening to her of course but also watching the faces of our community who had crammed into the pews of the round auditorium at Montreat Conference Center in North Carolina. The rain was pouring outside, the parking lot was a soup of mud, we were all cold, the logistics of the event were shaky at best, the coffee was dangerously close to running out in the lobby, but every face was turned toward her with expectation and warmth as she spoke to us in her East Tennessee accent about anglerfish, apocalypse, and evolving faith.* They laughed, they cried, they scribbled furiously in their notebooks. Her children were backstage with her husband and our friends, her sister was near the front with her own new baby daughter in arms, and it felt like a new beginning.

I remember thinking to myself, "God, I love her. I can't believe

---

* The message Rachel preached that morning is still available for you to hear through *The Evolving Faith Podcast*, Season 1, Episode 1, "Evolution, Apocalypse, and Remembering Rachel Held Evans," https://evolvingfaith.com/podcast/season-1/blog-post-title-four-dac6d.

I get to do such good work with such a good sister at my side. I hope we do this forever."

Just a few short months later, I was at her side when she died.

WHILE RACHEL WAS WORKING ON THE MANUSCRIPT that would become *A Year of Biblical Womanhood*, she became passionate about reclaiming Proverbs 31 as a blessing for women, rather than an impossible to-do list or an unattainable goal. That Hebrew phrase from the ancient poem—*eshet chayil*—was often translated as "a woman of virtue." But through her studies, Rachel discovered it was more accurate to say "woman of valor" and that, far from being an unattainable ideal or a measuring stick for failure, it was a way to celebrate who women already are and the work we do in the world. Rachel found this small shift both fascinating and freeing, so she began to affirm other women by using that phrase to celebrate our accomplishments from career to education, parenting to homemaking, activism, and peacemaking.* From ordinary victories like potty training toddlers to big ones like publishing a book, we could expect an all-caps *ESHET CHAYIL* text from Rachel, usually with half a dozen exclamation points (!!!!!!).

At the very end of her life in the small hours of the morning on May 4, 2019, both of my hands were steady when I placed them on her head. I prayed a cobbled-together version of the Catholic prayer for the sick and dying: "Go forth, beloved soul, from this world in the name of God the Almighty Father, who created you, in the name of Jesus Christ, Son of the living God,

---

* You can read more about this shift in chapter 4 of Rachel Held Evans, *A Year of Biblical Womanhood: How a Liberated Woman Found Herself Sitting on Her Roof, Covering Her Head, and Calling Her Husband "Master"* (Thomas Nelson, 2012).

who suffered for you, in the name of the Holy Spirit, who was poured out upon you, in the Love that you abide within. Go forth, woman of valor."

And she was gone.

THERE ARE A HUNDRED DETAILS OF THOSE AWFUL, awful days of Rachel's sickness and death and then the weeks of helping to plan her funeral that I will never forget and never share. Yet however traumatizing, painful, and sad, I hold all those moments like pearls in my memory because they are just as much a part of loving her as every joke, every phone call after the kids were down for the night, every long conversation of theology and work and our families, every email or message sent (usually with "*eshet chayil!!!!!!!*" traded back and forth), every bad selfie in that Nashville hotel bathroom vainly trying to re-create a movie still from *Thelma and Louise* together, every secret told, every comment on each other's blog posts or reply on Twitter, every moment of amused eye contact in a crowded room at a conference, every meal we shared (even that one ill-advised late-night sushi platter in central Kansas).

Being a writer is an odd thing because your words just *go on*, even after your life on earth ends. In the years since Rachel died, I've borne witness to how her powerful and brave words have continued to go forth, healing, empowering, strengthening, upsetting, and even bringing hope today. This book is one more way that Rachel's legacy of love and courage keeps going forth. She left us such an honest pathway to follow, straight to the love of our God. We are all, people and pages, still going forth, all of us held in the same Love that I deeply believe held Rachel throughout her entire life and now holds her always.

THANK YOU AGAIN TO OUR CONTRIBUTORS FOR YOUR beautiful memories, precious reflections, and gracious companionship. Thank you to the entire publishing team at HarperOne, particularly our kind and care-full editor Stephanie Smith. Thank you to Rachelle Gardner, Rachel's long-time literary agent and my own, yes, but also our friend and companion through every mountaintop and every valley. Thank you to our fellow troublemakers, the blogging community of the early aughts and 2010s, the Why Christian? and Evolving Faith communities, her followers on Twitter, even her critics and those concerned pearl-clutchers, really, thank you to every one of you who were alongside Rachel.

Thank you to her beloved Dan (who is still awesome) and the kids, as well as her extended family, friends, and wide community for trusting me to shepherd this work of hers into the world; it has been an honor, truly. Thank you for letting me claim my little spot at the shoreline of your wide sea of grief, to let me hold vigil with you. Thank you for sharing Rachel with us for all those years and now beyond.

And thank you to you, dear readers. You meant so much to Rachel. Whether you were alongside of us for those years or are just now getting to know her work, you are deeply loved. You were carried in her heart and then in mine as this book came together. Thank you for being part of this story, too. You were always kindred spirits.

And finally, Rachel. I miss you every single day. God, I love you. I still can't believe I got to do such good work with such a good sister at my side.

Go forth, woman of valor (!!!!!!).

Sarah

CONTRIBUTOR BIOGRAPHIES

Candice Marie Benbow (she/her) is a multihyphenate creative who situates her work at the intersections of faith, feminism, and culture. Candice is the author of *Red Lip Theology: For Church Girls Who've Considered Tithing to the Beauty Supply Store When Sunday Morning Isn't Enough* (Convergent, 2022). She is also a writing coach and literary agent with Gardner Literary Agency. You can find Candice online at candicebenbow.com.

Micha Boyett (she/her) is an author, writer, youth pastor, podcaster, Down syndrome advocate, barre enthusiast, and lover of proper cappuccinos. Her latest book is *Blessed Are the Rest of Us: How Limits and Longing Make Us Whole*. She has an MFA in poetry from Syracuse and makes her home in New Jersey with her husband and three sons. You can find her online at michaboyett.com.

Cindy Wang Brandt (she/her) is the author of *Parenting Forward: How to Raise Children with Justice, Mercy, and Kindness*. She is the host of the *Parenting Forward* podcast and conference. She's also the founder of the popular Facebook group Raising Children Unfundamentalist. Cindy lives in Kaohsiung, Taiwan, with her husband and two children. You can find her online at cindywangbrandt.com.

Alise Chaffins (she/her) is a film critic, author, and former blogger. She lives in West Virginia with her family. You can find her online at alisechaffins.substack.com.

Shane Claiborne is a bestselling author, well-known speaker, and activist. Together with his friend Tony Campolo, Shane founded Red Letter Christians, and he is also the visionary founder of the Simple Way in Philadelphia. You can find him online at shaneclaiborne.com.

Monica A. Coleman (she/her) is the author of six books, a renowned scholar, podcaster, speaker, and ordained minister. She is the John and Patricia Cochran Scholar for Inclusive Excellence and professor of Africana Studies at the University of Delaware, after nearly fifteen years of graduate theological education at Claremont School of Theology, the Center for Process Studies, and Lutheran School of Theology at Chicago. Dr. Coleman has earned degrees from Harvard University, Vanderbilt University. and Claremont Graduate University. You can find her online at monicaacoleman.com.

Kaitlin B. Curtice (she/her) is an award-winning author, writer, poet-storyteller, and public speaker. An enrolled citizen of the Potawatomi nation, Kaitlin's award-winning book *Native: Identity, Belonging, and Rediscovering God* won the 2020 Georgia Author of the Year award in the religion category. Kaitlin lives near Philadelphia with her partner, two dogs, and two kids. You can find her online at kaitlincurtice.com.

Shannon Dingle (she/her) is the Community Engagement Associate for Little Lobbyists and the author of *Living Brave: Lessons* *from Hurt, Lighting the Way to Hope*. She is a disabled activist, freelance writer, sex-trafficking survivor, young widow, and recovering perfectionist. She lives in Raleigh, North Carolina, with her six children. You can find her online at shannondingle.com.

Glennon Doyle (she/her) is the *New York Times* bestselling author of *Untamed* and *Love Warrior* (a 2016 Oprah's Book Club selection). The host of the award-winning podcast *We Can Do Hard Things*, she is an activist and lecturer, and the founder of the online community Momastery and the nonprofit organization Together Rising. She lives with her wife and family in California. You can find her online at momastery.com.

Dr. Peter Enns (he/him) is the Abram S. Clemens professor of Biblical Studies at Eastern University, St. Davids, Pennsylvania. He is the author of several books, including his most recent, *Curveball: When Your Faith Takes Turns You Never Saw Coming (or How I Stumbled and Tripped My Way to Finding a Bigger God)*. Pete is also the cohost of *The Bible for Normal People* podcast. You can find him online at thebiblefornormalpeople.com.

Kathy Escobar (she/her) is a pastor, spiritual director, speaker, organizational consultant, advocate, and author of several books, including *Practicing: Changing Yourself to Change the World* and *Faith Shift: Finding Your Way Forward When Everything You Believe Is Coming Apart*. She's also co-executive director and founder of #CommunityHeals: Making Spaces for Transformation Accessible for All. You can find her online at kathyescobar.com.

Kathleen Gleason (she/her) was one of Rachel Held Evans's best friends and her college roommate. She is an ESL teacher in adult education. Kathleen currently lives in Dayton, Tennessee, with her husband and two sons. You can find her on Instagram at @virgrockinout.

Lisa Sharon Harper (she/her) is an author, storyteller, podcast host, speaker, activist, and educator. Her latest book is *Fortune: How Race Broke My Family and the World—And How to Repair It All*. She is the founder and president of the consulting group FreedomRoad.us. You can find her online at lisasharonharper.com and freedomroad.us.

Austen Hartke (he/him) is the author of *Transforming: The Bible and the Lives of Transgender Christians*. He is also the founder and former executive director of Transmission Ministry Collective, an online community dedicated to the spiritual care, faith formation, and leadership potential of transgender and gender-expansive Christians. Austen is a graduate of Luther Seminary's Master of Arts program in Old Testament/Hebrew Bible Studies. You can find Austen online at austenhartke.com.

Jen Hatmaker (she/her) is a *New York Times* bestselling author of more than a dozen books, including her latest, *Awake: A Memoir*. She is also the host of the award-winning podcast *For the Love*, the curator of the Jen Hatmaker Book Club, and a popular speaker. She lives in Austin, Texas, with her family. You can find her online at jenhatmaker.com.

Dr. Peter Held (he/him) recently retired as professor of Christian Thought and Biblical Studies at Bryan College in Dayton, Tennessee, where he also served as senior fellow for Christian Worldview and vice president for Student Life. He now makes his home in Boone, North Carolina, with his wife, Robin. He is Rachel Held

Evans's and Amanda Held Opelt's father and the grandfather of four. These days, you can find him in one of Boone's many fine coffee shops.

Carol Howard (she/her) is a Presbyterian pastor, author, speaker, and painter. She lives in Madison, New Jersey.

Kristen Howerton (she/her) is the author of *Rage Against the Minivan: Learning to Parent Without Perfection*. She is a writer, speaker, podcast host, and licensed marriage and family therapist working with couples, families, and individuals. Kristen lives in Southern California with her four children. You can find her online at kristenhowerton.com.

Zack Hunt (he/him) is the author of *Unraptured: How End Times Theology Gets It Wrong* and *Godbreathed: What It Really Means for the Bible to Be Divinely Inspired*. Zack has spent the past decade writing and speaking about the interplay of faith and politics in the public sphere. He lives in California with his wife and their two daughters. You can find him online at zackhunt.net.

Emmy Kegler (she/her) is a pastor in the Evangelical Lutheran Church in America, currently on leave from call to care for her growing family. She is also the author of *One Coin Found: How God's Love Stretches to the Margins* and *All Who Are Weary: Easing the Burden on the Walk with Mental Illness*. She lives in Minnesota with her wife and two children. You can find her online at emmykegler.com.

Kathy Khang (she/her) is an author, writer, speaker, and yoga teacher. Her latest book, coauthored with Matt Mikalatos, *Loving Disagreement: Fighting for Community Through the Fruit of* *the Spirit*, was a 2024 ECPA Book Award winner and a 2023 winner of the *Christianity Today* Faith and Culture Book of the Year. You can find her online at kathykhang.com.

Mihee Kim-Kort (she/they) is a Presbyterian minister, agitator, speaker, writer, and slinger of hopeful stories about faith and church. She is co-pastor with her spouse of First Presbyterian Church in Annapolis, Maryland, and earned a PhD in Religious Studies at Indiana University. You can find them online at mkimkort.com.

Rachel Kurtz (she/her) is a queer singer, songwriter, artist, and single mom from Minneapolis, Minnesota. Her latest release is the single *Gay Kids*, now available. You can find her online at rachelkurtz.com.

Tanya Marlow (she/her) is a writer and speaker on the spirituality of suffering and a lecturer in pastoral theology. Her passion is combining biblical texts with honest theologies of disability and suffering. Based in Canterbury, England, she is mostly bed-bound with chronic illness and does let it limit her. Her books include *Those Who Wait: Finding God in Disappointment, Doubt, and Delay* and you can find her online at tanyamarlow.com.

Sarah McCammon (she/her) is a national political correspondent for NPR and cohost of *The NPR Politics Podcast*. Her recent book *The Ex-vangelicals: Loving, Living, and Leaving the White Evangelical Church* was an instant *New York Times* bestseller. She lives in Norfolk, Virginia, with her husband and two children. You can find her online at sarahmccammon.substack.com.

Mike McHargue (he/him) is a veteran executive and creative producer with more than twenty-five years of experience working with organizations with global impact. He's the chief operating officer of Wohler Chemical, a cofounding partner at Quantum Spin Studios, creator of World of Vesser, and the author of two bestselling books. His work can be seen on everything from the Marvel Cinematic Universe to Netflix. You can find him online at mikemchargue.com.

Scot McKnight has been married to Kris for more than fifty years and professor for more than forty years. Scot loves the church, with all its foibles and glories, and has spent his life pressing the church to inhabit the kingdom vision of Jesus. Scot and Kris love to go for long walks, looking for birds, and to travel to well-known as well as new places.

Brian D. McLaren (he/him) is an author, speaker, activist, and public theologian. He is dean of faculty for the Center for Action and Contemplation and cohost of the Southern Lights conference. Brian is married to Grace, and they have four adult children and five grandchildren. You can find Brian online at brianmclaren.net.

Mason Mennenga (he/him) is a podcaster, speaker, YouTuber, and the internet's youth pastor. He is also the podcast host of *A People's Theology* as well as *The BlackSheep Podcast*. You can find him online at masonmennenga.com.

Osheta Moore (she/her) is an author, activist, pastor, and peacemaker. Her latest book is *Dear White Peacemakers: Dismantling Racism with Grit and Grace*. She lives in Saint Paul, Minnesota, with her husband and their three children. You can find her online at osheta.com.

Shauna Niequist (she/her) is the *New York Times* bestselling author of *I Guess I Haven't Learned That Yet*, *Present over Perfect*, and other books. She lives in New York City with her husband, Aaron, and their sons, Henry and William. You can find her online at shaunaniequist.com.

Amanda Held Opelt (she/her) is an author, speaker, and songwriter. She lives in the mountains of Boone, North Carolina, with her husband and two young daughters. She is also Rachel Held Evans's younger sister. You can find her online at amandaheldopelt.com.

Matthias Roberts (he/him) is a queer psychotherapist and the author of *Holy Runaways: Rediscovering Faith After Being Burned by Religion* and *Beyond Shame: Creating a Healthy Sex Life on Your Own Terms*. You can find him online at matthiasroberts.com.

Matthew Paul Turner (he/him) is a force in the Christian children's book publishing world, with titles like the bestselling *When God Made You* and *When I Pray for You* beloved around the world. He is also the collaborator for Rachel Held Evans's *New York Times* bestselling children's books *What Is God Like?* and *What Is the Bible?* Matthew lives in Nashville, Tennessee, with his three children. You can find him online at matthewpaulturner.com.

Winnie Varghese (she/her) is an Episcopal priest.

Matthew Vines (he/him) is the founder and executive director of the Reformation Project and the author of *God and the Gay Christian: The Biblical Case in Support of Same-Sex Relationships*. In 2013, Matthew launched the Reformation Project, a Bible-based, Christian nonprofit organization that works to advance LGBTQ inclusion in the church while remaining grounded in a love for God, a love for the Bible, and a love for the church. You can find him online at matthewvines.com.

Kelsey Hanson Woodruff is a scholar of Christianity, gender, and media. She holds a PhD in religion from Harvard University. She is also an ordained minister in the Presbyterian Church (USA). She is writing a biography of Rachel Held Evans, forthcoming from Eerdmans Publishing. Kelsey is originally from California and now lives in Massachusetts. You can find her online at kelseyhansonwoodruff.com.